MYTH, MAGIC, AND MORALS

"And what is meant by intellectual honesty? Nothing but a refusal to allow other impulses, such as the love of gain, or of applause, or the desire to promote any other end which is not purely intellectual, to interfere with the operations of the intellect in ascertaining and systematising facts. The decisive superiority of the Copernican theory over the Ptolemaic lies, not in its superior ease in working, but in its greater utility for purposes of system and prophecy. Without it there would have been no prospect of the great advances in astronomical theory which have since been made, or of our greatly increased accuracy in predicting astronomical phenomena. Results of this kind are not to be expected by a thinker who misrepresents his facts, or distorts his theory in the interests of any end which is not purely intellectual."

—WILLIAM BENETT, *The Ethical Aspects of Evolution*, p. 68.

MYTH, MAGIC, AND MORALS

A STUDY OF CHRISTIAN ORIGINS

BY

FRED. CORNWALLIS CONYBEARE, M.A.

(LATE FELLOW AND PRAELECTOR OF UNIV. COLL. OXFORD; FELLOW
OF THE BRITISH ACADEMY; DOCTOR OF THEOLOGY, *honoris causa*,
OF GIESSEN; OFFICIER D'ACADÉMIE)

WIPF & STOCK · Eugene, Oregon

Wipf and Stock Publishers
199 W 8th Ave, Suite 3
Eugene, OR 97401

Myth, Magic, and Morals
A Study of Christian Origins
By Conybeare, F. C.
Softcover ISBN-13: 978-1-7252-8907-9
Hardcover ISBN-13: 978-1-7252-8909-3
eBook ISBN-13: 978-1-7252-8908-6
Publication date 10/9/2020
Previously published by Watts & Co., 1909

This edition is a scanned facsimile of
the original edition published in 1909.

SYNOPSIS OF CONTENTS

INTRODUCTION: ON METHOD

CHAPTER I.—PAUL

P. 1. PAUCITY of tradition and lack of contemporary information about Jesus of Nazareth—p. 2. Paul's Epistles contain the earliest mention of him—p. 3. Paul not interested in the historical Jesus, but only in the Jesus of his own ecstatic visions—p. 4. History of Paul—p. 6. He conceived of Christ as an ideal eternal being and Saviour of the world, and not of the Jews alone—p. 7. His conflict with the genuine Apostles of Jesus, who insisted on converts keeping the Law—p. 9. Paul silent about the moral teaching of Jesus—p. 11. The pact with James and John; Paul may preach to the Gentiles, if he will collect ample alms for the Church of Jerusalem—p. 12. In his visits to Jerusalem Paul avoided any general contact with the Church there—p. 15. Paul dogged in his missionary labours by Judaising emissaries—p. 16. Belief in the resurrection the only tenet he had in common with these opponents—p. 18. Paul's visions the first stage in the deification of the Jewish Messiah.

CHAPTER II.—THE GOSPELS COMPILATIONS

P. 20. The Fourth Gospel develops the Pauline view of Christ and elevates him into the Divine Logos—p. 21. Dependence on Mark of Matthew and Luke—p. 22. Plagiarism no reproach in ancient and mediæval literature—p. 23. Modifications of Mark's text made by Matthew and Luke—p. 24. The Non-Marcan source used by Matthew and Luke—p. 26. The First and Third Gospels compilations.

CHAPTER III.—MARK

P. 28. Chief episodes narrated by Mark—p. 32. His literary method —p. 33. He enables us to trace a development in the Messianic self-consciousness of Jesus; the esotericism ascribed to Jesus by Mark—p. 35. In Mark the disciples only gradually recognise Jesus to be the Messiah, and Jesus only gradually reveals himself as such, and that only to his intimates, and not to the Jews in general—p. 38. Peter's recognition of Jesus as Messiah in the traditional Jewish

SYNOPSIS OF CONTENTS

sense—p. 39. Jesus's figure of the Son of Man—p. 40. Philo's presages of a peaceful but triumphant Messiah—p. 43. The belief in the Messiah's return—p. 45. Why was Jesus sentenced to death? —p. 46. J. Wellhausen's appreciation of Mark.

CHAPTER IV.—STRUCTURE OF MARK'S GOSPEL

P. 51. Examples of double narratives in Mark: explanation of them—p. 57. Mark compiled his Gospel from pre-existing written sources, which sometimes coincided with the Non-Marcan source of Matthew and Luke.

CHAPTER V.—MATTHEW AND LUKE

P. 60. Mark supplies these evangelists with their general outline and framework of Jesus's history—p. 61. They correct Mark's Greek and omit his Aramaic idioms—p. 62. They also obliterate human traits related by Mark of Jesus, such as Jesus's rejection by his own fellow townsmen, his inability to cure unless the patients believed in him, his prohibition to others to call him good—p. 65. In all this the first and third evangelists anticipate the fourth—p. 66. Other examples of human traits of Jesus effaced in Matthew and Luke— p. 69. The accusations levelled against Jesus by the Scribes, that he had a devil; and, by his mother and brethren, that he was mad— p. 72. The pious frauds of the English Revised Version—p. 76. Matthew's exaggerations of, and Luke's improvements upon, Mark's narrative prepare the way for the Fourth Gospel—p. 77. But the twenty-first chapter of the Fourth Gospel enshrines some early traditions—p. 80. Prophetic *gnosis* in Matthew.

CHAPTER VI.—LUKE

P. 83. Luke freely adjusts Mark's narratives to his own dramatic ideals —p. 86. He manufactures the seventy or seventy-two disciples out of a doublet in his sources—p. 90. Later Christian literature furnishes biographies of these disciples, who yet only existed in Luke's fancy— p. 91. Examples of how Luke could invert and travesty his sources— p. 92. His account of the gift of speaking with tongues is proved from Paul's letters to be false—p. 100. His account of the resurrection a bold manipulation of Mark's text—p. 102. Harnack on Luke's pretensions to be an accurate historian—p. 104. But Luke, according to ancient standards of literary propriety, had a right to use a stray document as he chose.

CHAPTER VII.—THE NON-MARCAN DOCUMENT

P. 107. Of this source Matthew best preserves the language, and Luke the order and arrangement — p. 108. Professor Harnack's reconstruction of it.

SYNOPSIS OF CONTENTS

CHAPTER VIII.—THE NON-MARCAN DOCUMENT *(Continued)*

P. 127. Reasons for regarding it as a very old source: it ignores the death and resurrection of Jesus—p. 131. Its horizon wholly Jewish and Galilean—p. 132. It contains features alien and abhorrent except to the most primitive age—p. 133. It ignores the miracles of Jesus—p. 134. It takes a Jewish view of the Messiah—p. 135. It ignores church organisation—p. 136. Does it preserve the sayings of Jesus which, according to Papias, were collected by Matthew?—p. 137. How far can the sayings preserved in this document be regarded as authentic?

CHAPTER IX.—THE TRUE JESUS

P. 139. There is not enough material for writing a life of Jesus—p. 141. Luke's statement that Jesus and John the Baptist were almost exactly contemporaries improbable—p. 142. Jesus's activity as an exorcist illustrated by parallels from contemporary Jewish, pagan, and other sources—p. 148. The accusation that he was an agent of Beelzebub—p. 149. Their conviction that he was the promised Jewish Messiah was for his disciples the psychological basis of their visions of him after his death, and of their belief in his Second Advent.

CHAPTER X.—JESUS'S MORAL TEACHING

P. 152. Some of his precepts inapplicable to civil society—p. 153. Their seeming universality due, partly to the fact that in his age no Jewish State existed, and partly to his expectation of the immediate advent of the Kingdom of God—p. 154. Similar precepts addressed by Philo to Gentile proselytes cut off by their change of faith from family ties—p. 156. Wide adoption of the Jewish Sabbath—p. 158. Philo's testimony to the trials of Jewish proselytes—p. 160. Jesus did not address his precepts to such proselytes, but everywhere assumes his hearers to be Jews and monotheists—p. 161. He looked forward, like Philo, to a speedy, but peaceful, emancipation of the Jews from the Roman yoke—p. 162. The lofty intransigence of his teaching.

CHAPTER XI.—THE BAPTISM OF JESUS

P. 164. The psychology of conversion—p. 166. The descent of the Spirit as a dove—p. 167. The Bath Kol—p. 168. The parallel of Hillel—Philo on the Bath Kol—p. 169. Parallel from the Testament of Levi—p. 171. The light on the waters of Jordan—p. 172. Idea of the baptismal re-birth of Jesus explains his title of "the great fish"—p. 174. This idea was exploited by the Adoptionists—p. 175. The feast of the Epiphany or of the Baptism—p. 177. Why was the age of thirty chosen as that of Jesus at Baptism?—Parallel of Zoroaster—p. 178. Pauline view that Jesus became Son of God through his resurrection, and not at Baptism—p. 180. The Ebionites insisted on the Baptism, but did not deify the Messiah—p. 181. Probability that the early Roman Church held Ebionite views—p. 181. Minucius Felix, Lactantius, and Aphraates admit godhood of Jesus Christ in a catachrestic sense only.

CHAPTER XII.—BIRTH LEGENDS

P. 186. Waning of the legend of the Virgin Birth—p. 187. Mark implicitly denied the Davidic origin of Jesus—p. 188. "Joseph begat Jesus"—p. 190. The legend that Jesus was born at Bethlehem unknown to Mark and the author of the Fourth Gospel—p. 191. Criticism of Luke's stories of the Birth—p. 193. The star of the Magi —p. 194. Parallels to Matthew's Birth legend—p. 195. Virgin birth of Plato—p. 196. Virgin births among animals; Virgin birth of Julius Cæsar, of Alexander, of Perseus—p. 198. Virgil's fourth Eclogue—p. 199. Philo on virgin births—p. 200. Literary method of Luke in narrating the births of John and Jesus—p. 202. His text interpolated from the Protevangel—p. 204. The virgin mother in Revelation—p. 206. Mark's Gospel and the Ebionite churches of Palestine denied the virgin birth of Jesus—p. 207. Judas Thomas, the twin brother of Jesus—p. 208. Aquila and Theodotion corrected *virgin* to *maiden* in their Greek versions of Isaiah, vii. 14—p. 210. The legend was due to the encratism of the early Churches—p. 211. And especially to the institution of spiritual marriage, evidenced by Paul's letters—p. 215. Encratism of Revelation, of Acts of Paul and Thekla—p. 216. Due to the belief in the imminence of the Second Advent and end of this world—p. 217. Spiritual wives in the Pastor of Hermas, in Cyprian's letters, in Gregory of Nyssa, in the Syriac and Celtic Churches—p. 219. Survival of the institution in the Middle Ages—p. 220. Harris and Oliphant—p. 222. Chivalry—p. 223. Muratori on spiritual wives—p. 224. The legend of the virgin due to encratite influence—p. 226. Docetic influences worked even to a denial that Jesus was ever born at all—p. 229. The dogma of the Immaculate Conception; feasts of the Virgin—p. 230. Belief that the Virgin conceived through her ears—p. 232. Monophysite belief about Christ's flesh; the Pearl—p. 233. Meaning of Paul's precept that women must veil their heads.

CHAPTER XIII.—MAGIC USE OF NAMES

P. 235. In folklore the name embodies the personality—p. 236. Names of power—p. 238. Ra's secret name—p. 239. Use of Jesus's name in exorcisms—p. 243. In consecrations—p. 245. Binding and loosing—p. 248. Magic use of keys—p. 249. The cursing of the fig-tree similar to Roman *Fascinatio*.

SYNOPSIS OF CONTENTS

Chapter XIV.—THE EUCHARIST

P. 251. Paul's account communicated to him in an ecstasy—p. 252. He invoked the analogy of Pagan and Jewish sacrifice—p. 253. His idealism dashed with fetishism—p. 255. Kinship and communion in food—p. 256. The meaning of the drinking of the blood of Christ—p. 258. Blood-brotherhoods—p. 259. Communion with devils and with Christ—p. 263. Were the bread and wine in Paul's sacraments magical substitutes for Christ's body and blood?—p. 265. Paul viewed the sacrament as a rehearsal of the sacrifice of Christ on the Cross—p. 266. Accretions of fetish belief round the sacrament—p. 267. The accounts of the last supper in First and Second Gospels influenced by Pauline Epistles—p. 268. That in Luke directly interpolated therefrom. His original text was free from Pauline influence, and merely ascribed to Jesus a presage of the imminent Kingdom of God—p. 271. The Essene daily sacrament of bread and water and that of the Therapeutæ influenced Christian practice—p. 274. The cleansing of sin by blood, especially by human blood—p. 275. Wine as a substitute for blood—p. 277. Pagan analogies.

Chapter XV.—THE END

P. 279. The Gospel stories of the trial of Jesus coloured by Christian hatred of the Jews—p. 280. Anxiety of the Church to exonerate Pilate—p. 281. This exemplified from Luke—p. 283. And from the pseudo-Petrine Gospel—p. 284. Pagan analogies to the darkness over all the earth—p. 286. Descents into Hell—p. 287. The rending of the veil of the Temple—p. 288. Psychological antecedents of the belief in the resurrection—p. 293. Resurrection after three days—p. 294. Jewish and Egyptian belief in a bodily resurrection—p. 296. The burial of Jesus—p. 298. The Gospel stories of the empty tomb invented to confute the Jews—p. 300. Reasons for fixing the resurrection on Sunday morning—p. 301. Matthew's amplification of Mark's tale—p. 304. The appearance on the mountain in Galilee—p. 308. Pseudo-Peter's account of the resurrection probably conserves the lost ending of Mark's Gospel—p. 312. Narrative of the Acts of Pilate.

Chapter XVI.—BAPTISM

P. 313. Origin of Bishops—p. 314. The rite of name-giving on the eighth day from birth; the "churching" of the child on the fortieth day—p. 315. Tertullian's condemnation of the baptising of children reflects the feeling of the entire early Church—p. 316. The rite of sealing with the Spirit survived as the Cathar *consolamentum*—p. 317. Survival of adult baptism in the Order of the Bath—p. 317. Catechumenate and adult baptism in the early Church described—

p. 318. Origin of triple immersion—p. 319. Use of living water—p. 320. Use of holy water and salt; the belief that post-baptismal sin was inexpiable, being sin against the Holy Spirit, led men to defer baptism until moment of death—p. 321. Invention by Pope Calixtus of the rite of penitence—p. 322. Relative unimportance of priests in the early Church; communication of Spirit by imposition of hands, and analogies in Mithraism and in folklore—p. 324. Use of rings against demons—p. 325. Significance of baptism of Jesus obscured in the later Christology which grew up with infant baptism—p. 327. Stress laid in early Church on continuity of baptism.

Chapter XVII.—MARCION

P. 329. Charles Darwin on Jewish origin of Christianity—p. 330. Marcion's attempt to deny that origin; he rejected, rather than allegorise, the Jewish Scriptures, and denied them to be inspired by the good God—p. 332. He ascribed the creation of the universe and of man to a Demiurge, whom he identified with the vindictive God of the Jews—p. 333. He denied that Jesus upheld the Jewish Law—p. 334. He was the spiritual father of the Western Manicheans—p. 336. Progressive revelation an implicit denial of the claims of Christianity to be the one true religion—p. 340. The conception of an omnipotent, but merciful, God contradicts all experience—p. 341. Paul's comparison of the Creator to a potter—p. 342. The idea of a first cause criticised—p. 343. Matter and mind, subject and object.

Chapter XVIII.—DEVELOPMENT

P. 347. J. H. Newman's *Development of Christian Doctrine*—p. 348. Criticism of the New Testament a new science—p. 349. Comparison with the hagiological studies of the Bollandists—p. 350. The early Church and Jesus himself believed that the end of the world was close at hand—p. 352. Apostolic belief in the messiahship of Jesus conditioned the subsequent belief in his second coming—p. 354. The Church was born of the waiting for a Second Advent which never occurred—p. 355. Growth of Christology in the first two centuries—p. 356. Criticism of the idea of a Chosen People—p. 357. Cosmogony of the Church wholly mythical and antiquated—p. 360. In Italy and Spain the ingrained fetishism of the poor a greater obstacle to intellectual emancipation than official Catholicism—p. 361. Timidity of Anglican divines.

INTRODUCTION

Of all the great figures which look down upon us across the gulf and void of time, Jesus of Nazareth is the most gracious and winning of aspect; and, although his memory was soon associated with that policy of craft and exclusiveness, of cruelty and credulity, which in East and West styled itself orthodoxy, nevertheless his name has ever been for the poor and oppressed, for the despised and disinherited of the earth, a bond and symbol of union in peace and charity. It behoves us, then, more than ever in this age, when old faiths are loosening their hold on us, and new superstitions, like Spiritualism, Occultism, and Christian Science, threaten to imprison our minds afresh, to inquire carefully who Jesus of Nazareth was, what were his real aims and ideas, what the means at his command for realising them, how the great institutions connected with his name originated and grew up. This I have tried to do in the following pages, in as simple and straightforward a manner as I could, without ambiguity, but also without sarcasm or mockery. For these qualities of style could only enlist me readers in circles where I would rather not find them, and are in any case inappropriate in such a discussion.

The orthodox reader will probably here exclaim: Then why choose such a title for your book? Can it do otherwise than wound and shock Christian sentiment? I do not think it should do so, and can only entreat such readers to be patient and hear me out; especially if, like most Christians, they can allege no better reason for holding the faith they profess than they can for the colour of their hair being what it is. For it is undeniable that most people merely inherit their religious beliefs, accepting them without question, and never asking what was the previous history of these opinions before they floated into their minds; nor how they tally with the ascertained results of astronomy, geology, and zoology, of history, anthropology, and other new learning.

I have, then, chosen the words "myth" and "magic" because there is no other way of characterising certain beliefs and practices of the early Church which in this work I have chosen to describe; and they can only offend those who imagine that Christianity is the one religion in the world entitled to respect, and that all other religions are systems of fraud and imbecility. I hold, on the contrary, that every creed and rite, from which men have drawn comfort in their trials and strength to bear their sufferings, should be treated with respect. Let it be the faith of Mahomet or the following of Buddha, the spell of the Malay or the *Consolamentum* of the Cathars of Albi, we must not scoff at anything in which our fellow beings have found a refuge from elemental terrors, and a panacea—none the less real to them because to us imaginary—for the many pains and aches of the flesh.

A myth is a religious narrative that purports to be historically true, but is not; and magic may for our purpose be defined as any rite or religious operation which, in ignorance of true causes, seeks to realise ends, necessary or unnecessary to the well-being of society, by an appeal to occult or supernatural forces, no matter whether the latter be regarded as personal or not.

Let me illustrate my meaning by examples. We all talk of the myth of Danae, and no one to-day believes that Danae really conceived Perseus in a shower of gold poured out by Zeus. I may go further, and say that no one believes nowadays that Danae and Perseus and Zeus were ever real personalities at all. In the same way, those who reject the story of the virgin birth of Christ, as devoid of historical

INTRODUCTION   xiii

substance, have every right to call it what it is—namely, a myth. If it be answered that the story of Christ's birth is in the Bible, while that of Danae is not, I should answer that in modern Church Congresses clergymen constantly stand up and declare the contents of the first chapters of Genesis not only to be mythical, but to have been borrowed from older Assyrian myths. Yet Paul attached so much weight to the story of the Temptation and Fall of Adam and Eve as to make it the basis of his doctrine of Christ and of Christ's redemption of our race. Here, then, is myth no less in the New than in the Old Testament; and I am by no means the first to find it therein.

It will certainly be also argued that the evidence of the saints of the early Church ought to be accepted by us, because they derived their faith direct, or almost direct, from Jesus Christ. I should reply that, morally gifted as Jesus was above his contemporaries, he nevertheless shared with them the chief superstitions of his age. And I will add, what will be new to those who are not versed in the literature of the early Church, that the Christians of the first three or four centuries, though they renounced the religious uses and rites of the pagan societies among whom they were recruited, were far from renouncing pagan beliefs. They ceased to offer sacrifice to the old gods, but they continued to believe in them. They merely changed their names and titles, and called them wicked demons instead of gods. They continued to believe that Zeus and Apollo, Mars and Venus, Mithras and Cybele, were supernatural beings, gifted with superhuman faculties and knowledge; and the main argument adduced by Christian homilists against sacrificing to the ancient gods was ever this, that they were hungry ghouls clamouring to be fed with the blood and reek of victims slain in their honour. Stop the sacrifices, they argued, and the demons that masquerade as gods will be starved out and reduced to weakness and impotence. Intellectually, then, conversion to Christianity counted for

xiv INTRODUCTION

little, and involved but a slight advance; and yet we are asked to accept blindly "the faith delivered to the saints," as if the latter were infallible authorities. The present Dean of Canterbury has gravely proposed that the English Church should retain or revive, as a norm for modern Anglican belief and usage, whatever was catholic or universally received during the first six centuries; as if, along with much else that is alien to modern thought and manners, that would not include the practice of sacrificing animal victims, for this continued for centuries in Christian shrines, and still flourishes in the churches of Syria and the Caucasus.

I pass on to sacraments. I should be the last to deny that Christians derive from these a great deal of moral comfort and edification. None the less, when a priest undertakes by certain movements of his hands, by use of certain invocations, of certain names and forms of words, which must on no account be varied, to impart to bread and wine, to water, oil, salt, bells, or what not, certain occult qualities and values, which they had not before and could not otherwise gain, he moves in the realm of pure magic. That such rites are attended with exhortations to repentance from sin and purification of the will and character is indeed fortunate, and a matter upon which we may well congratulate those who assist; but it does not alter the character of such ceremonies, and there is no use in not recognising that the atmosphere of a church—where animistic belief is allowed to colour and shape the rite of communion, where the women come fasting and the officiating clergy wear white gloves in handling the elements, where a bit of bread is carried about in procession and exposed or elevated for the adoration of the faithful—is an atmosphere which, if we encountered it among the medicine-men of the Congo, we should not scruple to say was impregnated with a belief in fetish and taboo. If, then, we are too frank and candid to uphold one set of weights and measures for our own religion, merely because it is ours, and another set for all other faiths, we must avoid circumlocutions, and boldly schedule the survivals or revivals which are to be witnessed in so many of our ritualistic churches, just where they really belong in the scheme of a comparative study of religions—namely, among fetish cults. Now the germs of such a sacramentalism are beyond doubt present in the New Testament, especially in Paul's Epistles.

It will be urged against me that in this book I seldom give references in support of my statements. I have not done so because, in a work intended to be brief and popular, it was impossible. To have done so efficiently would have required a score of volumes of the same size. Behind my book, however, lie twenty years of close study of the Christian literature and rituals of the first five centuries; and I doubt if anyone who has pursued the same course of reading for an equal length of time, and with an open mind, will condemn many of my conclusions.

Some of my readers may also find fault with me for not having discussed methodically and more at length the date and authorship of each Gospel. On the whole, the traditional dating seems to me the most satisfactory. Thus I should set the composition of Mark's Gospel, as we have it, about A.D. 70, of Luke's at any time between 80 and 95, of Matthew's about 100, of John's about 110. I see little difficulty in supposing that the John Mark mentioned in Paul's Epistles drew up some time after Peter's death (as Irenæus affirms) the Gospel named after him; and I am inclined to think that Luke, the companion of Paul, really wrote the third Gospel and the Acts, though there is, of course, much to recommend the counter-hypothesis. The Gospel of Matthew is recognised even by conservative critics to be the work of an unknown writer; and the old view that the Fourth Gospel was written by an apostle and eye-witness is quite exploded.

How far back the Aramaic traditions exploited by Mark may go, we do not know. In estimating their age, however, we must bear in mind that it was not antiquarian or historical interest that led to their being collected and redacted. Had it been so, the world must have waited much longer; for few or none were interested to know about the brief ministry of a Messiah who was expected to come again, and that shortly. The eyes of believers were, up to the end of the first century, fixed on the future and not on the past; and the aim of the second evangelist was rather to prove, as against the Jews who denied it, that Jesus was Messiah and Son of God, than to set on record for posterity the facts of his earthly career. It is, therefore, merely incidentally that he supplies us with an outline of that career. Primarily his work was a party pamphlet. The sayings of Jesus must have been written down at an earlier stage, because they were wanted as a manual of moral teaching. They were rules which every candidate for the kingdom of God, soon to be manifested, had to lay to heart and observe. I should not, therefore, be surprised to learn that the Aramaic text of these sayings was current within a short generation after the death of Jesus.

Of the Epistles of Paul, very few are now disputed by competent critics. I am disposed to accept as authentic all of them, not excepting the ones addressed to Timothy and Titus. For the latter form a group, of which it is difficult to accept one member and not the others. Now it is quite inconceivable that a forger of Pauline Epistles, wishing, if not to honour Paul, at least not to bring him into disrepute, would attribute to his pen the statements that we find in the Second Epistle to Timothy—namely, that all the believers in Asia had "turned away from" him, and that at the very first hearing of his appeal to the Cæsar in Rome " no one took my part, but all forsook me." "May it not be laid to their account!" he adds, showing how reprehensible he felt their desertion of him to be. A forger would not thus have gone out of his way to reveal to us that the entire Church of Rome belonged to the Judaising party of James and John, and that their hatred of the Apostle of the Gentiles continued to be so intense that they abandoned him in his hour of need. I believe no one would ever have disputed the authenticity of this letter if a pagan had written it instead of Paul. If, then, it is authentic, the other two must be accepted also. A tendency set in very early among Christian writers to glose over and obliterate all traces of the quarrel between Paul and the pillars of the Church, which in the Epistle to the Galatians, probably the earliest of the letters of Paul, is so vividly described. In the Acts of the Apostles this tendency is very clearly exhibited, and any forger of Pauline letters would have been dominated by it. The Epistle to the Hebrews has never been seriously attributed to Paul, but it is clearly anterior to A.D. 70, and Tertullian was probably right in attributing it to Barnabas.

I have cited the Book of Revelation as a work of the last decade of the first century. This was the tradition of Irenæus, and the fact that a rescript of Domitian of the year 93 is cited in it verbatim confirms that tradition. This, however, does not preclude us from seeing in it a working up of an earlier document of about the year 68 or 69, to which date Renan assigned it.

It remains to acknowledge my indebtedness to the three greatest Christian scholars of our age—the Abbé Loisy, Prof. Adolf Harnack, and J. Wellhausen. I have here and there cited them by name; but those who are acquainted with their works will recognise their influence in almost every page of my book.

I fear most of my readers will find my first few chapters, in which I set forth the textual problem, stiff reading. If so, I need not be disappointed; for in the field of criticism no results can be worth much which do not involve hard study. Nothing is so contemptible as the facile orthodoxy which would fain raise no questions, and the exponents of which are accustomed to plead that it is so much simpler to take every statement in the Bible at its face value.

Such exhortations are in vain in the present day, when the dogmatic repose of earlier generations has been widely and ruthlessly disturbed. It cannot be restored. We must face the problems of our age, and adopt the solutions which an enlightened criticism provides. Those who decline to do so, and try to maintain in their minds what has aptly been called a water-tight compartment for their religious convictions, are in danger of ruining themselves as well as their fellows. For a man's character is all of a piece, and we cannot burke awkward questions, thrust our heads into the sand, and practise sophistry and make-believe in so intimate a concern as religious belief, without sooner or later forfeiting all round those qualities of manliness, honesty, and painstaking thoroughness which alone can enable Englishmen in these days of keen competition to hold their own.

F. C. C.

January 31st, 1909.

Chapter I.

PAUL

The late Master of Balliol, Benjamin Jowett, once wrote to a lady who sought his opinion, that the Gospels are fragments of unknown age, full of incredible things; and few will to-day maintain the narratives, which survived among the Christians, of the life of the founder, Jesus of Nazareth, to be as full, accurate, and authentic as the supposed importance of their subject-matter demands. Of Socrates, Plato, Aristotle, and many other teachers of antiquity, not to mention great military and political leaders, we can out of the records bequeathed to us construct lifelike pictures, can trace with certainty the gradual development of their minds and characters, and exhibit in detail their careers. Often we have their very letters and writings; and coins and sculptures preserve to us the lineaments of their countenances. Yet of Jesus, whose birth is supposed to have opened a new era, not only for this earth, but for the entire universe, we know all too little; and we have not enough material to write a life of him, in the sense in which we write lives of Julius Cæsar, of Cicero, of Augustus, and of many others who were nearly his contemporaries.

But the Gospels are not the earliest Christian documents which we possess; for the earliest of them —that of Mark—is nearly a generation later than the Epistles of Paul, of which several were written within a generation of Jesus's death. And this is not all. Paul was in personal relations—often strained, it is true, yet none the less actual—with Peter and John, the immediate disciples of Jesus, and with James, his brother, and first president of the Church of Jerusalem. Anxious to ascertain the facts of Jesus's life, it is to these Epistles that we naturally turn. We do so in vain! Paul had unique opportunities of informing himself about the earthly career of Jesus, of handing on this information to his converts; but of set purpose he declined to do anything of the sort. "*Even though we have known Christ after the flesh, yet now we know him so no more,*"[1] he writes to his flock at Corinth—words which imply that he had probably seen Jesus, and, if not that much, that he anyhow was acquainted with the facts of his life through others who knew him personally. Yet he deprecates such knowledge. If he ever saw Jesus in the flesh, he would fain forget that he did so, and have others forget it also. He attaches no importance to the fact, nor desires others to do so. On one event alone in Jesus's life he lays stress—namely, on his crucifixion. "*The Jews*," he writes to the same converts, "*ask for signs*"—that is to say, for miracles worked before their eyes; "*the Greeks seek after wisdom*"—that is to say, after a system of ethical philosophy and a rational synthesis of reality. Jesus the Messiah, or Christ, so he hints, could supply neither of these needs. "*We,*" he continues, "*preach Christ crucified, unto Jews a stumbling-block, and unto Gentiles foolishness.*"[2] In the real Jesus, in the humble teacher of men, the healer of their souls and bodies, Paul was

---

[1] 2 Cor. v. 16.   [2] 1 Cor. i. 23.

not interested. And yet this enthusiast's letters are not wholly barren, but reveal, though quite incidentally, the following facts about Jesus. We learn from them that he was *born of woman*—that is to say, like any other human being; that he was born *of the seed of David*, and was *under the law*—in other words, that he was an orthodox Jew; that he shared with us all the weakness and infirmities of the flesh; that he was *obedient unto death*, and died on the cross suffering as ordinary men suffer and die.

But this earthly life of Jesus, beginning with birth and ending with crucifixion, was, according to Paul, a mere incident in a larger divine life and existence. And at this point it is important to notice that Paul was pre-eminently a man of visions and dreams, prizing what in moments of ecstasy he beheld more highly than waking realities. The crucified Jesus, who had been raised from the dead, not in the corruptible flesh, but with such a spiritual and incorruptible body as, according to Paul, could alone inherit incorruption, had been seen after death by a multitude of his followers, and last of all had appeared and spoken to himself during his journey to Damascus. He even relates how, on this or perhaps some other occasion, he was *caught up into the third heaven, whether in the body or out of the body he knew not*.[1] Thus "*caught up into paradise*," he had "*heard unspeakable words, which it is not lawful for a man to utter.*" Lest he should *be exalted overmuch by the exceeding greatness of these revelations*, there had been given to him *a thorn in the flesh, a messenger of Satan to buffet him*. Of this he had prayed to be delivered; but the Lord

---

[1] 2 Cor. xii. 1 foll.

4   PAUL

had appeared to him and said, *My grace is sufficient for thee.*[1] The affliction in question was undoubtedly the epilepsy which often attends such temperaments.

From such incidents as the above we can understand the character of Paul's gospel. He was, like many a later saint, of a temperament naturally ecstatic, and perpetually saw Christ and conversed with him in visions; his words and actions, even his missionary movements, as he is careful to inform us, were inspired and directed not by reflection but "by revelation."

What was the previous history of this enthusiast? He was, so he tells us, a Jew of the Jews, and a Pharisee as well. As such he had, during his early manhood, sought to win the approval of a jealous God by meticulous observance of the taboos and prescriptions of the Mosaic law. At Tarsus, his native place, he learned to talk and write Greek, without, however, forfeiting his own Aramaic dialect, as did most of the Jews when once they were Grecised. In that part of Asia an enormous number of pagans, without adopting all the practices of Judaism, had yet assimilated Jewish monotheism, and his knowledge of this outer fringe of his religion taught Paul later on to remit for his converts the heavy yoke of the Jewish law.

After the death of Jesus, Paul, ever-zealous, whatever party he espoused, threw himself into the persecution of the followers of the new Messiah; yet not for long. Struck with the fortitude with which his victims met their death, he began to entertain misgivings of the righteousness of his cause. Christian Inquisitors have easily stifled such misgivings, if they

[1] 2 Cor. xii. 9.

ever felt them. But Paul was cast in another mould; his scruples, once excited, gathered force in his sensitive conscience, and ripened at last into a vision of Jesus on the road to Damascus, when he heard the voice of the risen Messiah calling to him from heaven: "*Saul, Saul, why kickest thou against the pricks?*" The pricks were those of his own conscience. It is untrue to say that from this crisis Paul emerged a different man, inspired with new ideals. He had already formed or imbibed from others the ideal of a universalist Messiah, perhaps even of a suffering saviour of humanity. This scheme lay ready in his mind; and he fitted it, not without some violence, on to Jesus of Nazareth, whose own teaching and example had so strongly impressed his personal followers. Their faith in their master impressed Paul in turn, and led him, as it were, to appropriate Jesus *nolens volens* as his own, and to superimpose on him all the transcendental *rôle* and cosmic importance which in previous training he had learned to assign to the expected Messiah. Thus conversion signified for Paul not an acceptance of new principles, but only a new application of old ones.

Let us illustrate this point. There is some uncertainty about the teaching of Jesus; but this much is clear, that he had no message except for his own countrymen, nor ever dreamed of any but Jews sharing in the heavenly kingdom whose near approach he proclaimed. He expressly forbad his disciples to missionise the heathen, or even the Samaritans, who yet in the Pentateuch reverenced the same sacred books as himself, and were in reality the most genuine Jews of that age. Paul, however, had, from early training, learned to conceive of the coming Messiah or Christ as a heavenly being, the power and wisdom of God, second only to the divine father, an uncorrupted image of God, an ideal type of humanity, such as was Adam before he clutched at equality with God and fell. The immediate followers of Jesus entertained no such lofty conception of the Messiah. He was to them a man sent from God, who had met with a cruel fate, but was still alive and was to appear again within their generation and restore the kingdom of David. But to Paul he was an ideal and eternal being, who had condescended to quit the right hand of God and to be found on earth in the likeness of sinful flesh, and, as the man Jesus, to die on the cross the death of a malefactor, in order that he might, as a perfect victim, conciliate the wrath of an angry God, and mediate the salvation, not of Jews alone, but of all mankind.

Thus Paul's Christ is an *a priori* construction of his own, owing to the historical man of Nazareth and to those who knew that man and cherished his memory little except the bare name of Jesus. Paul's Jesus is an ideal superhuman Saviour, destined, from the beginning of the world, to play an ecumenic *rôle*. Raised by the spirit of God from the dead, the saviour has left behind in the grave, together with the flesh now given over to corruption, all his Jewish exclusiveness, all his human traits, even his sex.[1] "*Ye are all*," writes Paul to the Galatians, "*sons of God, through faith, in Christ Jesus.......There can be neither Jew nor Greek, there can be neither bond nor free, there can be no male and female: for ye all are one in Christ Jesus.*" From such a standpoint there could obviously be no reason why Gentiles converted to Messianic Judaism

---

[1] Gal. iii. 26 foll.

should accept the Jewish law and undergo circumcision, why they should keep sabbaths, or observe the many ritual taboos which hedged in the dinner-table of the Jews and prevented their eating in the company of Gentiles. It was just here that Paul could not fail to come into conflict with Peter and James and John, and other personal followers of Jesus. The latter had indeed known how to interpret in a rational manner the rule of the sabbath, but had never dreamed of repealing it, any more than of repudiating circumcision or the Jewish sacrificial system. His followers, accordingly, could but resent Paul's denial that the law was binding for his converts, his allowing them to participate in the meals of Gentiles, his contempt for taboos in general. They denounced the short cut to salvation which he had invented for Gentiles, and insisted that there was no way into the impending messianic kingdom except through the very works and observance of the law which Paul reckoned unnecessary. The Messiah, they argued, was a Messiah of the Jews alone, not of the Gentiles, for whom the divine promises were never made, and between whom and Jehovah no covenant ever existed. Therefore a Gentile who desired to enter the kingdom must enter it through the narrow gate of Judaism. They asked what right had Paul to cloak his revolt against the law with the name of Jesus, who had, with his own lips, declared that he came not to abolish the law, but to fulfil it. By what right, they asked, did Paul attribute his own dreams and fancies to a Christ whom he had not known, and from whom he had never received any apostolic commission? They scoffed at his revelations, and, in the heat of the conflict, even went so far as to identify him with the anti-Christ.

The only answer Paul could make was to sneer at the exclusive pretensions of the twelve apostles, and to fall back on his own visions. He had, he argued, anyhow *seen* Christ—namely, the risen Christ—and had been commissioned by him to preach the gospel to the Gentiles. It was not Paul that spoke and acted, but the spirit of Christ dwelling within him, and constituting him its vehicle and mouthpiece. Here was a quarrel too deep to be healed until the generation of Palestinian Christians who had really known Jesus should pass away. For the present, thanks to Paul's tact, a truce was patched up, by the terms of which his Gentile converts were to be recognised as brethren if they would eat none but *kosha* meat, and subscribe liberally for the sustenance of the brethren in Jerusalem, who seem to have been much impoverished either by persecution or by their attempts to live communistically, or by both.

Only in Palestine could the Jews of that age practise the law with any strictness; in the Greek and Latin cities all round the Mediterranean they could not maintain it even among themselves, much less among their converts. Hence what has been termed Judaising Christianity—that is, the Christianity which insisted on circumcision, sabbaths, dietary taboos, and other rules of the Mosaic law—soon perished and was lost to view except within the narrow limits of Palestine. Even there it hardly survived the fall of Jerusalem in A.D. 70. The terms of the truce were thus to some extent imposed by hard facts on Peter and John and James.

It has been necessary to dwell so long on an early quarrel which nearly strangled the new religion in its cradle, because Paul's silence about the historic Jesus is otherwise unintelligible. He was well aware that the horizon of Jesus, like that of any other Galilean prophet of that age, was bounded by an exclusive regard for Judaism and Jewish nationality; that his sympathies had not overstepped these limits; that he had forbidden to his disciples the paths of the Gentiles and the cities of Samaritans; and, knowing as much as he did, he could hardly do otherwise than disparage, both for himself and his flock, all knowledge of Christ "*after the flesh.*" Instead of pondering the real facts of Jesus's life and ministry, he fixes his own gaze and that of his converts on the pattern laid up in heaven. This is why we seek in vain in Paul's letters for details of Jesus's earthly career. It did not interest him; nay, more, it was an awkward and unpleasant topic, which lay too near the accusations from which he had incessantly to defend himself. Quite incidentally, as we have seen, he records, or rather enables us to infer, a few general facts about the life of Jesus; but in general he abstains from mentioning it, and is absorbed in his own hallucinations and transcendental fancies—grandiose, it is true, but sorely baffling our modern curiosity.

And it is not merely the outward events and vicissitudes of Jesus's life, as even unsympathetic Jews must have witnessed them, that failed to touch and interest Paul; he is equally silent about the moral and religious teaching of the Master, and shows no acquaintance with the Sermon on the Mount or with the parables. And this is all the stranger because there are several fairly well-authenticated sayings of Jesus which would have stood him in good stead when he was combating the Judaising apostles.

For example, on one occasion at Antioch, Paul found himself "*resisting Peter to the face.*" The latter had been sitting down at table with Gentile converts, regardless of Mosaic commensal taboos. Before long there arrived spies from Jerusalem sent by James, the brother of Jesus, "*false brethren*"—so Paul calls them —"*privily brought in to spy out our liberty which we have in Christ Jesus.*" "*And when they came,*" continues Paul, "*Peter* [or Cephas] *drew back and separated himself, fearing them that were of the circumcision.*" Here, if anywhere, one would expect Paul to appeal to the saying: "*Not that which entereth the mouth defileth the man; but that which proceedeth out of the mouth, this defileth the man......the things which proceed out of the mouth come forth out of the heart; and they defile the man. For out of the heart come forth evil thoughts, murders, adulteries, fornications, thefts, false witness, railings; these are the things which defile the man; but to eat with unwashen hands defileth not the man.*"

Yet, often as Paul recurs in his Epistles to this question of food taboos, he never alleges in defence of the freedom which he claimed in Christ the actual teaching of the latter. The nearest approach is in the Letter to the Romans, xiv. 14: "*I know and am persuaded in the Lord Jesus that nothing is unclean of itself.*" But no one familiar with the Pauline style will interpret this as an appeal to special precepts uttered by Jesus and transmitted to Paul by those who listened thereto. On the contrary, in the particular context (Galatians ii.) where he relates this quarrel with Peter and James, he is careful to emphasise the complete independence of his gospel from theirs. His words are these: "*After the space of fourteen years I went up again to Jerusalem......by revelation; and I laid before them the gospel which I preach among the Gentiles.......But from those who were reputed to be somewhat (whatsoever they were, it maketh no matter to me; God accepteth not man's person)—they, I say, who were of repute, imparted nothing to me....... And when they perceived the grace that was given unto me, James and Cephas [i.e., Peter] and John, they who were reputed to be pillars, gave to me and Barnabas the right hands of fellowship, that we should go unto the Gentiles, and they unto the circumcision; only they would that we should remember the poor; which very thing I was also zealous to do."*

The situation is clear. The real companions of Jesus, James and Peter and John, obedient to their Master's tradition, obstinately refuse themselves to preach the gospel to uncircumcised Gentiles. Paul insists on doing so, and alleges in justification his own special revelations of Jesus. They on their side consent to allow him to go his way, and to disseminate outside the Jewish world the gospel which was his, yet not theirs nor their Master's, on one condition, that he and his converts send plenty of money to support the saints of Jerusalem. The "pillars" of the Church there are clearly anxious to be rid of Paul, and with truly Jewish practicality they name their terms. They will leave him alone with his Gentiles, but he must not forget the backsheesh. Nor did Paul forget it, for in his second Letter to the Corinthians two entire chapters are given up to the topic. In these he employs every art of rhetoric, flattery, and edification, in order to induce his converts to subscribe, and that handsomely. His anxiety about the matter is ever undisguised, and we discern clearly that in a heavy subsidy, oft repeated, lay his only hope of being able to keep on any sort of terms with the saints of Jerusalem.

Paul elaborated his gospel in the silence and solitude of Arabia. He declined from the very first moment of his conversion to resort to the brethren of Jerusalem and Galilee, in order to learn from their lips what had been their Master's life and teaching. Thus he writes to the Galatians (i. 11): "*For I make known to you, brethren, as touching the gospel which has been preached by me, that it is not after man.*"

This means that he had no human teacher, nor depended on any humanly transmitted reports of who Jesus was and what he taught. So he continues: "*For neither did I receive it from man, nor was I taught it, except by way of revelation on the part of Jesus Christ.*"

This indicates that Paul got his gospel through visions and private revelations of his own. It had nothing to do with what the companions and apostles of Jesus remembered of their Master's life and conversations. In the immediate sequel he reminds the Galatians of how he had begun life as an observing Jew, and of how he persecuted the Christians: "*For ye have heard of my manner of life in time past in the Jews' religion, how that beyond measure I persecuted the Church of God, and made havoc of it; and I advanced in the Jews' religion beyond many of mine own age among my countrymen, being more exceedingly zealous for the traditions of my fathers.*"

And then once more he emphasises the fact that his teaching had nothing in common, no connection, with the teaching of the historical Jesus as reported by his direct disciples: "*But when it was the good pleasure of God, who separated me from my mother's womb, and called me through his grace, to reveal his Son in me, that I should preach him among the Gentiles; immediately I conferred not with flesh and blood; neither went I up to Jerusalem to them which were Apostles before me; but I went away into Arabia; and again I returned unto Damascus."*

The revelation, then, with which he was graced was this, that he was to go and preach the Son of God among the Gentiles—preach, that is to say, not the historical Jesus, but *a priori* messianic conceptions of his own. Had he gone up to Jerusalem and condescended to ascertain from the *flesh and blood* companions of Jesus what manner of man the latter had really been, and what he had taught, he would have learned at the outset that Jesus had reserved the messianic kingdom for conforming Jews alone, and peremptorily forbidden the inclusion of uncircumcised Gentiles, whose idolatry he never once denounced, simply because they and their affairs lay so entirely outside of and beyond his horizon. Paul was aware that his initial revelation conflicted with the traditions of the earthly Jesus, and for that reason avoided Jerusalem and the apostles that were before him. We need not regret that his innate idealism launched him in the way of the larger and more liberal teaching. He had a soul above taboos, and so really had Jesus, who, if he had been a Jew of the Dispersion, and his horizon not confined to Galilee, might equally have cast off the slough of Jewish ceremonialism, and have opened his messianic kingdom to all who had become monotheists.

After three years thus given up to his own lucubrations, Paul did repair to Jerusalem in order to make the acquaintance of Cephas (Peter), with whom he stayed for the brief space of fifteen days. Paul was, on this occasion, in the midst of those who had followed Jesus, listened to his teaching, and received from him a commission to preach. Yet he makes no secret of how little he felt himself to be in sympathy with them. He tells us that he mixed with them, during that fortnight, as little as possible. "*But other of the apostles,*"[1] he writes, "*saw I none, but only James, the Lord's brother.*" Thus he avoided even the solemn meetings of the brethren for *the breaking of bread and for the prayers* (Acts ii. 42).

And lest such indifference should seem impossible to his converts, he adds: "*Now touching the things which I write unto you, behold, before God, I lie not.*" We see how morbidly afraid he was lest his converts in Galatia should suppose that he owed any part of his gospel to men of flesh and blood instead of to direct revelation. And he drives the point home by relating that at this time, three years after his conversion, he "*was still unknown by face* [*i.e.*, personally] *unto the churches of Judæa which were in Christ; but they only heard say, He that once persecuted us now preacheth the faith of which he once made havoc; and they glorified God in me.*" It is clear from the above that Paul rather shunned them than they him. What reason could he have for doing so except this, that he knew them to be out of sympathy with him on vital points?

Fourteen fresh years seem to have elapsed before Paul, according to the passage already quoted, again went up to Jerusalem, always "*by revelation*"; and

---

[1] Gal. i. 19.

in order "*to lay before*" the leaders of the Jerusalem fellowship "*the gospel which I preach among the Gentiles.*" This gospel he had evolved out of his own inner consciousness, so we are not surprised to learn from the next verse that he only laid it "*privately before them who were of repute.*" It was clearly so remote from the gospel with which the mass of believers were familiar in the very home and diocese of Christ himself that it was expedient not to communicate it to them. We infer that, if he had broached it to them, there would have been such a general outcry against him as would have deprived him of the "*liberty in Jesus Christ*" which he and his converts enjoyed; and he "*would be running*" in the future and "*have run*" in the past "*in vain.*" He relates with much complacency how, in the course of this second visit to Jerusalem, he found nothing to learn even from those "*who were reputed to be pillars of the church.*" They "*imparted nothing*" to him. After so many years it was rather late to try. And how delightfully ironical is Paul at the expense of the older apostles and kinsmen of Jesus! "*Whatsoever,*" he adds, "*they were matters not to me; God accepteth not man's person.*"

But if Paul succeeded when in Jerusalem in withholding the character of his gospel from the mass of the believers there, he could not prevent Palestinian missionaries from penetrating into Galatia and other districts which he claimed for his own, and there announcing another gospel, more authentic—let us not scruple to own it—than that which he had evolved out of his own ecstatic consciousness, though less attractive to Gentiles, who naturally preferred to believe that the Jesus in whose name Paul appealed to them was just a monotheistic teacher with a special message for Gentiles. We know exactly what was Paul's attitude to the more genuine exponents of Christian tradition. He has himself set it on record in the same Epistle to the Galatians, ch. i. 6 foll.: "*I marvel that ye are so quickly shifting from him* [God or Paul] *that called you, by the grace of Christ, unto a different gospel; which is not another, only there are some that trouble you, and would pervert the gospel of Christ. But though we, or an angel from heaven, should preach unto you any gospel contrary to that which we preached unto you, let him be anathema* [i.e., cursed]. *As we have said before, so say I now again, if any man preacheth unto you any gospel other than that which ye received* [i.e., from Paul], *let him be anathema.*"

From such words as these we can see how sure Paul felt of his own revelations, and how remote it was from his purpose to learn from those who had known Jesus personally. He had his own ideas of what part a Messiah must play in heaven and on earth, and he was not going to abandon them for anyone. Accordingly, he writes triumphantly of the results of his visit after fourteen years to Jerusalem as follows: "*Did we give way so as to submit* [to the false brethren privily brought in, who came in privily to spy out our liberty]? *No, not for one hour.*"

Was there, then, no common position and ground, nothing in which Paul could agree with the older disciples? There was indeed such a position; but, characteristically enough, it is no episode or fact belonging to the earthly life and career of Jesus, nothing the cognisance of which can be described as a knowledge of Christ *after the flesh*. He shared with them the belief that Jesus had been raised from the dead and promoted to a first throne in heaven, whence he would in a brief space return on the clouds of heaven to earth, to judge all men.

In the first Letter to the Corinthians (ch. xv.) Paul enumerates the appearances of the risen Jesus thus: "*Now I make known unto you, brethren, the gospel which I preached unto you, which also ye received. ......For I delivered unto you first of all that which also I received, how that Christ died for our sins according to the scriptures; and that he was buried; and that he hath been raised on the third day according to the scriptures; and that he appeared to Cephas; then to the twelve; then he appeared to above five hundred brethren at once, of whom the greater part remain until now, but some are fallen asleep; then he appeared to James; then to all the apostles; and last of all, as unto one born out of due time, he appeared to me also.*"

Such testimony as the above stands or falls with a number of other equally well authenticated ghost-stories. That the appearances recorded by Paul were subjective, in the sense that Jesus only appeared to those who already believed in him, is declared to have been the case in the Acts of the Apostles. It is impossible to collate apparitions, and we know not in what guise Jesus appeared to Paul, who had never enjoyed his personal acquaintance, and in whose case, therefore, were absent those psychological materials and conditions of an apparition which were amply present in the case of the others whom he enumerates. However, these considerations are alien to our present purpose, which is to point out how important a part these visions of Christ played in the development of Paul's Christology. It was only too easy to clothe a phantasm with sublimest attributes, to promote it to the dignity of *Power and Wisdom of God*. That the other apostles already believed at this stage that Jesus *died for our sins* is not likely, for, in the earliest strata of evangelic tradition, we have no trace of such an idea. They may have believed Jesus to be the Messiah, who was to come again; but it would appear from a passage in Paul's Epistle to the Romans (ii. 16) as if his future *rôle* of judge of the quick and the dead was not yet fixed in their minds.[1] However this may have been, the messianic *rôle* was a purely human one, which Mohammed's personal followers might equally have assigned to him. On the other hand, the celestial figure which Paul beheld in his dreams, and which spoke to him in the third heaven, was much more than a Messiah of the Jews. It is not too much to say that his apparitions formed the first step in the deification of Jesus, and that they are the basis and beginning of all the transcendental speculations about him which ultimately crystallised into the dogmas and creeds of the Church.

One point more. Paul knew that Jesus died a Jew, sharing the ordinary prejudices of Jews, and excluding uncircumcised Gentiles from the blessings of that future kingdom which he went to prepare in heaven. He believed, however, that in being raised by the spirit from the dead he was, in some mysterious manner, promoted to be the saviour of all mankind,

---

[1] Rom. ii. 14–16: "For when Gentiles which have not a law do by nature the things of the law, these, having no law, are a law to themselves, in that they show the work of the law written in their hearts, their conscience bearing witness therewith, and their thoughts one with another accusing or else excusing them; in the day when God shall judge the secrets of men, *according to my gospel*, by Jesus Christ." We may infer that it was only according to Paul's gospel that Jesus Christ was to act as judge of all men, Gentiles as well as Jews. Probably the point is that the genuine apostles regarded Jesus as the destined judge of Jews alone—an idea attested by Matt. xix. 28.

and became a universalist teacher, bearer of a name of power before which all angels and demons, both in heaven and hell, must prostrate themselves. He died a human being, he was raised a divine life-giving and recreative spirit. The real disciples of Jesus enjoyed apparitions enough of him after death, but we do not hear that they invested the figure they saw with the majestic *rôle* and cosmic attributes of the Pauline vision. It is certain they did not, and could not do so; for they had known him in the flesh, and were trammelled by what Paul stigmatised as carnal memories. Had Paul also so known him, his visions could not so lightly have soared into the empyrean. His Christ would have remained a mere human Messiah of the Jews. But in that case Christianity would have fallen stillborn on the world, and have vanished as it began—an obscure sect of messianically-minded Galileans.

CHAPTER II.

THE GOSPELS COMPILATIONS

THE New Testament of the Christians contains four Gospels, named respectively *according to* Matthew, Mark, Luke, and John,[1] of which the first three as much agree with one another in style and contents as they differ from the fourth. They are party documents, so far as their manifest aim is to show that Jesus was, what the majority of Jews denied him to be, the Messiah; nevertheless they are, on the whole, transparently sincere documents embodying naïve traditions, mostly collected from the mouths of the people of the districts about which he had wandered and taught, of his wonder-workings, teaching, and death. The fourth Gospel, as we have remarked, contrasts with these three in style and attitude; it inverts the sequence of the chief events of Jesus's ministry as narrated in them, transforms his teaching beyond all recognition, turns him into the Logos or Divine Reason, and in other respects shows itself to be a religious romance embodying speculations about him, later much than Paul, but of which Paul's ecstatic thinking was the *fons et origo*. This fourth Gospel enshrines, no doubt, many noble thoughts, but is, on the whole, frigid, insincere, and full of exaggerations. We may safely neglect it in any attempt to get back to the earliest traditions of Jesus.

[1] I refer to these in the sequel as Mt, Mc, Lc, Jo.

THE GOSPELS COMPILATIONS

If the reader will take a red pencil and underline in the Gospels of Mt and Lc all the phrases, sentences, and entire narratives which are in verbal agreement with Mc, he will find very little left of the latter which is not in them; so that, if we had not Mc's gospel preserved to us, we could yet reconstruct nearly the whole of it out of the agreements of the other two. A single example will illustrate this. Let us take Mc ii. 13–17 and confront it with Mt ix. 9–13 on one side and Lc v. 27–32 on the other, italicising in them every word in which they agree with Mc:—

LUKE.	MARK.	MATTHEW.
27. *And* after this *he went forth* and he beheld a *customs officer, by name Leveis, sitting at the customs house,* and said *to him, Follow me.*	13. And he went forth again unto the sea, and all the people came to him, and he was teaching them. 14. And as he passed along he saw Leveis, the son of Alphæus, sitting at the customhouse, and says to him, Follow me. And he arose and followed him.	9. And Jesus, *as he passed along* thence, saw a man *sitting at the customs house,* called Matthew, *and says to him,* Follow me. And he arose and followed him.
28. *And* having left everything, *he arose and followed him.* 29. And Leveis made a great entertainment for him *in his house.* And there was a crowd *numerous of customs officers* and others who *were* with them *lying down to eat.*	15. And it happens that he lies down to eat in his house, and numerous customs officers and sinners lay down with Jesus and with his disciples; for they were numerous and were following him, (16) and scribes of the Pharisees. And, seeing that he ate with customs officers and sinners, they said to his disciples, that with the customs officers and sinners he does eat and drink.	10. *And it happened,* as he was *lying down to eat in the house,* why lo, *numerous customs officers and sinners* came and *lay down to eat with Jesus and his disciples.* 11. *And* the *Pharisees seeing said to his disciples,* Why *with the customs officers and sinners* eateth your teacher?
30. And the *Pharisees* and their *scribes* grumbled unto *his disciples, saying,* Wherefore *with the customs officers and sinners* do ye *eat and drink?* 31. *And Jesus* answered, and spake		

22 THE GOSPELS COMPILATIONS

to *them, They have not need* that are healthy *of a physician, but they that are badly.* 32. *I have not come to call the just, but sinners,* to repentance.	17. And Jesus, having heard, says to them, They have not need who are strong of a physician, but they that are badly. I came not to call the just, but sinners.	12. But he, *having heard,* said, *They have not need who are strong of a physician, but they who are badly.* 13. But go ye on your way and learn what this means ; I will have mercy and not sacrifice. For *I came not to call the just, but sinners.*

The original texts here translated are, of course, Greek ; but the point to be apprehended can be made clear in a literal translation like the above. It is this, that Mt and Lc have merely appropriated the narrative of Mc, altering it and retouching it here and there, as they liked. And there is nothing in all these alterations to show that Mt knew of Lc's text, or *vice versâ*. We infer that they worked independently of each other.

In the present age there is a prejudice against an author who takes another's book, copies it out, and publishes it as his own. We call him a plagiarist, and there is no reviewer but would ridicule him as a literary thief. But in earlier ages, when there was no printing-press, and authors did not expect to make money by their works, there was no such prejudice. A man wrote a book for a small circle of friends, perhaps even for his own private edification. It passed in hand-written copies from reader to reader, and anyone who thought he could improve on what thus fell into his hands, scrupled not to recast and even to re-write. Thus books were made out of books; and authors, if they did not appropriate the works of others entire, yet never hesitated to borrow incidents, episodes, descriptions of men's appearance and character, and to weave these loans into their own works. Thus a medieval biographer, writing a life of Charlemagne, would copy out the picture of an ancient Cæsar, drawn by Suetonius eight centuries before, and make it do duty for his hero, even as the later Ephesians, when they desired to honour the patriots of their age, would chisel the name of an ancient celebrity off his statue in the public square and replace it with the name of the more modern celebrity.

We must not, then, condemn the authors of the first and third gospels for appropriating the text and matter of the second ; for, in doing so, they merely followed the literary custom, as of their own, so of preceding and subsequent ages. It is more important to remark that, having before us in Mc the main authority used by the two later evangelists, we can judge of their literary methods and discern how they used their sources. By way of example, let us take the section of triple text, transcribed above, and verse by verse compare Mt and Lc with Mc, their common source. In verse 13 of Mc the itinerary of Jesus is given : he went forth *unto the sea.* The copyists skip this detail, as they do the point that the people were flocking to Jesus to hear his teaching. Lc adopts the phrase that *he went forth ;* Mt the other, *as he passed along.*

In verse 14 both omit the name of the officer's father, *Alphæus,* and Mt substitutes *Matthew* for *Leveis* (or Levi). Lc improves on his source by explaining that Leveis *left everything,* with proper apostolic renunciation of this world's goods. It does not appear, however, that he gave up his house and cook.

In verse 16, for Mc's *scribes of the Pharisees* Lc substitutes *Pharisees and their scribes,* Mt *the Pharisees* simply, omitting *scribes.* In Lc it is the disciples who are reproved in the second person plural for eating with publicans, etc. In Mc the complaint is addressed to the disciples that Jesus does so, and here Mt is faithful to Mc. Lastly, in v. 17, Mt introduces the saying *But go ye*, etc., and Lc makes the addition *to repentance*. On the whole, Mt and Lc reproduce their source in this passage with a fair amount of fidelity; but both omit touches of local colour, and neither scruples to amplify and add to the utterances of Jesus. Mt in particular changes the name Levi into Matthew.

I would invite my readers to continue this line of research for themselves. It only needs a coloured pencil and a sixpenny text of the gospels. Let them also ask themselves what becomes of the dogma of the literal inspiration of the Scriptures, in view of the light which such research throws on the way in which at least two of our gospels were compiled.

So far, then, we have established that Mt and Lc had at least one source in common—namely, Mark. But if we take a blue pencil, and underline the matter that Lc and Mt have in common, but which is not to be found in Mc, we detect in them a second common source, which critics to-day distinguish as the non-Marcan document. Let us choose as an example the story of the temptation of Jesus after his baptism. Lc and Mt relate the first part of this story in the words of Mc, but then continue it from a non-Marcan document which told the story at somewhat greater length. This document is lost, but we can reconstruct it out of what Lc and Mt jointly have preserved of it. In printing their texts let us distinguish by italics as before what they borrow from Mark, and by capital letters what they severally copied from the other or non-Marcan source, which to-day is lost to us, and only recognisable by a comparison of them.

THE GOSPELS COMPILATIONS

Matthew.	Mark.	Luke.
1. Then Jesus was led up *into the wilderness* by the *spirit*, to be *tempted* by the devil, (2) and having fasted *forty days* and forty nights, afterwards he hungered.	12. And immediately the spirit sends him forth into the wilderness. 13. And he was in the wilderness forty days being tempted by Satan, and he was with the wild beasts, and the angels ministered unto him.	1. But Jesus full of a holy *spirit* returned from the Jordan, and was led in the *spirit* in *the wilderness*, (2) *forty days* being *tempted* by the devil; and he ate nothing in those days, and when they were completed he hungered.

Matthew.

3. And the tempter came up and said to him, If thou art Son of God, speak that these stones become loaves.

4. But he answered and said, It is written, not by a loaf alone shall man live, but by every word issuing forth by mouth of God.

5. Then the devil taketh him along into the holy city, and stood him upon the wing of the temple, (6) and says to him, If thou art son of God, cast thyself down. For it is written that he shall give his angels charge concerning thee, and on hands they shall bear thee up, lest ever thou dash thy foot against a stone.

7. Jesus said to him, Again it is written, thou shalt not tempt the Lord thy God. (8) Again the devil taketh him along on to a mountain high exceedingly and shows him all the kingdoms of the universe and the glory of them. (9) And he said to him, These things all will I give thee, if thou wilt fall down and worship me. (10) Then saith to him Jesus, Begone, Satan! For it is written, the Lord thy God shalt thou worship, and him alone shalt thou serve. (11) Then the devil letteth him go, and Lo, *angels* came up and *ministered unto him*.

Luke.

3. But the devil said to him, If thou art son of God, speak to this stone that it become a loaf.

4. And Jesus made answer to him, it is written that not by loaf alone shall man live.

5. And having led him up he showed him all the kingdoms of the world in a moment of time.

6. And the devil said to him, to thee will I give all this authority and the glory of them, for to me it hath been given over, and to whomever I will, I give it.

7. Thou then, if thou wilt worship before me, it shall all be thine. (8) And Jesus, answering, said to him, It is written, Thou shalt worship the Lord thy God, and him alone shalt thou serve. (9) But he led him into Jerusalem and stood him on the wing of the temple, and said to him, If thou art son of God, cast thyself down hence. (10) For it is written that he shall give his angels charge concerning thee to guard thee, (11) and that on hands they shall bear thee up, lest ever thou dash thy foot against a stone. (12) And Jesus answering him said, It hath been said, thou shalt not tempt the Lord thy God. (13) And having completed every temptation, the devil quitted him for a season.

Here we see that Mt and Lc have copied out from a document, which is lost to us, a longer form of the story than Mc supplied them with. In this longer form of the legend Jesus is tempted by hunger, and there is a *crescendo* of temptations, more clearly brought out by Mt than by Lc, who inverts the second and third. In Lc verse 6 the words *of them* refer back to *kingdoms*, which he omits, substituting *all this authority*. Here again, then, Mt has best preserved the underlying source. Mt has a thought in his verse 4 which Lc omits, and Lc in his verse 6 is careful to inform us that all temporal power belongs to the devil. In Mt verse 8 the devil takes Jesus up into a mountain, and in verse 10 the words *Begone Satan* are peculiar to this evangelist. In verse 11 Mt brings the episode to an end in the same way as Mc, whereas Lc sends the devil away for a time only, as if he was to come back again.

When we have deducted from Mt and Lc all the matter which they borrow in common from these two sources, there is left very little peculiar to the Gospel of either. They have, in fact, both compiled their Gospels, all except an insignificant portion, from two older Greek documents, of which the one remains to us and is called Mc's gospel, while the other has perished. This second document contained the stories of the Baptism and Temptation, and some few other episodes; but it mainly contained moral sayings and aphorisms. Out of it came the so-called Lord's Prayer and the Sermon on the Mount. Many of the aphorisms must have been loosely strung together in it, for Mt, as we shall see later on more in detail, often sets a saying in one context or background, Lc in another. It is possible also that Mt included matter from this last source which Lc left out, and *vice versâ*, just as the one of them sometimes keeps from Mc matter which the other omits. It is probable also that Lc had a third source from which he took a few striking parables peculiar to himself. Why Lc— who, at the beginning of his Gospel, assures us that "many had taken in hand to draw up a narrative" (of Christ's ministry)—should have used just the two earlier documents used by the author of the first Gospel, we do not know. If we had not his assurance, we should naturally presume that only those two were in circulation in the districts or district in which they moved.

It follows that the first and third gospels are not original works, but mere compilations of earlier books; and the compilers have certainly compressed or expanded one of their sources—viz., Mc—as they pleased, and, in not a few cases, have tried to improve upon it by omitting traits of simple humanity which still remain therein, but which offended a later generation as being out of keeping with the growing legend of the divinity of Jesus. The old traditional view that the Gospels are original documents, independently thrown off by their authors in the heat of inspiration, must be given up; nor is it any longer held even by divines accounted orthodox.

CHAPTER III.

MARK

BUT, before noticing in detail the modifications of Mark's narrative indulged in by the two other evangelists, it is well to examine a little more in detail this Gospel itself, the earliest sketch of the incidents of Jesus's ministry which we possess.

It begins with a notice of John, a Jewish ascetic whose activity is independently attested by the Jewish historian Josephus, and who, some time in the third decade of the Christian era, "baptised in the wilderness and preached the baptism of repentance for the remission of sins." It was widely believed that the Messiah was about to appear and restore in Palestine the golden age of the Jews. Those who had not repented and washed away their offences against the Mosaic law would be excluded from the restored kingdom of David. Mark relates that penitents flocked to hear John's preaching from all over Judæa and from Jerusalem, that they confessed their sins and washed themselves in the cleansing waters of Jordan.

Among those who thus came to be baptised was one Jesus from Nazareth, of Galilee. As he went up out of the water, he saw the heavens rent asunder, and the spirit, as a dove, descend upon him; and a voice from heaven cried, "Thou art my beloved son, in thee am I well pleased." Thus Jesus became a vehicle of the divine spirit, and was acclaimed from heaven as the Messiah, or son of God. His temptation by the evil one, of which the narrative has been given above, at p. 25, immediately followed upon his baptism. Having triumphed over the devil, Jesus was now ripe for the work of his ministry, and, John having been imprisoned or slain by Herod Antipas, Jesus took up his master's work, proceeded to Galilee, and began to preach. We learn nothing of his age, appearance, or previous life, nor why he went to Galilee. We do hear, however, that, instead of proclaiming himself to be the Messiah, he merely delivered the same message as John, saying, *The time is fulfilled, and the kingdom of God is at hand; repent ye.*

The next episode is the call of four fishermen of Galilee, Simon (Peter), and Andrew, James and John, the two sons of Zebedee, to be disciples. Jesus sees them in boats casting their nets, and, without preface or ceremony, says: *Come ye after me, and I will make you fishers of men.* Whereupon they abruptly forsake their nets and follow him.

This anecdote cannot be from the lips of an eye-witness, but has been arranged as a background against which Jesus can utter his aphorism about fishers of men. In its childish simplicity, this story of the call of the four chief apostles reminds me of a question once put to me by my little boy, aged four. "Father, how did you come to know Uncle Gus?" I hesitated a moment to reply, and the child promptly supplied his own solution: "I suppose you met him in the street one day, and spoke to him, and liked him so much that you asked him in to tea." That is a child's way of making friends with other children; and Mark's idea of how Jesus made disciples is almost equally naïve.

The first act of Jesus, now that he has got a following, is to expel an unclean spirit from one who was possessed. Spirits were popularly supposed to have second sight, and know more than human beings; and, accordingly, this spirit, when Jesus approached, recognised him at first sight and cried out: *What have we to do with thee, thou Jesus of Nazareth? Art thou come to destroy us? I know thee who thou art, the holy one of God.*

The literary motive of the writer is clear. Jesus had been acclaimed as the Son and Messiah at his baptism by a voice which was only heard by himself; now he is recognised as such by the devils or evil spirits, who henceforth are arrayed against him as a counter kingdom of evil. The "*authority*" he here displays over the demons who obey him excites general comment, "*and the report of him went out straightway everywhere into all the region of Galilee round about.*"

This interview with the evil spirits had taken place in the public synagogue at Capernaum on a sabbath. On the evening of the same day Jesus repairs to the house of Simon and Andrew, and heals Simon's mother-in-law of a fever; and at even *they brought to him all that were sick or had devils*, to be cured. But this time "*he suffered not the devils to speak, because they knew him.*" So anxious was he to hide the fact that he was the promised Messiah.

Whence this reticence on the part of Jesus? We are not told; but during the next few chapters, in which the typical teaching of Jesus and a number of cures and miracles are given, the same silence is enforced. "*See thou say nothing to any man*," he says to the leper he had healed (Mark i. 44). And then, in open contradiction of himself, he adds, "*but go thy way, and shew thyself to the priest, and offer for thy cleansing the things which Moses commanded for a testimony unto them.*" If to the priest it was to be thus solemnly attested that the leper was cleansed, and so fit to be admitted afresh into the synagogue, how could others not hear of it? We are therefore not surprised to learn that the leper at once "*went out and began to publish it much and to spread abroad the matter, insomuch that Jesus could no more openly enter the city, but remained outside in desert places.*"

In the last verses of ch. iv. Jesus stills a storm on the lake of Galilee, and the same miracle is repeated at the close of ch. vi. The interval between these two great nature miracles, which we shall presently discuss more in detail, is filled up with two stories, the one of them telling of the grotesque miracle of the Gadarene swine, the other of the raising from the dead of Jairus' daughter. These miracles are the chief thaumaturgic feats of Jesus during his Galilean ministry. Yet he wishes them to be kept quiet, and we read, as before, that "*he charged them much that no man should know this.*" Nevertheless, when in the next chapter he returns with his disciples to his own country, we are told that his fame had spread thither, so that many were astonished, and asked how he came to work such mighty works. So regularly does our author stultify himself!

The cure of a woman with a bloody flux is thrust into the midst of the Jairus story, which is followed in ch. vi. by a visit of Jesus to his own home, where his own family flout him. There follows, first the giving of a commission to the twelve apostles, already named in ch. iii. 14-19; then the story of John's beheadal (incidentally suggested by a mention of Herod and of his attitude towards Jesus), and then a first edition of the miracle of feeding thousands of people on nothing at all. Mark thus crowds incident on incident, miracle on miracle, into this first sabbath day at Capernaum, but is silent about the events of the next few months which Jesus spent in the same region. It would seem as if he only cared to sketch a few striking scenes appropriate to the delivery by Jesus of certain aphorisms, mostly directed against the pharisees and scribes. Such are the following:—

> The Son of Man [*i.e.*, any man whatever] hath power on earth to forgive sins.
>
> They that are whole have no need of a physician, but they that are sick: I came not to call the righteous, but sinners.
>
> The sabbath was made for man, and not man for the sabbath: so that the Son of Man [*i.e.*, any man whatever] is lord even of the sabbath.
>
> A prophet is not without honour, save in his own country, and among his own kin, and in his own house.

We have noticed above how constantly in this Gospel Jesus enjoins those he cured to let no man hear thereof, and it is probably historically true that he began his career by merely proclaiming the kingdom of heaven to be at hand and the Messiah about to appear. It would seem as if he only gradually acquired confidence in himself, and finally accepted the conviction that he was himself the Messiah only when his disciples and followers forced the *rôle* upon him. If there is any truth in the picture given in all three Gospels of John the Baptist— and it is in a manner attested by Josephus—then he, too, had some trouble to persuade the enthusiastic crowds who flocked to hear him preach that he was not himself the Messiah, but only his forerunner and herald. These injunctions of secrecy, therefore, are intelligible as part of a tradition already waning that Jesus did not make his *début* as Messiah, but assumed the *rôle* little by little; the other evangelists servilely copy them out from Mark, yet stultify them by insisting that Jesus was from the first acclaimed as Messiah both by himself and by others. They therefore leave no room for growth and development in his own and other men's ideas, and are, so far, less entitled to credence than Mark.

Another characteristic of Mark's narrative is harder to explain—this, namely, that he constantly assigns, as the reason why Jesus taught in parables, the desire not to be understood by those who heard him. Thus, when the disciples ask him, in private, the meaning of the parable of the Sower, in ch. iv., he prefaces his explanation with these words: "*Unto you is given the mystery of the kingdom of God; but unto them that are without all things are done in parables: that seeing they may see, and not take in; and hearing they may hear, and not understand; lest haply they should turn again, and it should be forgiven them.*"

In other words, Jesus used the parable in order to conceal his meaning from his hearers; and though, like Jonah, he taught repentance to his generation, he was, nevertheless, as anxious as was that hero of senseless fable that his hearers should, after all, not repent and become worthy of the messianic kingdom of promise.[1] And yet, in ch. vi. 34, we read that on

[1] The book of Jonah was favourite reading in the days when the Gospels took shape. As Jonah's preaching was a sign to his genera-

another occasion Jesus "*saw a great multitude and had compassion on them, because they were as sheep not having a shepherd: and he began to teach them many things*"; and in ch. iv. 33 it is indicated that many understood him, for such is the sense of the words, "*with many such parables spake he the word unto them, as they were able to hear it: and without a parable spake he not unto them. But privately to his own disciples he explained all things.*"

The pretence of esoteric mystery ascribed to Jesus in the first quoted passage is surely as stupid as it is unworthy of a teacher who, if he used parable at all, undoubtedly used it as the best way of getting at the hearts and understandings of the poor and ignorant. The additional explanation, that it was to prevent his hearers from turning again and being saved, betokens on the part of the narrator an almost incredible smallness of mind. It is worthy of Mark, who elsewhere would fain persuade his readers that the withering of

tion, so was that of Jesus; and, as Jonah was in the belly of the fish three days and three nights, so for a like space of time Jesus lay in the tomb. It may be one of the Scriptures to which Paul appealed when, in 1 Cor. xv. 4, he declares that Jesus *was buried and raised on the third day according to the Scriptures*. The saying that *the Son of Man must be killed and after three days rise again*, which Mark viii. 31 puts into the lips of Jesus, probably had the same origin. It is therefore probable that Mark's grotesque fancy that Jesus taught in parables, not in order to be understood of the Jews, but in order that he might not be understood, was partly suggested by the legend of Jonah, whose story was, briefly, as follows: Jonah iii. 1 foll.—And the word of the Lord came unto Jonah....saying, Arise, go unto Nineveh, that great city, and preach unto it the preaching that I bid thee. So Jonah arose....and began to enter into the city....and he cried, and said, Yet forty days, and Nineveh shall be overthrown. And the people of Nineveh believed God; and they proclaimed a fast and put on sackcloth.....And God saw their works, that they turned from their evil way; and God repented of the evil, which he said he would do unto them; and he did it not. But it displeased Jonah exceedingly, and he was angry.....And the Lord said, Doest thou well to be angry?....Should I not have pity on Nineveh, that great city?....

a fig-tree, in consequence of curses hurled at it by Jesus for not bearing fruit out of season (Mark xi. 13), is a palmary example of prayer answered and faith in God rewarded! Here we have jarring notes, vulgar dissonances, in the narrative, that may or may not have marred it in its original form. For, as it stands, the Gospel of Mark is a redaction only, and a rather clumsy one, too, of earlier narratives, taken without acknowledgment from some earlier writers, just as the first and third evangelists took from Mark.

The crisis and turning-point in the career of Jesus is supposed by Mark to have been reached when Peter, in answer to Jesus's question, "*Whom do men say that I am?*" replied, "*Thou art the Christ.*" Jesus instantly "*charged them that they should tell no man of him.*"

So much is clear about the intentions of this writer: he wishes to convince his readers that Jesus was Messiah and Son of God. First the voice from heaven, at the baptism, assures Jesus himself of this; then the demons recognise him as such. His works of power equally manifest him. His teachings, as explained to the inner circle of his disciples, prepare their minds for the great truth. Then Peter, as spokesman of his fellows, affirms it; and the cycle of evidence is completed at the Transfiguration (in ch. ix.), when the three favoured apostles—Peter, James, and John—having accompanied him "*up into a high mountain,*" see him in a nimbus of glory conversing with Elijah and Moses. Supreme assurance of the great truth is now vouchsafed to them also, for a voice from heaven (this time addressed to them) declares: "*This is my beloved Son. Hear ye him.*" But here once more the accustomed caution is enforced by Jesus thus: "*And as they were coming down from the mountain he charged them that they should tell no man what things they had seen, save when the Son of Man should have risen again from the dead.*"

Mark would have us discern in Jesus from the outset that Messiahship which was only gradually recognised by the disciples, and which, to the Jewish contemporaries of Jesus, was never revealed at all.

What is behind all this mystification? Mark does not expressly take us into his confidence, but the following explanation has been suggested. The Messiahship was a Jewish conception, for it was the future Messiah's *rôle* to liberate the Jews from the moral servitude of sin and from physical subjection to Gentiles. It was, therefore, a terrible impediment to the diffusion of the Christian religion among Gentiles, that the Jews, almost *en masse*, would not hear of the claims advanced in favour of Jesus. The earliest literature of the Church was mainly written to prove that Jesus had fulfilled the Scriptures, and therefore *was* the Messiah. Now Mark—as his frequent explanations of Jewish names and customs prove—wrote for Gentiles; and Gentiles might well ask: "How can we be expected to believe that Jesus is Messiah, when the very Jews as whose Messiah he came deny it?" Mark's answer is, in effect, as follows: The voice in Jordan proclaimed him Messiah, but only to himself. The demons, through their supernatural insight, detected him, but "*he suffered them not to speak, because they knew him.*" Similarly, his miracles and cures were not to be divulged. He taught in parables, lest the Jews should understand him and turn again. Least of all might his disciples speak of what they saw on the mount of transfiguration or reveal his Messiahship, patent at last to themselves. This is all by way of explaining why the Jews, as a race, did not accept Jesus as their Messiah. Jesus had never wished them to do so, nor given them a chance. The expedient is clumsy, and, no doubt, violates the documents and traditions which the evangelist inherited, and according to the original tenour of which the miracles and teachings of Jesus excited the utmost enthusiasm and the most widespread rumour among the people. Thus Mark stultifies himself in every paragraph, and, incidentally, supplies the Jews with the amplest justification of their negative attitude. It is an apologetic method so favourable to them that no subsequent Christian writer ever resorted to it.

The above is probably the true explanation of the atmosphere of secrecy and mystery in which—as against the Jews, though not as against his readers and Jesus's own disciples—Mark seeks to shroud the sayings and doings of Jesus. At the same time there may be a kernel of historical truth in it all; for what other motive, except fear of Herod Antipas, the murderer of his master John, can have led Jesus to quit that prince's tetrarchate (in which lay Galilee and Capernaum), and to migrate into the neighbouring province of Herod's brother Philip and into the Decapolis? Messiahs were many in that age, and met with a cruel fate when they fell into the hands of Roman governors or of members of the Herodian dynasty friendly to Rome. Jesus may well have shrunk from assuming the name and *rôle* of Messiah.

With this migration, anyhow, begins the second period of Jesus's ministry; and it is, perhaps, Mark's own literary device, as he introduced the Capernaum ministry with popular questionings as to who and what Jesus was, so to begin the epoch of his wanderings with similar questions, put first into Herod's lips (Mark vi. 14) and then into those of Jesus (Mark viii. 27). By this time Jesus has reached the town of Cæsarea, at the foot of Mount Hermon, in Philip's province. Peter is now made to answer the question; and his answer is confirmed from heaven in the transfiguration scene. But it is intimated that, when Peter answered Jesus and said, "*Thou art the Christ,*" he still regarded the Messiah as a warrior after the style of Mohammed, commissioned by heaven to head a successful revolt against the Romans to liberate Israel. In Acts i. 6, after the Resurrection, the first thought of the faithful is still that the Lord will now at last *restore the kingdom to Israel*, and achieve the task of a purely Jewish Messiah. This was the ideal of a Messiah which filled Peter's mind, and led him openly to rebuke Jesus when the latter, by way of answer to his recognition of him, "*began to teach them that the Son of Man must suffer many things, and be rejected by the elders and the chief priests and the scribes, and be killed, and after three days rise again.*" Jesus, when he draws near Jerusalem, after wandering through the region beyond Jordan, repeats this prophecy in greater detail, declaring even that the Son of Man shall be condemned to death and *delivered up to the Gentiles, who shall mock him, and shall spit upon him, and shall scourge him, and shall kill him, and after three days he shall rise again.*

These specific prophecies were not, of course, uttered by Jesus, but are put into his mouth after the event by the author or authors of our document. That the followers of Jesus, whenever they first acclaimed him as Messiah, intended the title in its military or martial sense is certain, from the above passage of Mark as from many others. Even after the Crucifixion they still believed that he would come again and perform the warlike feats popularly expected of the Messiah.

From the moment of his being acclaimed as Messiah by Peter, Jesus is repeatedly made to speak of himself in the third person—as *the Son of Man*. About this title's real meaning there is much uncertainty, and the following account of it is only probable:—

In the first section of the Gospel of Mark this phrase, the Son of Man, seems to bear its ordinary Semitic meaning of a human being—man in general; but in the transfiguration episode, and throughout the rest of the Gospel, it bears the meaning already assigned to it in the Book of Daniel (some 200 years B.C.), wherein (ch. vii. 13) we read as follows:—"*I saw in the night visions, and behold, there came with the clouds of heaven one like unto a son of man, and he came even to the Ancient of days, and they brought him near before him. And there was given him dominion and glory, and a kingdom, that all the peoples and nations and languages should serve him: his dominion is an everlasting dominion, which shall not pass away, and his kingdom that which shall not be destroyed.*"

In the last section of this Gospel Jesus is very pointedly identified with Daniel's phantom form. He has been arrested, and all his followers have fled, even Peter denying all knowledge of him. The high priest challenges him to declare who he is: "*Art thou the Christ, the son of the blessed one? And Jesus said, I am; and ye shall see the Son of Man sitting at the right hand of power, and coming with the clouds of heaven*" (Mark xiv. 62).

And in an earlier passage (xiii. 24), where Mark is describing in words borrowed from a lost Jewish apocalypse what is to occur at the end of the world, we read what the Son of Man is to achieve when he comes again : "*But in those days, after that tribulation, the sun shall be darkened, and the moon shall not give her light, and the stars shall fall from heaven, and the powers that are in the heavens shall be shaken. And then shall they see the Son of Man coming in clouds with great power and glory. And then shall he send forth the angels, and shall gather together his elect from the four winds, from the uttermost part of the earth to the uttermost part of heaven.*"

In such passages as the above we get a glimpse of the hopes and aspirations of the Jews in Palestine, where the rule of Rome pressed most heavily upon them and was most acutely felt to be a violation of their traditions and religion. But the same daydreams floated also before the mind of the Jews of the Dispersion, and in a work, entitled *About the Curses*,[1] of the Alexandrian Jew Philo, we have a vivid record of them, which has all the more value for us because, as a rule, the messianic aspirations of the Jews are voiced in apocryphal works like the Book of Enoch and the Testaments of the Twelve Patriarchs, of which we can fix with any precision neither the age nor the authorship. Here is a testimony, however, written, it would seem, not before 35 A.D. and not after 42 A.D. by a Jew of Alexandria deeply versed in old Greek philosophy and literature, and so Hellenised that he could not understand his own tongue. Yet he shared in the Zionist dreams of his compatriots. In Palestine

---

[1] *De Exsecrationibus.*

he sees realised in all their dreadful intensity the
curses proclaimed in Deut. xxviii. against those who
break the statutes and law of Jehovah. Fire and
sword, hunger and panic, drought and disease, the
men carried captive to far lands, the women the toys
of their captors—in all this the pious Jew discerned
the wrath of God against a chosen people who had
turned away from him to worship idols, and neglected
to observe the sabbaths. But, although the stalks are
consumed, yet the root remains, and Philo dreams of
a time when his countrymen, overcome with shame and
remorse, will be converted, will upbraid themselves for
their errors, will confess and acknowledge with purified
hearts the sins they have committed against themselves, and win afresh the goodwill of their God and
saviour, who, from the first, implanted reason in them,
and made them kinsmen of his own Logos or Word. The
sudden conversion of their Jewish serfs to virtue and
goodness will so impress their Roman oppressors and
masters that the latter will set them free, ashamed to
hold in captivity men so openly superior to themselves.
Forthwith, as if by concerted arrangement and in one
day, all Jews enslaved even at the ends of the earth
will be freed beyond all expectation. Those who a
little before were dispersed over Greece and Italy,
over islands and mainland, will rise up as one man,
and hurry, one from here, another from there, to the
appointed spot, led on like guests by a vision of a face
too divine to be accounted merely human, invisible to
others, and revealed to them that are saved alone.
In that moment the lost and erring Israelites are
reconciled to their divine father through his mercy
and through the intercession of their holy ancestors,
who, as disembodied spirits, offer up to him, in spirit

and truth, adoration and prayers, which cannot fail of their effect. But what shall most provoke the grace and pity of the offended God is the change of heart in those now led on to a fresh covenant. Out of a trackless wilderness they have, with the least difficulty, found a path and set their face to their true goal, which is nothing else than to please God, as children may please their father. And when they reach their destined goal the cities, erewhile desolate, flourish again, and the earth, that was sterile, brings forth her fruits in abundance. And the change is wrought all on a sudden, for God will turn his curses against the enemies of the repentant race who were all jubilant over its calamities, making them a cause of bitter jibes and reviling.[1]

Philo's language, of course, is largely a paraphrase of the eloquent chapters of Deuteronomy; yet he writes as if he believed that these chapters had a present application. A pious Jew, he resented the Roman rule, the brutal violation of his temple, the coarse

---

[1] In yet another passage—namely, in the treatise *About Rewards and Punishments*—Philo reveals the same thought. He dwells on the necessity for a really good man to follow the holy laws every day of his life. "If there be but one such man in a city, he will tower above that city; if the entire city be equally good with him, it will stand out among the inhabitants of the land around; but, if a race exhibits such virtue, it will overtop all other races, as the head overtops the body to the eye of the beholder, and will not merely enjoy a commanding reputation, but will benefit all who witness." He goes on to remark that the spectacle of a holy race devoted to the practice of the law will stimulate surrounding races to emulate its example, and after a little uses the following significant words: "As then God could easily bring together men settled afar in the remotest regions by a single word of command, and gather them from the ends of the world into any place he chooses, so with the intelligence which, from long error, has utterly lost its way and been overcome by pleasure and lust, the Saviour can no less in his pity easily bring it back from the trackless waste into the way of salvation," and so forth. Here he distinctly glances at the current belief that the faithful among the Jews were to be miraculously restored to their land.

assaults on his religion by such satirists as Apion. He had no confidence in the power of the Jews to get rid of the alien by force of arms. His only hope was in a supernatural liberator, descending from heaven and rescuing from their oppressors the chosen race of Israel. But Israel must first repent and fulfil all righteousness —that is, discharge faithfully all the works of the law; in particular, keep the sabbaths holy and observe the rule of circumcision. Then, and not before, will the heavenly Messiah appear and establish on earth the kingdom of David. No material preparation for this blessed consummation is of any use. The kingdom of heaven cannot be taken, or rather won and established, by force, but only by moral and social reformation. Only Jahveh and his messenger, the Messiah, can establish it by a sort of *coup d'état* from the clouds. When these roll away the Jews will be seen in their resplendent utopia, their enemies and oppressors in Tartarus. Supernatural signs, an enumeration of which, from some Jewish apocalypse, is in Mark xiii. put into the mouth of Jesus, will precede the Messiah's advent, but it will not come as any result of an historical evolution.

When Jesus died on the cross the confidence of his followers in him, the belief that he would restore the kingdom of David, suffered an eclipse. But this was only temporary, and it revived in their breasts when, in Galilee and elsewhere, he appeared to them in their dreams and visions as a heavenly figure transported to heaven like Enoch or Elias.

We cannot to-day trace out with any certainty the development of ideas in the earliest Christian community of Galilee and Jerusalem. It would seem, however, as if the disciples who fled back into Galilee when Jesus was arrested and condemned were first roused from the despair which had overtaken them by visions of their Messiah raised from the dead and alive in heaven. That these visions were subjective only is certain, from the fact that they were moulded by ancient ideas of heaven and earth and hades, and still more from Luke's admission, Acts x. 41, that God, when he resuscitated Jesus, manifested him, not to all the people, but only to a few pre-ordained persons. If we can believe (what all the Gospels again and again affirm) that Jesus himself asserted that he was to be raised from the dead after three days—that is to say, before his spirit definitely quitted the vicinity of his corpse (and according to ancient belief it did not do so until three days had expired)— we need go no further in search of a psychological explanation of their visions. They were begotten of a belief which Jesus himself held and implanted in them. But, although their confidence in Jesus, so rudely shaken, was thus restored, there was, nevertheless, as yet no sign of the restoration of the kingdom of Israel. Jesus had been promoted to a place of dignity in heaven; but the dreams of Jewish patriotism were left unfulfilled. Hope, once resuscitated, could not again be extinguished. No real enthusiast ever admits that he has been deceived. He must needs fortify himself, and rise to still higher flights. Accordingly, the leaders of Christian speculation discovered, on the one hand, that it was predicted by Isaiah and other ancient prophets that the Messiah was to be persecuted, to suffer and be slain by the unjust (perhaps Jesus himself taught as much), and, on the other hand, the Messiah so slain was to come again in glory, as Daniel's Son of Man, to punish his enemies and reward his just ones. Thus the heavenly Messiah was to make good the defects which Peter in the scene at Cæsarea Philippi discovers in the suffering earthly one. The belief in a speedy return of Jesus the Messiah in glory was one of the few real ties between Paul and the other apostles. When exactly after the Crucifixion it arose we do not know, but it was very early and very general; for Paul attests that the commonest form of Christian prayer in his day was *marāna tha*—*i.e.*, Come thou, O Lord; and the belief left its impress in a hundred ways on the manners, institutions, and liturgies of the earliest Church.

The last six chapters (xi.–xvi.) of Mark contain the story of the Crucifixion, told with so much detail that it fills as many pages as the entire year of the Galilean ministry. Jesus's movements are recorded day by day, and from the moment of his arrest events are related hour by hour according to the watches of day and night. But, although the narrative is so detailed, it is often very obscure. Jesus is crucified on the Paschal feast-day, although, two days only before the feast, the chief priests and scribes have arranged to take and kill him *before* the said feast begins, "*lest haply there shall be a tumult of the people*" (Mark xiv. 2). If he was really crucified on the feast-day, it follows that the last supper was the Passover meal. If, however, the priests and scribes carried out their programme, it was not.

Another inconsequence in the narrative is this: Jesus is ostensibly condemned by the priests as *king of the Jews*, and because he owned himself to be the Messiah, the son of the blessed one. And yet it was no offence to the mind of pious Jews that a prominent teacher should give himself out to be the Messiah. Indeed, his doing so was as eminently calculated to win their sympathies as it was likely to procure his condemnation by a Roman administrator as a mischievous political agitator. The real Jewish gravamen against Jesus is hinted at by Mark, but relegated to the background. It was his prophecy of the destruction of the temple—an event which any clear-sighted observer of the growing hostility between Jew and Roman must have foreseen.

I feel that any dispassionate critic, trained in the study of ancient historical documents, will agree with the following appreciation of Mark's Gospel; it is that of the *doyen* of Old Testament scholars, J. Wellhausen, who thus sums up his impressions of the first five chapters:—

> In the same measure as the first day in Capernaum is crowded with incidents, the year in Capernaum and the whole Galilean epoch is barren of them. It has to its account half-a-dozen miracles and a handful of other events. In chs. ii. and iii. a few weighty and more or less paradoxical aphorisms are grouped together, rather because they resemble each other than because they were uttered at one time. Each of them is elicited by some definite incident or occasion which is carefully described, and they are all of them aimed at the Scribes or Pharisees or other persons who came into conflict with Jesus, not excepting his own family in Nazareth. Upon these follow in ch. iv. the parables of the Sower, and a longer address to the people delivered from the boat in which he sat on the lake. Without any change of scene there follows closely a group of three miracles, of which one is wrought during the passage over the lake, a second after landing on the other side, a third on returning to

MARK 47

Capernaum (iv. 35–v. 43). That is all. Names of persons are seldom given, even Jairus being omitted in D.[1] Among the *dramatis personæ* Jesus is the only one who properly speaks or acts. His opponents merely draw him out; his disciples are supernumeraries. But of his comings in and goings forth, how he supported himself, how he lived, ate and drank, of his intercourse with his intimates, we learn nothing. It is related that he taught on the sabbath in the synagogue, but we are not allowed to form an idea of what he taught; we only get a hint of what he said outside the synagogue, generally in view of some particular incident which required him to say something. Ordinary events are not recorded, only a few extraordinary ones. This cannot be wholly explained by supposing that Mark was not writing for the instruction of future generations, and therefore left unsaid incidents with which, as being almost contemporary, his first readers were well acquainted. Even if we allow for this, the meagreness of the tradition is remarkable. From our verdict that the Gospel of Mark, as a whole, lacks the characteristics of a genuine history we cannot exempt the story of the Passion. Our curiosity is left unsatisfied. Nothing is motived in it, nothing explained as arising out of what goes before. There is no background, no causal connection of one incident with another. Of chronology there is no trace; nowhere is a fixed date given. Clear geographical indications, it is true, are supplied, and the scene is, as a rule, depicted, though too often in a loose way, as taking place in some house or other, on a mountain, in a lone place. But there is as little attempt to trace out what happened from place to place, to supply an itinerary, as there is

---

[1] The Cambridge uncial codex, which belonged to Beza.

to trace it from point to point of time. The scene shifts from place to place; but rarely, if at all, do we learn through what places Jesus passed on the way. Particular narratives are often graphic and lively, yet without owing anything to fictitious or merely rhetorical devices; these, however, are mostly strung together as anecdotes, *rari nantes in gurgite vasto*, and do not suffice as materials for a Life of Jesus. Nor do they leave on us the impression of their being based on accounts of people who, having eaten and drunk with him, had tried to impart to others a picture of his personality. Not that characteristic features are altogether wanting. He watches, for example, the people as they drop their money into the treasury. He knows men and men's hearts. Friend and enemy alike feel his superiority without his needing expressly to manifest it. He towers in solitude above those who surround him, even over his disciples, about whom one feels a certain surprise at his needing them at all. At the same time his is no cold, dispassionate nature; its note is warmth of moral feeling, intense sensibility. He yields to holy sympathy in his anger with the authorities of the people, and his sympathies are all with the humble. Sympathy and desire to succour inspire not only his miracles, but his teaching; he cares for soul and body of the needy, is at once teacher and physician, and, if needs be, host as well.

In Mark, however, this sympathy is seldom put forward as the motive for his miracles of healing; they are intended to be, before everything else, works of power, proving him to be the Messiah. Mark does not write *de vita et moribus Jesu*, nor is he concerned to give us an idea, still less a picture, of his person. His personality is lost sight of in his divine vocation, and Mark's only desire is to demonstrate that he was the Messiah. His disciples, it is true, only recognise him as such after the journey to Jerusalem has begun; but, in point of fact, he was Messiah from the baptism onwards—from the very beginning of his public ministry—and, if his own words did not prove him such, anyhow his works did so. They were seen, if not at the time, in any case in the sequel, to be the outcome of his Messianity; and it is in this guise that Mark presents them—namely, as examples which prove his thesis, and so have a place in the Gospel of Jesus Christ. It is true that he does not obtrude this point of view; and, in confirmation of the impression which, in his opinion, the mere facts ought to create, he uses only the utterances of the demons who see more clearly than the disciples. He never resorts to Matthew's argument from Scripture: This happened in order that the Scripture might be fulfilled, etc.

But it was hardly Mark himself who, from a mass of earlier material which he had before him, chose out such portions as suited his purpose, and rejected the rest. The oral tradition which he had at his disposal had already been winnowed and condensed under the guidance of the same point of view which inspires his own method. He passes over in silence this or that detail with which he could assume his readers to be acquainted—*e.g.*, the names of Jesus's parents. All the same, he has not left much that is genuinely historical for his successors to glean, and what they know, but he did not, is of doubtful value. The tradition which he exploits is relatively rich for Jerusalem, but on the other hand poor for Galilee; just as tradition about Mohammed is rich for Medina, but poor for Mecca. Here is a contrast which is inexplicable, supposing the tradition goes back to the original disciples. Nor are the Galilean narratives, as a rule, of such an internal texture that they can be referred to them. How can Peter have been the authority for the sudden call of the four fishers of men? How can he have testified to the walking on the waters, or to the driving of the evil spirits into the swine, to the healing of a woman with an issue of blood by the power attaching to a garment, of dumb and blind people by application of spittle? And why do we not learn more details, and those more credible, of the intercourse of the Master with his disciples? It would rather seem as if the narrative handed down in Mark did not proceed primarily from those who were in the intimacy of Jesus; for the most part it is rude and popular in character, as if it had long circulated from mouth to mouth among the people, and, in doing so, acquired the abrupt and forcible story-telling form in which we have it to-day. Popular taste delights in miracles and expulsions of demons, in the repeated recognition of Jesus by demons; and, as signs of Messiahship, such incidents were perhaps found by missionaries of the gospel to be the most telling and to "draw" most among the classes from which Christianity was chiefly recruited. Mark took up what tradition provided him with; but the arrangement of the material in three main sections is his work, and, of course, involved a process of editing. To this may be ascribed the introductions and conclusions, the transitions, short summaries, lists, as well as the names and descriptions of persons to whom Jesus is made to address his sayings.

Chapter IV.

STRUCTURE OF MARK'S GOSPEL

There are many stars in the firmament which to the eye appear single, but which, if we use a telescope, are seen to be not one star, but two, or even three. So, if we turn the telescope of critical analysis on to Mark's Gospel, it can be resolved, like a compound star, into two or even more documentary layers. In ancient documents compiled from earlier sources we regularly meet with what critics call textual doublets —that is, parallel narratives of the same incident, which have been copied out one after the other. That the same event, or group of events, should happen twice over is anyhow improbable; and, if the two narratives are to any extent in verbal agreement, we can be quite sure that we have got before us, not two distinct stories, but two textual variants of one and the same story, naïvely copied out, one after the other, by one who failed to see that his sources overlapped.

Mark's Gospel contains several such doublets; we are sure, therefore, that he was a compiler, who used up pre-existing documents which he had somehow come across. Let us take an example, setting in opposite columns the two parallel narratives, and italicising the two texts wherever, in the Greek, they verbally agree:—

52 STRUCTURE OF MARK'S GOSPEL

MARK vi. 30–45.

And the apostles gather themselves together unto Jesus; and they told him all things, whatsoever they had done and taught. And he saith to them, Hither ye yourselves apart unto a desert place and rest awhile. For many were they who were coming and going, *and they had no* opportunity even *to eat.* And they went away into a desert place in the boat apart. And they saw them going, and many recognised (them), and they ran hither and thither by land from all the cities and forestalled them. And he came forth and beheld a *great multitude, and he had compassion on them* because they were as sheep without a shepherd: and he began to teach them many things. And when the day was now far spent, his disciples came unto him, and said, *The place is desert,* and already the hour is late. Send them away, that they may go into the hamlets around, and villages, and buy themselves what to eat. But he answered and said to them, Give ye them to eat. And they say to him, Shall we go and buy for two hundred pennies loaves, and give to them to eat? *And he saith to them, How many loaves have ye?* Go and see. And when they knew, they say, Five, and two *fishes.* And he commanded them that all should recline company by company on the green grass. And they lay down rank by rank, by hundreds and by fifties. *And he took the* five *loaves* and the two fishes, and, *having* looked up to heaven, he *blessed* and *brake* the loaves; *and he gave to the disciples to set before them;* and the two fishes he divided to all. *And they all ate and were filled. And they* took up broken pieces, twelve

MARK viii. 1–13.

In those days, when there was again a *great multitude, and they had nothing to eat,* he called unto him his disciples, and saith unto them, *I have compassion on the multitude,* because they continue with me now three days, and have nothing to eat. And if I send them away fasting to their home, they will faint by the way; and some of them are come from far. And his disciples answered him, Whence shall one be able to fill these men with loaves here *in a desert place? And he asked them, How many loaves have ye?* And they said, Seven. *And he commandeth the multitude to lie down* on the ground: *and he took the* seven *loaves,* and having given thanks, he *brake and gave to his disciples, to set before them;* and they set them before the multitude. And they had a few small *fishes:* and having *blessed* them, he commanded to set these also before them. *And they did eat and were filled: and they took up of broken pieces* that remained over, seven *baskets. And they were* about four thousand : *and he sent them away. And straightway he entered into the boat* with *his disciples,* and came into the parts of Dalmanutha.....And he left them, and again *entering into* (the boat) departed *to the other side.*

basketfuls, and the same of the
fishes. *And they* that ate the
loaves *were* five thousand men.
And straightway he constrained
his disciples to *enter into the boat*,
and to go before him *unto the
other side* to Bethsaida, while *he
himself sent the multitude away.*

Here we have two versions of one and the same
story, told twice over in nearly identical words. The
only question which can be raised is, whether it was
Mark who thus juxtaposed them, or whether he
already found the doublet in an earlier source, and
copied it out. The latter is probably the case, for it
is unlikely that the compiler who found the two
narratives separately in two different sources, and
united them in one book, would place in Jesus's
mouth the following review of them both (Mark
viii. 19, 20): "When I brake the five loaves among
the five thousand, how many baskets full of broken
pieces took ye up? They say to him, Twelve. And
when the seven among the four thousand, how
many basketfuls of broken pieces took ye up? And
they say unto him, Seven. And he said unto them,
Do ye not yet understand?"

The author who invented this soliloquy must surely
have already found the double narrative before him.
If so, we can detect at least four stages of development
in this part of Mark's Gospel:—

1. A single original narrative of a miraculous
feeding of several thousand people in a desert place
off a handful of loaves and fishes.

2. This narrative, being carelessly copied, developes
into the two slightly different stories which we have
before us; in the one, Jesus is taken to Dalmanutha
after he has worked the miracle, in the other to

54 STRUCTURE OF MARK'S GOSPEL

Bethsaida. In the one he feeds 4,000, in the other 5,000.

3. A later compiler puts together these two parallel narratives in the same document, mistaking them for two stories of two separate events.

4. A still later author, Mark—or whoever redacted this Gospel in its present form—copied out the two-fold narrative and added the soliloquy in which Jesus insists on the separateness of the two miracles. It is a good example of how conversations were invented for Jesus and his disciples. It has been argued that for a document to develop through so many stages a long time, perhaps as many generations as there are stages, would be necessary. But no one would so argue who has studied the transmission of popular tales in the ages which preceded printing. Four years would be quite enough for the development above traced in the narrative of Mark; for all depends on how many were reading and copying out the book —in a word, on the amount of vogue it enjoyed; and that it was widely dispersed may be inferred from the fact of two evangelists independently using it.

It should be remarked also that the overlapping in this part of Mark is not confined to this miracle, but affects other incidents as well, as the following table of doublets shows :—

vi. 30–34 Feeding of the 5,000	=	viii. 1–9 Feeding of 4,000
vi. 45–52 Passage over lake to Bethsaida. Jesus walks on the water	=	viii. 9–13 Passage over lake to Dalmanutha. Cp. iv. 35–41
vii. 31–37 Cure of a deaf and dumb person by use of spittle	=	viii. 22–26 Cure of a blind man by use of spittle

Here are two sets of events which are parallel and follow in the same order, though in the passage to Dalmanutha there is no miracle of walking on the water. At vi. 53–vii. 30 other matter has been inserted in the first half of the doublet, as it has been at viii. 14–21 in the second half.

At first sight the miracle of healing the blind man, viii. 22–26, would appear to be a different miracle to vii. 31–37, where it is a deaf and dumb person who is healed; but if the two passages are set side by side, they are seen to be mere variants of one and the same original. Let us so set them, italicising them where they present a literary connection with each other:—

MARK vii. 31–36.	MARK viii. 22–26.
And again he went out from the borders of Tyre, and came through Sidon unto the sea of Galilee, through the midst of the borders of Decapolis. *And they bring to him one* that was deaf and had an impediment in his speech; *and they beseech him to lay his hand on him. And he took him* aside from the multitude privately, and put his fingers into his ears, and he *spat* and *touched* his tongue; *and he looked up* to heaven, and sighed, and saith unto him, Ephphatha, that is, Be opened. And his ears were opened, and the bond of his tongue was loosed, and he spake plain. And he charged them that they should tell no man; but the more he charged them, so much the more a great deal they published it.	And they come into Bethsaida. *And they bring to him a* blind man, *and beseech him to touch him. And he took* hold of the blind man by *the hand*, and brought him out of the village; and when he had *spit* on his eyes, and *laid his hands on him*, he asked him, Seest thou aught? *And he looked up*, and said, I see men; for I behold (them) as trees walking. Then again he laid his hands on his eyes; and he looked steadfastly, and was restored, and saw all things clearly. And he sent him away to his home, saying, Do not even enter into the village.

The verbal identities which connect the above narratives and prove them to be mere variants of a single original are more obvious in the Greek than in a translation. But even in it we realise the identity in the two incidents of *mise en scène* and locality; for *Sidon*, as Wellhausen has shown, is an error for Saidan—*i.e.*, Bethsaida. In both places they bring the patient to Jesus and beseech him to lay his hand on him, or—what is the same thing—to touch him. In both cases Jesus takes the patient apart from the throng or away from the village, and uses his own spittle as a remedy, putting his fingers in the one case into the ears, in the other laying them on the eyes. In the one case it is Jesus who looks up, in the other the patient; but the Greek phrase is identical. Both stories end with the same injunction of secrecy.

Such doublets as the above must perplex half-educated people who have been brought up to believe that the Gospels are documents specially inspired, essentially true in what they relate, incapable of error, and not to be classed with the rest of ancient biographical literature. For they show that the Gospels have grown up very much in the same manner as other half-legendary histories of popular heroes. In the Alexander romance, in any life of a popular saint, in any collection of folklore tales, we are sure to find one original story told in two or more different ways. The two variants generally arise through oral repetition of the tale; but they may be engendered almost as easily inside of the written tradition. In either case a later story-teller—especially one who, like the compiler of the narratives before us, is anxious to relate as many miracles of his hero as he can—is sure, sooner or later, to incorporate in his book both forms of the one story as if they were separate stories of distinct episodes.

We have selected, as illustrations, the two most striking examples to be found in Mark of overlapping narratives; but others exist. Thus in ix. 36 Jesus "*took a little child and set him in the midst of them, and, taking him in his arms, he said to them, Whosoever shall receive one of such little children in my name,*

STRUCTURE OF MARK'S GOSPEL 57

receiveth me," etc. Another form of the same story meets us in the very next chapter, x. 13: "*And they brought unto him little children.......And he took them in his arms*" and said, "*Whosoever shall not receive the kingdom of God as a little child,*" etc.

And in another way it can be shown that Mark's Gospel is not an original document, but one compiled from earlier sources. Just as inside of it there are narratives which overlap each other, so there are parts of it which overlap, and are in literary agreement with, parts of the non-Marcan document as it may be reconstructed from the first and third Gospels. Let us consider an example:—

MARK xii. 38-40.	MATTHEW xxiii. 1, foll.	LUKE xi. 37, foll.	LUKE xx. 45-47.
And in his teaching, he said, Beware of the scribes, which desire to walk in long robes, and *salutations in the market-places, and chief seats in the synagogues*, and chief places at feasts: they who devour widows' houses, and for a pretence make long prayers; these shall receive greater condemnation.	Then spake Jesus to the multitudes and to his disciples, saying, The scribes and the Pharisees sit on Moses' seat... ..But all their works they do to be seen of men: for they make broad their phylacteries, and enlarge the borders (of their garments), and love the chief places at feasts, and the chief seats in the synagogues, and salutations in the market-places..... Woe unto you, Scribes and Pharisees, for ye are like	Now as he spake, a Pharisee asked him to breakfast with him, and he went in and sat down to meat..... Woe unto you Pharisees! for ye love *the chief seats in the synagogues, and the salutations in the market-places*. Woe unto you! for ye are as the tombs which appear not, and the men that walk over know it not.	And in the hearing of all the people he said unto his disciples, BEWARE OF THE SCRIBES, WHO DESIRE TO WALK IN LONG ROBES, AND LOVE SALUTATIONS IN THE MARKET-PLACES, AND CHIEF SEATS IN THE SYNAGOGUES, AND CHIEF PLACES AT FEASTS; WHICH DEVOUR WIDOWS' HOUSES, AND FOR A PRETENCE MAKE LONG PRAYERS: THESE SHALL RECEIVE GREATER CONDEMNATION.

| unto whited sepulchres, which outwardly appear beautiful, but inwardly are full of dead men's bones, and of all uncleanness. Even so ye outwardly appear righteous unto men. |

In the above, notice that Luke, in xx. 45–47, copies integrally Mark xii. 38–40, and sets the saying in the same background as Mark. But in xi. 43 he has already had the saying about chief seats and salutations, appending to it the saying about tombs, which Matthew, though changing somewhat its purport, also associates therewith. It hardly admits of doubt that Luke found the saying about chief seats and salutations twice in his sources—once in Mark, and again in the non-Marcan document—and copies both passages out. Matthew also found the saying twice, but rolls up into one the two sources which here overlapped one another. But, if so, there must have been some common document underlying both Mark and the non-Marcan source. The two overlap in the same way in the story of the Baptism, of the Temptation, and in sundry other passages, two of which we considered above (pp. 54, 55, 56).

Enough has been said. Mark, the main source of the first and third evangelists, is himself no original writer, but a compiler, who pieces together and edits earlier documents in which his predecessors had written down popular traditions of the miracles and passion of Jesus. Their interest had lain more in the wonders worked by Jesus than in his teaching, of which Mark

STRUCTURE OF MARK'S GOSPEL

preserves but little. The traditions thus collected were at first framed in the Aramaic tongue; for Jesus and his first followers, being Galileans, spoke that dialect, and Mark's Greek is so full of Aramaic phrases, names, and idioms as to justify the contention of Wellhausen and other competent Semitic scholars that the documents which he inherited were translations of Aramaic originals; and the same remark holds good of most of the material contained in the non-Marcan source.

CHAPTER V.

MATTHEW AND LUKE

WE have seen in the previous chapter how slender, and also how uncritical and popular, were the traditions of Jesus which underlay the Gospel of Mark; and yet this Gospel supplied the historical framework of the longer Gospels associated with the names of Matthew the apostle, and of Luke the companion of Paul. To the order in which the chief events of the ministry, passion, and death of Jesus followed one another, these later evangelists had no clue except such as Mark supplied; for the non-Marcan document —apart from its account of Jesus's baptism and temptation—was not a history, but a collection of aphorisms and parables uttered by Jesus. For the where and when and what of Jesus's actions these later writers depended on Mark; and from him is derived the historical plan of their Gospels. They forsake it occasionally, though never in unison; and whenever they do so, they soon return to it. That this is so is apparent if we set out in parallel columns the sections of Mark which each reproduces, preserving the order in which they do so. Here is the table:—

IN MATTHEW.	IN LUKE.
Mark i. 1-20.., i. 40-45.., i. 29-34.., iv. 35-41, v. 1-20, ii. 1-22, v. 21-43.., iii. 13-19, vi. 7-13. ., ii. 23-iv. 34. ., vi. 1-6, vi. 14-ix. 50. ., x. 1-31. ., x. 32-xii. 12. ., xii. 13-xiii. 37.., xiv. 1-xvi. 8.	Mark i. 1-15.., i. 21-39. ., i. 40-iii. 19.., iv. 1-25, iii. 31-35, iv. 35-43, vi. 7-44, viii. 27-ix. 50.., x. 13-52.., xi. 1-xvi. 8.

In the above the double dots signify additions made by these two evangelists to the scheme of Mark. The matter added is usually taken from the lost non-Marcan source, and consists mainly of parables and sayings. Luke, however, adds in his chapters ix.–xix. much matter of his own which cannot be traced in Matthew, and is probably taken from some other than the non-Marcan source which he shared with Matthew.

It is not our object to analyse the whole of the three Gospels into their sources, but only to show that they are all three compilations from earlier sources. We also need to inquire how these compilers used their sources, how they regarded evidence, how they conceived of history. This train of investigation is especially important in the case of Luke, because from his pen we have got, beside his Gospel, a lengthy history of Peter and Paul and of the early missions of the Church, called Acts of the Apostles. If we can determine from an examination of his Gospel his general character and calibre as an historian, and can estimate how he used his sources, we shall be in a better position to appreciate the historical value of Acts.

Matthew a little and Luke still more smooth down the somewhat rough Greek of Mark, and eliminate from it uncouth forms. They also remove from it Aramaic names and phrases, though they retain Mark's translations of the same. For example, in Matthew ix. 18 the name Jairus is left out, in xv. 5 the word Corban; in repeating Mark v. 41 both Matthew (ix. 25) and Luke (viii. 54) omit the words *Talitha cumi*, which mean: Maiden, I say to thee, Arise. They omit many indications of place given by Mark; and Luke in particular reveals complete ignorance of Palestinian geography, making Galilee part of Judæa, and bringing Jesus into Jerusalem by way of Jericho after he has descended thither through Samaria. Here Mark had brought Jesus down from north to south through Peræa, on the east side of Jordan, and quite rightly made Jericho his last halt before entering the holy city. Luke, however, for reasons of his own, takes him through Samaria to the west of the river, yet copies blindly out from Mark the last section of the itinerary, forgetting or not knowing that it is no longer possible.

It is specially instructive to note differences in Matthew and Luke due to alteration and development of the beliefs and ideas which Christians entertained about Jesus. In Mark, it is true, Jesus had already become a prophet and wonder-worker, walking on the waters, feeding thousands off nothing, raising the dead, and, in general, giving those signs of his Messiahship which, according to Paul, the Jews demanded of him, but demanded in vain. Nevertheless, Mark has still many stories to tell of him which are very human, and go far to set him on a level with other prophets. In Matthew and Luke, however, the process of deifying him before death, as Paul only deified him after death, has already begun. They both try to sublimate his character, and to eliminate traits of common humanity retained by Mark. In so doing they point the way for the fourth Gospel, in which the divine Reason, or *Logos*, masquerades across the stage in human form, an insipid figure muttering oracles over the heads of his audience, a Christ who no longer weeps or prays except to the gallery. Painters of sacred pictures are apt to delineate as

Christ a weak, vapid, languid Syrian. As a man of flesh and blood, as one who is good because he had it in him to be bad, they are not at liberty to picture him; as God, they obviously cannot. The wishy-washy Christ they are left with is the Christ of the fourth Gospel. This process of emasculation, then, has already begun in Matthew and Luke, and we forthwith give examples of it.

Mark vi. 1-6 contains the following text: (1) *And he went out from thence; and he cometh into his own country; and his disciples follow him.* (2) *And when the sabbath was come, he began to teach in the synagogue: and many hearing him were astonished, saying, Whence hath this man these things? and, What is the wisdom that is given to this man, and such mighty works wrought by his hands?* (3) *Is not this the carpenter, the son of Mary, and brother of James, and Joses, and Judas, and Simon? And they were offended in him.* (4) *And Jesus said unto them, A prophet is not without honour, except in his own country, and among his own kin, and in his own house.* (5) *And he could there perform no mighty work, save that he laid his hand on a few sick folk, and healed them.* (6) *And he marvelled because of their unbelief.*

Here we have a graphic picture. The fame of Jesus's doings in Capernaum has reached his own home and village. He goes there, but finds even his own family unsympathetic. His miracles are scoffed at. They have known him from childhood; they know his mother and brothers and sisters. Familiarity breeds contempt. They pronounce Jesus to be an upstart, and make light of him and his works. The first condition of faith-healing is wanting, with the result that he is unable to do any mighty work there.

Here is a frank admission that faith on the part of the sick was as essential to the cures of Jesus as it is to those of Lourdes. But such an admission seemed sorely to derogate from the dignity of Jesus in a later generation, when he was becoming more divine than human. Luke, accordingly, omits the passage altogether, unless his ch. iv. 16–30 be an echo of it. Matthew, as usual, is more faithful to his source; but he is compelled to minimise the force of Mark's words, and, accordingly, for verse 5 substitutes this (xiii. 58): "*And he did not many mighty works there because of their unbelief*"—suppressing the fact that he *could* not. He also substitutes the words "*Is not this the carpenter's son?*" for "*Is not this the carpenter?*" probably because he deemed it derogatory to attribute so humble a calling to so exalted a person as Jesus.

It is, moreover, to be noticed that even the text of Mark has been retouched in this passage; for how could the same persons be astonished in verse 2 who are offended at him in verse 3, and have no honour or respect for him in verse 4, no faith in him in verse 6? It is clear from the context that, far from admiring his teaching and reputed miracles, they made light of them, and were outraged at the claims made in his behalf. It follows that some such words as "scoffed at him" or "mocked" must have originally stood in the text, and have been changed to "*were astonished.*"

Again, in Mark x. 17, 18, we read that "*there ran one to him, and kneeled to him, and asked him, Good teacher, what shall I do that I may inherit eternal life? And Jesus said unto him, Call thou me not good. None is good save one, even God.*"

Here we read in the manuscripts of Mark's Gospel: "*Why callest thou me good?*" instead of the downright prohibition: "*Call thou me not good.*" But the latter stands in many citations of the passage found in authors older by two hundred years than our earliest manuscripts; and therefore I have adhered to it in my translation. Long before A.D. 200 Jesus was exalted in most circles of believers to the rank of the sinless Word or Logos of God, the spotless lamb offered for men's sins; and it was already blasphemous to suggest that he ever sinned or was capable of sin. Accordingly, Matthew garbles his source as follows (xix. 16): "*And behold, one came to him and said: Master, what good shall I do, that I may have eternal life? And he said unto him, Why askest thou me about that which is good? One there is who is good.*"

Here, then, in the original text, Jesus, with the humility which characterises a really great teacher, deprecated the hasty homage of an impetuous youth, and hesitated to accept an epithet which a Jew could apportion to the divine being alone. Matthew suppresses all this, and would have us believe that, in Jesus's opinion, no one was able to instruct another about good and evil except God, because the latter alone is good. In the same spirit, as we shall see later on, Matthew pretends that John declined at first to baptise so superior a being as he recognised Jesus to be, and since he cannot, after all, suppress a fact so well established, he omits, in iii. 4, the statement put in the forefront by Mark—namely, that the baptism preached by John was one of repentance for the remission of sins, and therefore superfluous for the sinless.

Here is another example: Mark i. 32 relates how, at Capernaum, at even "*they brought unto him all that were sick and those possessed by devils,......and he healed many that were afflicted with various diseases, and cast out many devils."*

Here Matthew cannot tolerate the implication contained in the words *all* and *many* that the power of Jesus to heal knew any limits; and so he corrects Mark thus: *" They brought to him many possessed with devils, and he cast out the spirits with a word, and he healed all that were afflicted; in order that there might be fulfilled what was spoken by Isaiah the prophet, He took himself our infirmities and bare our diseases."*

Matthew therefore alters Mark's *all......many* into *many......all;* and this short passage exemplifies two other peculiarities of this writer. He adds *de suo*, "from his own store," the detail that Jesus healed the sick by mere word of mouth, because he does not wish his readers to suppose that so exalted a being polluted his hands by touching the sick. And this is probably why he omits to copy out the two cures by combined use of touch and spittle which Mark records (vii. 31–37 and viii. 22–26), and which are criticised above (p. 55). Perhaps, however, it was rather the magic use by Jesus of spittle than the actual touching that shocked him; for he seems to have regarded touching the sick as a magical practice, different from the act of laying hands on them; and where Mark x. 13 says that *" they brought to Jesus little children that he should touch them,"* substitutes (xix. 13) *"that he should lay his hands on them and pray."* In the same way the sick were in this country healed by king's touch, and the Anglican Prayer-book formerly contained a corresponding rite. This is no longer printed, for religious people nowadays regard it as superstitious, though they retain laying on of hands or ordination by a bishop, regardless of the fact that both rites really belong to the same order of ideas, as I shall point out later on.

Another peculiarity of Matthew which characterises this passage is the appeal to prophecy, to which we return lower down (p. 80).

The Christ of Mark is still so far human that he is ignorant of the date even of the most important of future events—namely, the Second Coming; and accordingly, in Mark xiii. 32, we have the following: "*When ye see these things coming to pass, know ye that he is nigh, even at the doors. Verily I say unto you this generation shall not pass away, until all these things be accomplished.......But of that day or that hour knoweth no one, not even the angels in heaven, neither the Son, but only the Father. Take ye heed, watch and pray: for ye know not when the time is.*"

Here, then, Mark, envisaging Jesus as the Son, sets him on the same dead level of ignorance as the rest of men. Matthew repeats the above passage textually from Mark; but, if we may trust the oldest manuscripts, omits the words "*neither the son.*" Luke also rewrites the passage, and most carefully strikes them out. The ascription of human ignorance to Jesus was no longer tolerable when they compiled their Gospels.

Again, as if it were derogatory, Matthew xix. 15 suppresses the fact recorded by Mark x. 16, that Jesus took little children *in his arms;* and where Mark records that Jesus, looking on the over-zealous youth that called him good, "*loved him,*" Matthew merely says, "*Jesus said unto him.*" So in xii. 13 Matthew suppresses the demonstration of human feeling recorded by Mark iii. 5. Here the Jews in the synagogue have blamed Jesus for healing on the sabbath, "*and when he had looked round about on them with anger, being grieved at their hardness of heart, he saith unto the man, Stretch forth thy hand,*" etc. Matthew substitutes: "*Then saith he to the man, Stretch forth thy hand.*" So in Mark i. 43 Jesus "*sternly charged*" one whom he healed to say nothing of it to any man; but Matthew tones down the text to this: "*Jesus saith unto him, See thou tell no man.*" And the pedantry of suppressing merely human traits in Jesus extends even to the least details. Thus (Mark ii. 5) Jesus addresses a palsied man who believed in him as follows: "*Child, thy sins are forgiven*"; and in x. 24, in addressing his disciples, he begins "*Children.*" This seemed too familiar to Matthew, and in the corresponding passages (ix. 6 and xix. 24) he omits *child* and *children*. Conversely, in Matthew and Luke the disciples are made to address Jesus by grander titles than in Mark. Thus, in Mark iv. 38 they say during the storm when they have waked him from sleep: "*Teacher* (didaskalos), *art thou not concerned lest we perish?*" Luke, transcribing the passage, substitutes "*Master, master* (epistatês), *we are perishing*"; for "*teacher*" seemed too familiar to him. Matthew, transcribing the passage, still further improves on it, and substitutes "*O Lord* (Kyrie) *save us, we are perishing.*" Similarly, in Mark ix. 5 Peter says: "*Rabbi, it is good for us to be here.*" But Luke already regarded Jesus as better than a mere Rabbi, so he substitutes, as before, the word *epistatês*, which means master or over-lord; and Matthew, as before, substitutes Lord. Such alterations may seem insignificant, but to the careful student they are as straws which show which way the wind is blowing; and in the last two decades of the first century, when the Gospels of Matthew and Luke were compiled, it was blowing hard towards the deification of Jesus. The Christian world was rapidly losing sight of the historical man of Nazareth, and beginning to substitute a theological figment.

One of the most striking and authentic passages in the Gospel is Mark iii. 20–35. Jesus, in his missionary enterprise, has achieved great success in Galilee, whither many from such far regions and cities as Jerusalem, Idumea, from beyond Jordan, from Tyre and Sidon, flock to witness his exorcisms of evil spirits; for he exercised such an authority over these and received from them such homage and acknowledgment as none of the Scribes and Pharisees, who yet presumed to lay down the law for the people. Be it observed in passing that many of the latter must, as educated men, have regarded the popular belief in devils as a vulgar superstition; and Philo, the literary Jew of Alexandria, an exact contemporary of Jesus, did so; so also did the author of the fourth Gospel, who scrupulously banishes them from his romance. John, to be quite accurate, ascribes the belief not to Jesus, but to the Jews, whom he represents as accusing Jesus of *having a devil* and *being mad* (John x. 20; cf. John vii. 20, viii. 48–52). Of Jesus's many exorcisms of demons, and of all his parleys with them, this Gospel contains not a word. Its author deemed contact with lower spirits to be derogatory of the dignity of the *Logos* or *Word* incarnate, and rigorously suppresses all memory of this aspect of Jesus's ministry.

Demonological superstition, however, is almost wholly absent from the Old Testament; and this was an additional reason why the Scribes and Pharisees, who were nurtured on the Jewish Scriptures, should neither have practised the exorcistic art nor have encouraged the beliefs which underlie it. But Jesus was certainly by his followers regarded as the vehicle and agent of a pure power or divine spirit of which the unclean spirits or demons were afraid; and an early tradition held that he received this power at baptism, and perfected it during the forty days of temptation in the wilderness. He was probably gifted to excess with that mysterious faculty of influencing the nervous system and the emotions (rather than the reason) of others with which we are to-day familiar in the case of so-called mesmerists.

In the same way Mohammed claimed that the spirit of God worked through him and led him on in whatever he did; and it was only because the clans of Arabia coalesced in this belief, and combined to have faith in him in this sense, that, on the eve of his death, they were able to forget their feuds and unite their forces for the conquest of an unbelieving world.

Now, there is only one way in which a prophet advancing such claims can be combated, so to speak, with his own weapons; and that is by declaring him to be mad; for this charge is at once an admission that a higher than human spirit and will animates him and utters itself through him, and a denial that the said spirit is a pure or divine, or, as we say nowadays, a sane spirit. And this, it appears from Mark, was the very charge now made against Jesus by his own household, by his own mother and brethren. The following is the passage, Mark iii. 20 foll.: "*And he cometh into a house. And the multitude cometh together again, so that they could not so much as eat bread. And when his family heard of it, they went out*

MATTHEW AND LUKE 71

to take and restrain him; for they said, He is out of his mind."

Here is inserted in the text a digression suggested by the last words, to the effect that the Scribes of Jerusalem declared that Jesus himself was possessed by Beelzebub, the prince of devils, and as such was able to cast out devils. Jesus answers that there is too much solidarity among the demons for their ruler to take part against his own minions. He has first bound the strong one, Satan, or he could not despoil his mansion. He adds that all blasphemies against God shall be forgiven, but that they who accuse him of having an unclean spirit shall never be forgiven, because they have blasphemed the holy spirit, the finger of God (Luke xi. 20) of which he is the vehicle and organ. In very similar terms Mohammed rebuked those who alleged him to be possessed by an evil spirit. The family of Jesus, in asserting him to be out of his mind, launched the same accusation against him, and so were guilty of the same unforgivable offence as the Scribes. Accordingly, Mark now returns to the family, and describes how they came to take him, as follows (iii. 31): "*And there come his mother and his brethren, and, standing without, they sent unto him, calling him. And a multitude was sitting about him; and they say unto him, Behold, thy mother and thy brethren without seek for thee. And he answereth them, and saith: Who is my mother and my brethren? And looking round on them which sat round about him, he saith: Behold, my mother and my brethren! For, whosoever shall do the will of God, the same is my brother, and sister, and mother.*"

And this is not the only passage in which Mark records the indifference, even the hostility, to the young prophet of his own family. In vi. 4 (see p. 63) he allows Jesus to comment with extreme bitterness on the reception accorded him in his own village: "*A prophet is not without honour save in his own country, and among his own kin, and in his own house.*" We have seen that Matthew garbles, and Luke omits the latter passage. Let us see how they deal with the one before us. In the first place, then, they both omit Mark iii. 19-21, for in their generation it was become scandalous to suppose that his own family could have set out to restrain Jesus as a madman. How acutely the scandal is still felt by orthodox Christians may be measured by the fact that the authors of the revised English version, recently issued by the Episcopal Churches of England and America, have falsified the text of Mark iii. 21, rendering the Greek words οἱ παρ αὐτοῦ by *his friends* instead of *his household* or *his family*. Yet the old authorised version of 1611 correctly sets in the margin Wycliff's rendering *his kinsmen*.

The revisers, in their preface, declare their aim to be to keep to the older text, "and to introduce as few alterations as possible, consistently with faithfulness." Their "faithfulness" has in this case not prevented them from trying to deceive English readers who cannot read Greek. Dr. Swete, Regius Professor of Divinity in the University of Cambridge and author of a learned commentary on this Gospel, rightly observes, in his note on this passage, that the Greek phrase admits of no other interpretation than "those of his own family," and weakly seeks to palliate the conduct of the mother of Jesus by supposing that, on this occasion, she allowed herself to be over-persuaded by his brethren.

After suppression of verse 21, the subsequent episode, Mark iii. 31–35, could be related with less scandal; for the bitter sense of the contrast drawn between the physical kinsmen and those who do the will of God is hidden from the reader, and it admits of being read as a bit of mere edification. Accordingly, Matthew and Luke retain these verses, though not without modification. Thus Matthew (xii. 46) turns Mark iii. 31 thus: "*While he was still speaking to the multitudes, behold his mother and brethren stood without seeking to speak with him.*" So they have not come to arrest him, but merely to converse with him. According to Mark, "*they sent to him calling him,*" as if he was still young enough to be amenable to their authority. Luke equally conceals the real object of their mission, for he writes thus (viii. 19, 20): "*And his mother came nigh him, and his brethren, and they could not reach him because of the crowd. And it was told him, Thy mother and thy brethren stand without, desiring to see thee.*"

Secondly, we must notice the changes here made by Matthew and Luke in the order of the narrative. In Mark the accusation preferred by his family against Jesus that he was mad, and their attempt to restrain him, gain in point and significance by the intercalation of verses 22–30, which relate how the scribes had already come from Jerusalem on the same occasion, and, as it were, uniting forces with his mother and brethren, "*said, He hath Beelzebub,*" and, "*By the prince of the devils he casteth out the devils.*" Matthew, no doubt in order to remove the sinister effect of Mark's narrative, separates the remarks of the scribes (for whom he substitutes *Pharisees*) and Jesus's answer to them from the visit of his mother and brethren

(Mark iii. 31–35 = Matthew xii. 46–50) by verses 33–45 of his ch. xii., in which the sign of Jonah the prophet and other matters are spoken of; and he causes the Pharisees to adduce their calumny in two passages which really duplicate one another, first on the occasion of Jesus's healing a deaf and dumb man, thus (Matthew xii. 22) : "*Then was brought unto him one possessed with a devil, blind and dumb: and he healed him, insomuch that the dumb man spake and saw.......But when the Pharisees heard it, they said, This man doth not cast out devils but by Beelzebub, the prince of the devils,*" etc.; and again, on an earlier but similar occasion, ch. ix. 32–34, where he seems to reproduce the non-Marcan source which he shares with Luke.

Luke, however, wholly separates the visit of the mother and brethren (Mark iii. 31–35) from the passage about Beelzebub, and brings it in as a sort of appendix to Mark iv. 1–25, so inverting Mark's order, for Mark iii. 31–35 = Luke viii. 19 to end, and Mark iv. 1–25 = Luke viii. 4–18. Luke brings in the accusations about Beelzebub later on in ch. xi. 14–26, and does not, like Matthew, duplicate them; he, in effect, combines Matthew ix. 32–34 (= Matthew xii. 22–24) with Matthew xii. 25–29 and xii. 43–45 in a way that shows that he had a common source with Matthew which recounted the whole episode somewhat as Mark does, and so overlapped Mark. The correspondences of the three Gospels may be represented as follows:—

Matthew (nil)	Mark iii. 20, 21	Luke (nil)
Matthew ix. 32–34 = Matthew xii. 22–24	Mark iii. 22	Luke xi. 14, 15
Matthew xii. 24–29	Mark iii. 23–27	Luke xi. 17–22
Matthew xii. 30 (non-Marcan source)	Nil	Luke xi. 23
Matthew xii. 31, 32	Mark iii. 28–30	Luke xii. 10

| Matthew xii. 43–45 (non-Marcan source) | Nil | Luke xi. 24–26 |
| Matthew xii. 46–50 | Mark iii. 31–35 | Luke viii. 19–21 (= Luke xi. 27–28, ?non-Marcan source) |

It is clear that Luke has preserved in its right place the paragraph in which the non-Marcan source threw Jesus's repudiation of the physical mother who had voted him to be insane. It is as follows (Luke xi. 27, 28): "*And it came to pass, as he said these things, a certain woman out of the multitude lifted up her voice, and said unto him, Blessed is the womb that bare thee, and the breasts which thou didst suck. But he said, Nay, rather are blessed they that hear the word of God, and keep it.*"

Here Jesus rebukes his mother in even bitterer terms than he uses in the Marcan form of the story. I have dwelt at such length on this episode, because it so well illustrates the growth of opinion about Jesus which went on in the early Church and the interrelations of the earliest documents. The passage, Mark iii. 21, is of extreme interest in view of the legends which soon sprang up about the mother of Jesus. I do not wish to throw stones at the Catholic religion, and rather sympathise than otherwise with a Jewish friend who remarked to me once that, if he were minded to say his prayers to another human being, he would as lief address them to a Jewess as to a Jew; at the same time I may be pardoned for drawing the reader's attention to the wide gulf which separates these passages from the Mariolatry which has been the staple of the Christian cult ever since the fifth century.

Faithful to this tendency in certain passages of

Matthew, the text of Mark is not merely changed, but added to, in order to magnify the supernatural power and *rôle* of Jesus. Thus Mark xiv. 47 relates that, when Jesus was arrested by a multitude sent out against him with swords and staves by the chief priests and scribes and elders, one of the partisans of Jesus "*drew his sword and smote the servant of the high priest and struck off his ear.*" That is all that Mark had to tell of the episode. But Matthew cannot let it end there, and invents the following speech for Jesus as appropriate to the occasion: "*Then saith Jesus unto him, Put up again thy sword into its place: for all they that take the sword shall perish by the sword. Or thinkest thou that I cannot beseech my Father, and he shall even now send me more than twelve legions of angels? How, then, should the Scriptures be fulfilled, that thus it must be?*"

And, as we are concerned with this episode, we may notice that Luke, equally with Matthew, felt himself called upon to improve on the story, and so he makes this addition (Luke xxii. 51): "*But Jesus answered and said, Suffer ye thus far. And he touched his ear, and healed him.*"

The Greek text implies that he instantly set the man's ear on again! Luke is careful to tell us just before (verse 49) that the swordsman had asked permission of Jesus to commit the assault: "*Lord, shall we smite with the sword?*"—a pure invention of his own.

We are not dealing here with the fourth Gospel, but we may note how, in this scene of Jesus's arrest, it excels Matthew and Luke in fanciful exaggeration; for, when the band of soldiers and officers appear to arrest him, Jesus asks, "*Whom seek ye?* They *answer, Jesus of Nazareth. Jesus saith unto them, I am he"* (John xviii. 5). "*When therefore he said unto them, I am he, they recoiled and fell to the ground.*" So powerful was the effluence of Jesus's majesty that a whole cohort of soldiers, when they draw nigh to arrest him, are hurled backward by it and thrown to the ground! In the same strain of exaggeration the fourth Gospel relates that Nicodemus, in anointing the corpse of Jesus, used up about 100 litres of myrrh and aloes—enough for the interment perhaps of ten ordinary mortals. In the same way, according to this Gospel, he turned as much water into wine at Cana of Galilee as would fill several modern watering-carts. Matthew is more interested than Mark in Jesus's teaching, yet he is not less fond of marvels, and does not scruple to improve upon his source in this respect. Thus, in Mark vi. 45-52, we have a story of how the disciples, alone in a boat by themselves by night on the lake of Galilee, were beset by a headwind; and about the fourth watch of the night Jesus came *walking on the sea*, with the intention of passing by them and reaching their destination before them. And they saw him walking on the sea, and thought it was a ghost, and cried out. But he answered, "*Be of good courage; it is I, be not afraid.*" Then he embarked on the ship with them, and the wind fell. This is all Mark relates; but Matthew sees his way, at this point, to "point a moral and improve a tale," and after the words "*be not afraid*" adds the following: "*But Peter answered him and said, Lord, if it be thou, bid me come unto thee upon the waters. And he said, Come. And Peter got out of the boat, and walked upon the waters and came to Jesus. But, seeing the wind, he was frightened; and, beginning to sink, cried out, saying, Lord save me. And instantly Jesus stretched forth his hand and took hold of him and said, O thou of little faith, why didst thou hesitate? And when they had embarked in the boat the wind fell.*"

There is a passage in the 21st chapter of the fourth Gospel—a chapter added later than the rest by some early editor—which seems to contain the germ of this miraculous story. It is this: "*Simon Peter saith unto them* [the other disciples], *I go a-fishing. They say unto him, We also come with thee. They went forth, and entered into the boat; and that night they caught nothing. But when day was now breaking Jesus stood on the beach: howbeit the disciples knew not that it was Jesus. ......That disciple therefore whom Jesus loved saith unto Peter, It is the Lord. So when Simon Peter heard that it was the Lord, he girt his coat about him (for he was naked) and cast himself into the sea. But the other disciples came in the little boat—for they were not far from the land, but about 200 cubits off—dragging the net full of fishes.......Simon Peter therefore went up (into the boat) and drew the net to land.*"

The above story corresponds too closely with Matthew xiv. 22–33 for us to suppose that it is of independent origin. In both the disciples are in a boat on the Sea of Galilee; Jesus approaches, and at first they fail to recognise him; but, when they do, Peter jumps into the sea. But in the Johannine form the particular miraculous element disappears which characterises Matthew. The boat is close to shore, and Peter jumps in with the intention of wading through the shallow water. Had he meant to swim he would not have put on his coat. Nor does Jesus walk on the sea, but stands on the shore. It is dangerous to try to rationalise any of the wonderful stories which the Synoptists relate; we may rather marvel that, in narratives which arose in so credulous an age and country, miracles are not more plentiful. Nevertheless, it really looks as if the author of this additional chapter of the fourth Gospel had got hold of a tale which is the *prius* of Matthew's story. If, in the Greek text of Mark, we change the preposition *epi* into *para*, we should get the meaning that Jesus came walking *along* the shore of the sea, and not *on* the sea. As the wind was against them, he might well catch them up and outdistance them; and Peter's object in jumping out would be to join Jesus on the land, which must have been close at hand for them to discern the figure of Jesus during the night. Perhaps *para* was the original reading. There can be no doubt, however, that Matthew wished to enhance the miracle as he found it related in Mark.

In another passage Matthew accumulates stupendous miracles where his source, Mark, is comparatively modest. The latter relates (xv. 38) that, when Jesus breathed his last on the cross, "*the veil [or screen] of the temple was rent asunder from top to bottom.*" Matthew (xxvii. 51-52) repeats this verbally, and adds, out of the fulness of his own store, the following: "*And the earth did quake; and the rocks were rent; and the tombs were opened; and many bodies of the saints that had fallen asleep were raised; and coming forth out of the tombs after his resurrection they entered into the holy city and appeared unto many.*"

Of this group of miracles Mark had never heard, nor Luke, though they are as addicted to wonders as Matthew. Even from the author of the fourth Gospel, who is inclined to "break the record" in such matters, it was still hidden when he wrote in the last decade of

the first century or in the first decade of the second.
One feature of Matthew's narrative remains to be
noticed—namely, what has been called his prophetic
gnosis; that is, the perpetual attempt to see in what
Jesus did, or said, or suffered, the fulfilment of old
Jewish prophecies of the Messiah. This style of
argument is, of course, addressed to Jews who hesitated
to accept Jesus as the Christ or Messiah. We do not
encounter in Mark this argument from prophecy, as
it is called; but Matthew caps almost every incident
which he copies from Mark with some Old Testament
text or other, always mangled, misunderstood, and
misapplied, in order to make it seem to fit. In a few
cases this leads to the strangest results. Let us take
as an example the triumphal entry of Jesus into Jerusalem shortly before his crucifixion, for his account of
which Matthew had no source other than Mark:—

MARK xi. 1–7.	MATTHEW xxi. 1–7.
(1) And when they draw nigh unto Jerusalem....he sendeth two of his disciples, and saith unto them, Go your way into the village that is over against you; and straightway as ye enter it, ye shall find a colt tied, whereon no man ever yet sat; loose him, and bring him. And if anyone say unto you, Why do ye this? say ye, The Lord hath need of him; and straightway he will send him back hither. And they went away, and found a colt tied at the door without in the open street; and they loose him. And certain of them that stood there said unto them, What do ye, loosing the colt? And they said unto them even as Jesus had said, and they let them go. And they bring the colt to Jesus, and they cast on him their garments; and he sat upon him.	And when they drew nigh unto Jerusalem....Jesus sent two disciples, saying unto them, Go into the village that is over against you, and straightway ye shall find an ass tied, and a colt with her; loose (them) and bring (them) unto me. And if anyone say aught to you, ye shall say, The Lord hath need of them; and straightway he will send them. Now this is come to pass, that it might be fulfilled which was spoken by the prophet, saying:— Tell ye the daughter of Sion, Behold, the king cometh to thee, Meek, and riding on an ass, And upon a colt the foal of an ass. And the disciples went, and did even as Jesus appointed for them, and they brought the ass, and the colt, and put on them their garments; and he sat upon them.

It is well to premise that you probably could not ride into the ancient Jerusalem, any more than into the modern, on any animal but an ass, so narrow and low are oriental streets and gateways. Moreover, in those lands in ancient times, as in modern, everyone who could afford it rode on an ass. It was, therefore, nothing exceptional for Jesus to enter the city in that manner. But to Matthew all he did was exceptional; his least action must fulfil some prediction or another about the Messiah to come uttered in ages long past. He therefore searched the Scriptures, and hit upon this text of Zechariah ix. 9. Now Zechariah, like other Hebrew poets, threw his wisdom into groups of two or three balanced clauses, of which, as a rule, the second and third repeat, though in different words, the gist of the first. Thus the passage before us, if rightly translated from the Hebrew, begins thus:—

> *Rejoice greatly, O daughter of Zion;*
> *Shout, O daughter of Jerusalem.*

These two clauses say the same thing in different words, for the daughter of Zion is no other than the daughter of Jerusalem, and one who rejoiced greatly shouted with joy. By the same rule, a Hebrew poet could not speak simply of an ass; that was too prosaic. He must add epexegetically that it was a colt and foal of an ass; and the Hebrew rightly turned here has the following sense: "*and riding on an ass, even upon a colt the foal of an ass.*"

Matthew, not understanding the methods of Semitic poetry, commits the mistake of supposing Zechariah to have intended two distinct animals, a she ass and its foal; and, on the basis of this error, he boldly sets out to rewrite Mark's account. The two disciples will find not a single ass, but *a she ass tethered and her colt with her.* The Lord needs *them* both. Their owner will send *them.* The disciples lead back the she ass and her colt, they lay their garments on both of them, and, mounted on both of them, according to Matthew, Jesus makes his entry into Jerusalem!

The revised version renders the last of the Greek words in this passage—*epanô autôn*—by *thereon*, as if it was on the clothes, and not on both animals, that Jesus sat. But here Mark has *epautôn*, "on *him*"— *i.e.*, on the ass. It follows that Matthew's phrase means "on the asses." In any case, the clothes had been laid on both animals; so that, if Jesus sat on the clothes, he sat on the asses as well. Here, as often, these revisers were barely honest.

CHAPTER VI.

LUKE

It remains to exemplify Luke's method of handling his sources. We have already seen that he shows the same tendency as Matthew to sublimate the figure of Jesus and eliminate from the record all manifestations of human emotion and weakness, at the same time that he magnifies the gifts of intuition and second sight which he supposes his hero to derive from his spiritual illumination in the Jordan. One great difference is at once apparent. In Mark, the Messiahship of Jesus is at first latent. He, indeed, receives it at baptism through the anointing with the Spirit, but only the demons, with their superhuman keenness of vision, can recognise it; it is hidden from his disciples, and not until the end of the Galilean ministry does Peter acclaim him Messiah, and even then in a manner that shows him to be alien to the profounder and more spiritual conception of a suffering Messiah which, if not Jesus himself, at any rate Paul had adopted. Luke will have none of this latency, nor will he permit Jesus to begin his ministry and achieve his first successes in Capernaum. On the contrary, he relates that Jesus began his career by standing up in the synagogue of his own village of Nazareth, and there and then proclaiming himself to be the Messiah foretold by the prophet Isaiah. He opened the roll of the prophets, we are told, and read the words: "*The spirit of the Lord is upon me, because he hath anointed me to preach good tidings to the poor,*" etc. Then he addressed the congregation, who sat with their eyes fastened on him, and said: "*To-day hath this Scripture been fulfilled in your ears.*"

The sequel of this narrative reveals, by its self-contradictions and inconsequences, the fancifulness of the entire incident. "*All,*" so we read, "*bare him witness, and wondered at the words of grace which proceeded out of his mouth.*" What more in the way of acknowledgment could Jesus desire, even though they did add the words, "*Is not this Joseph's son?*" But Jesus is not satisfied with their universal approval, and launches himself at once into the following outburst, as petulant as it is, under the circumstances, inept: "*Doubtless ye will say unto me this parable, Physician, heal thyself: whatsoever we have heard of as done at Capernaum, do also here in thine own country. And he said, Verily I say unto you, no prophet is acceptable in his own country.*"

Observe how, without giving his countrymen time to accept him, he thrusts a quarrel on them, and talks himself into a rage, when as yet they have done nothing but wonder at his words of grace. In the reference to Capernaum, however, verse 23, Luke fairly betrays himself. For, according to his own text, Jesus only goes to Capernaum later on in verse 31, when he is expelled by force from Nazareth. How does Luke know of Jesus's brilliant achievements in Capernaum? Only from Mark, who takes him to Capernaum first, and then to Nazareth. It follows that in the Nazarene synagogue they could not have heard of achievements which at this stage, even of Luke's narrative, much more of his informant's, were not yet achieved. The words, then, "*Whatsoever we have heard of as done at Capernaum,*" attributed to those who listened to him in the synagogue at Nazareth, involve a *hysteron proteron*, or, as we say, put the cart before the horse; but, if this is so, then this entire scene in the home synagogue is a literary fiction rather carelessly contrived. We note also that Luke could not get away, even when he would, from the ground-plan of events laid down for him by Mark, his dependence on whom will out, even when he waves aside his order of narrative.

In the rest of his speech Jesus continues to upbraid his countrymen, contrasting them unfavourably with the pagans of Syria, and indicating his preference for the latter. Small wonder that his words goad his audience, which had begun by admiring his words of grace, into indignation: Verses 28-31: "*And they were all filled with wrath in the synagogue, as they heard these things; and they rose up, and cast him forth out of the city, and led him unto the brow of the hill whereon their city was built, that they might throw him down headlong. But he passing through the midst of them went his way. And he came down to Capernaum, a city of Galilee.*"

It was more dramatic to set the rejection of Jesus by his own people before the Capernaum ministry rather than after it, as Mark had done. But in doing so Luke bungles his story in such a manner as to reveal his ultimate dependence on Mark for his order of events; and so we are put on our guard. We shall suspect him, whenever he departs from Mark's order, of inventing scene and conversation alike, as here. From the very beginning, then, of his Gospel Luke appears as a picturesque writer seeking for effect; and the speeches put into the mouth of his *personæ dramatis* are as freely invented as the incidents. It is useless for certain scholars and archæologists to extol him as a Christian Thucydides. This single example of his method serves to put us on our guard against extravagant eulogiums. He shares with Thucydides a good style and the faculty of inventing speeches, but nothing else. But let us proceed to further examples of his skill in inventing incidents, and even institutions. Mark relates, in iii. 13-19 and vi. 5-13, how Jesus chose out twelve apostles, and laid down certain precepts which they were to follow in their missionary journeys. The non-Marcan source, used by Matthew and Luke, also related the same episode. Now, Matthew, when he found the same incident described in both his sources, was accustomed to weave them together into a single narrative; and we can usually, thanks to our possession of Mark and Luke, separate, without much difficulty, from one another the sources used by Matthew in such compound narratives. We can do so here. Luke, on the other hand, was prone to keep the Marcan and the non-Marcan accounts apart; and, if he could, to turn them into separate histories of distinct events. This he does here; but how could twelve apostles be chosen and instructed about their missions twice over? Luke gets out of this difficulty in this way. He keeps the Marcan record of the appointment of twelve apostles, but turns the non-Marcan record of the same incident into the story of a call and appointing of seventy disciples, who were to missionise the seventy tribes into whom the whole world of Gentiles was popularly supposed to be divided, just as the twelve were to missionise the twelve tribes of Israel. If we confront the texts of the three Gospels, we see at once that the mission of the seventy was originally no more than a textual variant of the mission of the twelve; is, in fact, just a creation of Luke's inventive fancy. In the following table the Marcan element is given in italics, the non-Marcan in capitals:—

MATTHEW ix. 37, 38.	MARK iii. 14 foll.	LUKE vi. 13 foll.
THEN SAITH HE UNTO his disciples, THE HARVEST TRULY IS PLENTEOUS, BUT THE LABOURERS ARE FEW. PRAY YE THEREFORE THE LORD OF THE HARVEST, THAT HE SEND FORTH LABOURERS INTO HIS HARVEST.	And he appointed twelve, that they might be with him, and that he might send them forth to preach, and to have authority to cast out devils, whom also he named apostles..... (the names follow).	And when it was day, he called his disciples: and he chose from them twelve, whom also he named apostles..... (the names follow).

MATTHEW x. 1 foll.	MARK vi. 7–13.	LUKE ix. 1–6.
And *he called* unto him his *twelve* disciples, and GAVE THEM *authority over unclean spirits*, to cast them out, and to HEAL all manner of DISEASE and all manner of sickness. Now the names of the twelve apostles are these....... These twelve Jesus *sent forth*, and charged them, saying, Go not into any way of the Gentiles, and enter not into any city of the Samaritans; but go rather to the lost sheep of the house of Israel. And as ye go, PREACH, saying, THE KINGDOM OF HEAVEN IS NIGH. HEAL THE SICK, raise the dead, cleanse the lepers, cast out devils: freely ye received, freely give. Get you no gold, NOR SILVER, *nor brass in your belts; no wallet*	And he called unto him the twelve, and began to *send* them forth two by two; and he gave them authority over unclean spirits; and he charged them to take nothing for their journey, save a staff only; no bread, no wallet, no brass in their belt, but (to go) shod with sandals: and (said he), put not on two coats. And he said unto them, Wheresoever ye enter into a house, there abide till ye depart thence. And whatsoever place shall not receive you, and they hear you not, as ye go forth thence, shake off the dust that is under your feet for a testimony unto them. And they went out, and preached that men should repent. And they cast out	And he *called the twelve* together, and GAVE THEM power and *authority* over all devils and to HEAL DISEASES. And *he sent* them *forth* TO PREACH THE KINGDOM of God, and to cure the sick. And he said unto them, *Take nothing for your journey, neither staff, nor wallet, nor bread*, NOR SILVER; *neither have two coats*. And *into* WHATSOEVER *house ye enter, there abide*, and *thence depart. And as many as receive you not*, WHEN YE DEPART FROM THAT CITY, *shake off* THE DUST from *your feet for a testimony against them*. And they departed and went throughout the villages, preaching the Gospel, and healing everywhere.

for your journey, neither *two coats*, NOR SHOES, *nor staff:* for the LABOURER is worthy of his food. AND INTO WHATSOEVER CITY or village YE SHALL ENTER, search out who in it is worthy; and *there abide till ye go forth.* And as ye enter into the house, salute it. AND IF the house BE worthy, let YOUR PEACE come UPON IT: BUT IF it be not worthy, let your peace RETURN TO YOU. *And whosoever shall not receive you, nor hear your words,* AS YE GO *forth* out of that house or *that* CITY, *shake off* THE DUST *of your feet.* Verily I SAY TO YOU, IT SHALL BE MORE TOLERABLE FOR the land of SODOM and Gomorrah in the day of judgment, THAN FOR THAT CITY. BEHOLD, I SEND YOU FORTH AS SHEEP IN THE MIDST OF WOLVES.

many devils, and anointed with oil many that were sick, and healed them.

LUKE X. 1-12.

Now after these things, the Lord appointed seventy others, and *sent* them *two and two* before his face into every city and place, whither he himself was about to come. And HE SAID UNTO them, THE HARVEST IS PLENTEOUS, BUT THE LABOURERS ARE FEW: PRAY YE THEREFORE THE LORD OF THE HARVEST, THAT HE SEND FORTH LABOURERS INTO HIS HARVEST. Go your ways; BEHOLD, I SEND YOU FORTH AS LAMBS IN THE MIDST OF WOLVES. Carry no purse, NO WALLET, NO SHOES: and salute no man on the way. And INTO WHATSOEVER house YE SHALL ENTER, first say, PEACE be to this house. And if a son of peace be there, YOUR PEACE shall rest UPON HIM: BUT IF NOT, it shall TURN TO YOU AGAIN. And in that same house remain, eating and drinking such things as they give: for the labourer is worthy of his hire. Go not from house to house. And INTO WHATSOEVER CITY YE ENTER, and they receive you, eat such things as are set before you: and HEAL THE SICK that are therein, and say unto them, THE KINGDOM OF GOD IS COME NIGH unto you. But INTO

WHATSOEVER CITY YE SHALL ENTER, and they receive you not, go out into the streets thereof, and say, Even THE DUST from your city, that cleaveth to our feet, do we wipe off against you: howbeit, know this, that THE KINGDOM OF GOD IS COME NIGH. I SAY UNTO YOU, IT SHALL BE MORE TOLERABLE IN THAT DAY FOR SODOM, THAN FOR THAT CITY.

Examining the above, we see that large blocks of text which Luke applies to the seventy are by Matthew applied to the twelve, though in conjunction only with Marcan matter. Luke, on the other hand, uses the Marcan matter of the twelve alone, without mixing it up with non-Marcan. The only exception is the phrase *two and two*, which must have stood in the non-Marcan source as well as in Matthew. Now, if the non-Marcan text had here related the calling of seventy disciples instead of twelve apostles, Matthew would almost certainly have kept it apart as a separate episode, instead of blending it with Mark's account. The idea of seventy disciples must therefore have originated with Luke, who thought that, as the twelve tribes of Israel had each an apostle, so the seventy races of the Gentiles must each have a disciple to convert them. And this explains their not being named, as are the twelve, for Luke, having invented them as a Gentile counterpart to the twelve, had no tradition of their names. Eusebius, the learned historian of the Church, who had read a mass of early Christian writers now lost, including Papias and Hegesippus, writing about A.D. 300, significantly remarks that "of the seventy disciples no list whatever is anywhere to be found in circulation"; and this statement accords wonderfully well with the results of modern textual criticism.

There were many analogies to suggest to Luke the story. Seventy, or more strictly seventy-two, translators were said to have rendered the Old Testament into Greek for Gentile readers and Greek Jews; and Typhon chose himself seventy-two associates in his conspiracy against Osiris. In the Sanhedrim there were seventy Jewish elders; to balance whom Luke perhaps invented his seventy disciples.

Although it does not directly belong to the topic before us to do so, it is worth remarking that the *lacuna* or gap in Christian tradition which Eusebius thus noticed was filled up very soon after his age; for one of the most widely dispersed documents of the fourth and fifth century is a list of the seventy disciples attributed to an otherwise unknown author, Dositheus. In this list not only their names and parentage are given, but brief histories of their missions. We learn to what race each of them carried the gospel, and how they died, many of them as martyrs of the faith. Thus, in proportion as we are removed in time further and further from the first age of the religion, the volume of information about it grows and swells. Believers wanted to hear what became of everyone whose name was furnished, or whose mere existence was hinted at in the New Testament, and suitable biographies were soon supplied to order. Nor was this literary superfetation of the second, third, and following centuries confined to biography. Testaments or wills of Jesus, constitutions and canons of the apostles, and similar documents were fabricated, often at enormous length, in which customs and institutions of the churches which had grown up subsequently to the close of the New Testament were described and boldly attributed to Jesus and the apostles, whose authority was thus by a literary trick obtained for masses of clerical and monastic regulations wholly alien to the spirit of an earlier age.

Luke x. 25–37 also furnishes a good example of how this evangelist could recast his material and invert its original drift. Let us confront the two texts :—

MARK xii. 28–34.	LUKE x. 25–37.
And one of the scribes came, and heard them questioning together; and knowing that he had answered them well, asked him, What commandment is the first of all? Jesus answered, The first is, Hear, O Israel, the Lord our God, the Lord is one: and thou shalt love the Lord thy God with all thy heart, and with all thy soul, and with all thy mind, and with all thy strength. The second is this, Thou shalt love thy neighbour as thyself. There is none other commandment greater than these. And the scribe said unto him, Of a truth, Master, thou hast well said, that he is one; and there is none other but he...... And when Jesus saw that he answered discreetly, he said unto him, Thou art not far from the Kingdom of God. And no man after that dared ask him any question.	And behold a certain lawyer stood up tempting him, saying, Master, by doing what shall I inherit eternal life? But he said unto him, In the law what is written, how readest thou it? And he answered and said, Thou shalt love the Lord thy God with all thy heart and in all thy soul and in all thy strength and in all thy mind, and thy neighbour as thyself. But he said to him, Thou hast well answered. This do, and thou shalt live. But he wishing to prove himself just said to Jesus, And who is my neighbour? Taking him up, Jesus said, A certain man was going down from Jerusalem to Jericho, and fell among robbers. ....(There follows the parable of the Good Samaritan.)

Here we note (1) that this dialogue of Jesus with the scribes, as related in Mark, took place in Jerusalem, just before the crucifixion. Luke, however, sets it on the way up to Jerusalem, in Samaria, where scribes were far less likely to encounter Jesus than in the Holy City.

(2) Mark sets the summary of the law in the mouth of Jesus; Luke transfers it to the lips of the lawyer.

(3) In Mark Jesus assures the scribe that he is *not far from the kingdom of God*, because he has *answered discreetly*. Luke, on the contrary, relates the incident as if the lawyer were actuated by mere hostility: *"he stood up to tempt Jesus"*—*i.e.*, to draw Jesus into making some answer which would compromise him. Luke also appends, quite artificially, the parable of the Good Samaritan, and so turns his answer to the question: *Who is my neighbour?* into a backhander against the Jews in general, and this lawyer in particular.

Our next example of Luke's unreliability, of his tendency to invent marvellous episodes out of nothing, shall be taken from his second book addressed to Theophilus, usually called the Acts of the Apostles. In Paul's Epistles we have whole chapters devoted to the theme of speaking with tongues. Religious emotion, like other emotions, if it reach a certain intensity, dismantles the intelligence and overpowers the larynx and vocal organs. The patient falls as it were into a trance or ecstasy, loses control of his voice, and breaks out into a series of inarticulate or half-articulate sounds and meaningless exclamations. In many ancient cults drugs were administered, especially to women, to make them " prophesy " in this way, and the priests who ran the shrines interpreted the mysterious oracles thus delivered in such a manner as to please the superstitious pilgrim and fill their own pockets. Such speaking with tongues is still an everyday phenomenon in the half-barbarous cults of Asia and Africa, and is not unknown among ourselves, as witness the following testimony of George Greville in his *Memoirs*, vol. iii, ch. xxii. :—

> Dec. 2nd, 1833 : I went yesterday to Edward Irving's chapel, to hear him preach, and witness the exhibition of the tongues.......After these three Spencer Perceval stood up. He recited the duty to our neighbours in the catechism, and descanted on that text in a style in all respects far superior to the others. He appeared about to touch on politics, and (as well as I recollect) was saying, " Ye trusted that your institutions were unalterable, ye believed that your loyalty to your king, your respect for your nobility, your "——— when suddenly a low moaning noise was heard, on which he instantly stopped, threw his arm over his breast, and covered his eyes, in an attitude of deep devotion, as if oppressed by the presence of the spirit. The voice, after ejaculating three " Ohs," one rising above the other, in tones very musical, burst into a flow of unintelligible jargon, which, whether it was in English or in gibberish I could not discover. This lasted five or six minutes, and, as the voice was silenced, another woman, in more passionate and louder tones, took it up. This last spoke in English, and words, though not sentences, were distinguishable. I had a full view of her, sitting exactly behind Irving's chair. She was well dressed, spoke sitting, under great apparent excitement, and screamed on till, from exhaustion as it seemed, her voice gradually died away, and all was still. Then Spencer Perceval, in slow and solemn tones, resumed, not where he had left off, but with an exhortation to hear the voice of the Lord, which had just been uttered to the congregation, and after a few more sentences he sat down.

Such a gruesome spectacle as the above could be witnessed in almost any meeting of the early Christians; and, as there were persons by temperament specially apt to fall into this morbid state, so there were others who were credited with the faculty of interpreting their ecstatic utterances. Paul, in his first Epistle to the Corinthians, xii. 28, includes *kinds of tongues* in his list of the gifts conferred by divine grace on the Church, other gifts being the apostolate, prophecy, teaching, helps, government. He discerned in the Church a divinely ordained division of labour, in that some had one gift, some another. "*Are all apostles? are all prophets? are all teachers? are all powers* [*i.e.*, mediums or controls]? *have all gifts of healings? do all speak with tongues? do all interpret?*" And in verse 10 of the same chapter he has already made a similar enumeration of the gifts of the spirit, mentioning first those which have an intellectual aspect—*e.g.*, the *word of wisdom*, the *word of knowledge*, *faith*, and then the merely pathological affections, as we should call them to-day, between which and the intelligence *faith* supplies the bridge of transition. The latter are as follows: *gifts of healing, workings of powers, prophecy, discernings of spirits, kinds of tongues, interpretation of tongues.* Of the above, one *rôle*, that of *discerner of spirits*, is omitted in the later list, yet he was an important person in an age when everyone believed in possession; for an unclean spirit, perhaps of a pagan god or hero, might insinuate itself into a believer, and impose on the body of the faithful, if there was no one at hand to discern and detect him. Paul was apt to depreciate the merely pathological aspects of spiritual possession, save, indeed, so far as he could appeal to them in proof of his own direct apostleship and revelations of Jesus Christ, and turn them against the older apostles and Judaizers who rejected his new gospel. Accordingly, in a subsequent chapter (xiv.), he begs his readers to bear in mind that "*he that speaketh in a tongue speaketh not unto men, but unto God; for no man understandeth: but through the spirit he speaketh mysteries.*" With such a gift Paul contrasts *prophecy*, whereby one *speaketh unto men edification and comfort and consolation*, presumably because his predictions of the future stimulate their hopes and enthusiasm. "*But now, brethren,*" continues Paul, "*if I come unto you speaking with tongues, what shall I profit you, unless I speak to you either by way of revelation, or of knowledge, or of prophesying, or of teaching ?......So also ye, unless ye utter by the tongue things easy to be understood, how shall it be known what is spoken ?......If then I know not the meaning of the voice, I shall be to him that speaketh a barbarian,*[1] *and he that speaketh will be a barbarian unto me.......I thank God, I speak with tongues more than you all: howbeit in the church I had rather speak five words with my understanding, that I might instruct others also, than ten thousand words in a tongue.......Wherefore tongues are for a sign, not to them that believe, but to the unbelieving: but prophesying* [is for a sign] *not to the unbelieving, but to them that believe. If therefore the whole Church be assembled together, and all speak with tongues, and there come in men without gifts or unbelieving, will they not say that ye are mad ?*"

And in the sequel Paul tries to lay down some rules for the regulation of this dangerous gift, which threatened to turn the assembly of the saints into a

[1] The Greek word *barbaros* signifies one who spoke an unintelligible tongue.

pandemonium, as follows: "*If any man speaketh in a tongue, [let it be] by two or at the most three [at a time], and [that] in turn; and let one interpret: but if there be no interpreter, let him keep silence in the church, and let him speak to himself and to God. And let the prophets speak by two or three, and let the others discern. But if a revelation be made to another sitting by, let the first keep silence. For ye can all prophesy one by one, that all may learn, and all may be comforted;...... for God is not [a god] of confusion, but of peace; as in all the churches of the saints.*"

In such passages as the above we breathe the very atmosphere of the earliest Church, and seem to have our finger on its pulse. We can realise the danger there was of emotion, ecstasy, and impulse swamping the slender barque. How far removed were such meetings from the Catholic services of to-day, whereat a priest and deacon work a little harmless magic up at an altar all by themselves for the good of a lot of lounging spectators! Paul was saner than the rest, and was for that reason more influential. Above all, he silenced the female ecstatics: "*Let the women keep silence in the churches: for it is not permitted unto them to speak; but let them be in subjection, as also saith the law.*"

So the law was, after all, good for something. How intensely naïve and human is the document we quote. "*Since ye are zealous of spirits,*" writes Paul to his converts, "*seek that ye may abound unto the edifying of the church.*" This implies that not a few of the believers were over-addicted to the use of their spiritual gifts, and, as long as they could show off, were not too solicitous of order and decency. "*If any man thinketh himself to be a prophet or a pneumatic* [*i.e.*, a medium], *let him bear in mind the things which I write unto you, that they are the commandment of the Lord."* Paul then had had a private, but eminently sensible, revelation on the point direct from Jesus Christ. In spite of abuses, however, he is not disposed to crush out such manifestations of the spirit; and his final advice is as follows: *"Wherefore, my brethren, desire earnestly to prophesy, and forbid not to speak with tongues. But let all things be done decently and in order."*

It is wonderful that, out of the emotional chaos which Paul's letters reveal to us, religious organisers, whose very names are unknown to us, could, in the next hundred years, evolve a system of episcopally governed churches in which all manifestations of the spirit had been repressed and crushed out, and the order of prophets replaced by a carefully graded hierarchy.

Probably the divers *kinds of tongues* recorded in Paul's letters were already, save in a few out-of-the-way communions, reduced to silence as early as the decade 85–95, during which Luke seems to have penned his book of the Acts. Was this writer ignorant of the true nature of the gifts of tongues, or did he sacrifice the truth in order to portray a miracle? We cannot say; but, anyhow, he gives, in Acts ii. 1–13, an account of the speaking with tongues wholly incompatible with Paul's. It was the first Pentecost after the ascension of Jesus, and his followers were met together in Jerusalem. *"And suddenly there came from heaven a sound as of the rushing of a mighty wind, and it filled all the house where they were sitting. And there appeared unto them tongues distributing themselves, like as of fire; and it sat upon each one of them. And they were all filled with the holy spirit, and began*

98 LUKE

to speak with other tongues, as the spirit gave them utterance.......And when this sound was heard, the multitude came together, and were confounded, because every man heard them speaking in his own language. And they were all amazed and marvelled, saying, Behold, are not all these which speak Galileans? And how hear we every man in our own language, wherein we were born? Parthians and Medes and Elamites, and the dwellers in Mesopotamia, in Judæa and Cappadocia, in Pontus and Asia, in Phrygia and Pamphylia, in Egypt and the parts of Libya about Cyrene, and sojourners from Rome, both Jews and proselytes, Cretans and Arabians, we do hear them speaking in our tongues the mighty works of God; and they were all astounded and perplexed, saying the one to the other: What can this mean?"

Luke is a delightful story-teller, and is quite wasted on the dull people who mistake him for a grave, accurate, and diligent historian. What was the use of tongues which were unintelligible except to God, of inspired utterances which yet had no meaning, and did but render him that spoke a barbarian to his hearers, and them in turn barbarians to him? Surely this could not have been the gift of a holy spirit which was to illuminate the seventy different races of the Gentiles? What was needed among the immediate followers of Jesus was rather a miraculous ability to talk their seventy languages. Such a faculty would really be a *sign to the unbelieving*. Accordingly, Luke turns the truth upside down and inside out, never suspecting that epistles of his master, Paul, would survive and contradict his pretty story eighteen centuries later.

A truer artist in fiction would have finished his story at this point; but Luke, in his search for picturesque detail, continues it in such a manner that the end of it entirely contradicts the beginning, as follows: "*But others mocking said, They are filled with new wine.*"

And this scoff supplies Peter with the argument of the speech which he forthwith delivers: "*For these men are not drunk, as ye suppose, seeing it is but the third hour of the day; but this is that which hath been spoken by the prophet Joel: 'And it shall be in the last days, saith God, I will pour forth of my spirit on all flesh: And your sons and your daughters shall prophesy, And your young men shall see visions, And your old men shall dream dreams,'*" etc.

All this conflicts with what precedes, for a sudden and miraculous mastery of foreign languages is the last thing we associate with drunkenness, so that it is absurd and inept to attribute such a scoff to any who witnessed the display. On the other hand, it would be neither absurd nor inept if the gift of tongues had been described as Paul—who spoke with tongues more than all of them (1 Cor. xiv. 18)—describes it. He asserts that "*if the whole church be assembled together and all speak with tongues and there come in men without spiritual gifts or unbelieving, they will say, Ye are mad.*"

Substitute *drunk* for *mad*, and we have the very episode and situation which Luke has travestied in this second chapter of Acts. It would be well if we could accept the second part of his story, which so well accords with Paul's testimony, and reject the first part, which conflicts therewith. But we have no alternative but to regard the entire scene as fictitious. How grotesque, for example, and materialistic is the idea of the holy spirit filling the house like a rushing wind!

Of the tongues of fire—a familiar fancy in pagan stories! In the oldest Syriac versions of the passage it is added that a sweet odour pervaded the house, and this feature was, perhaps, eliminated by the Greek editors of Luke's text; it was, however, a familiar idea among ancient pagans that the epiphany of a god was attended with a sweet smell, and that he left behind an odour of sanctity. Hence the line of Ovid : " *Mansit odor. Posses scire fuisse deam* " ("An odour remained. You could tell that a goddess had appeared").

Let us take one more example of how Luke handles his evidence. At the close of his Gospel Mark relates how certain women, when the sabbath was over, *brought spices* in order to *anoint* the corpse of Jesus. "*And they came very early on the first day of the week to the tomb at sunrise, and they said to themselves, Who shall roll away for us the stone from the door of the tomb? And on looking up they see that the stone has been rolled away, although it was so big.*"

So far Luke is fairly faithful to his source, save that (according to the old form of text in D) he adds (in xxiii. 53) that he set a stone upon the tomb, so huge that twenty men could barely have rolled it along. Let us contrast his text from this point with that of Mark. It is the episode of the women's visit :—

MARK xvi. 5–8.	LUKE xxiv. 4–9.
And having gone into the tomb, they saw a youth sitting on the right hand, clothed in a white garment, and they were astonished beyond measure. But he saith to them, Be ye not so astonished. Ye seek Jesus of Nazareth, the crucified one. He is risen, he is not here. Behold the place where they laid him. But go ye, tell	But having gone in, they found not the body of the Lord Jesus. And it came to pass as they were perplexed about this, behold men twain stood before them in gleaming apparel. And, as they were affrighted and bowed their heads to the earth, they said to them, Why seek ye him that liveth among the dead? He is not here,

his disciples and Peter that he goeth before you into Galilee. There shall ye see him, as he told you. And they went out and fled from the tomb. For a trembling and ecstasy had possession of them, and they said nothing to anyone, for they were afraid.

but is risen. Remember how he spake unto you while he was still in Galilee, saying that the Son of Man must be delivered up into the hands of sinful men, and be crucified, and the third day rise again. And they remembered his words, and returned from the tomb, and told all these things to the eleven, and to all the rest.

Note how Luke speaks of the *Lord* Jesus, a phrase never found in Mark. Next *the youth in a white garment* is multiplied like a vision of Falstaff into *two men in gleaming apparel*. The simple words of the youth in Mark are tricked out into the rhetorical question, "*Why seek ye him that liveth among the dead?*" Then the statement of Jesus, recalled to the women, that he would precede his disciples into Galilee, and that they should see him there, is altogether set aside; and for it is substituted the commonplace prediction of his crucifixion and resurrection formerly uttered by Jesus in Galilee. For Luke, in opposition to Matthew and Mark, will have it that Jesus was seen after death by the disciples in Jerusalem, and not in Galilee; and to make this possible he suppresses the circumstance that at the crucifixion they fled back thither. Lastly, in flagrant contradiction with his source, Mark, who asserts that *they said nothing to anyone*, Luke declares that the women returned from the tomb and announced *all these things to the eleven and to all the rest* (of the faithful).

If we found Thucydides or Polybius or Dio Cassius or any other ancient author playing fast and loose with his sources as Luke here and elsewhere does with his, we should regard them as untrustworthy authors, incapable of transmitting faithfully to their readers the evidence which lay before them. In almost every case in which we can thus compare Luke with Mark, we find the same loose treatment of his evidence. He is a picturesque story-teller, who does not understand or desire historical accuracy. We must not blame him; for his main concern is to edify, and very few writers of that age, even among pagans, had any idea of what truth and accuracy in narrative mean. If anyone is to blame, it is the orthodox divine who imagines that because Luke was an evangelist he was exempt from the ordinary faults of his age. So low was his standard of historical truth that he sets up pretensions to being more trustworthy than his predecessors in the preface to his Gospel, as follows: "*It seemed good to me also, having traced the course of all things accurately from the first, to write unto thee in order, most excellent Theophilus, that thou mightest know the certainty concerning the things which thou wast taught by word of mouth.*" In his Gospel where he puts forward these claims of superiority we can control his statements, because we have got his sources before us. If we had not them almost entire, we could never have divined that a writer who talks in this way about certainty was a mere compiler, and inexact at that.

In the book of Acts we can, unfortunately, but rarely control his narrative, and must therefore use great caution in reading it. The well-known German scholar Adolf Harnack, Professor of Church History in the University of Berlin, in his minute study, *Luke the Physician*,[1] forms a like estimate, for he writes as follows, p. 112:—

> St. Luke is an author whose writings read smoothly;

[1] Williams and Norgate, 1907; English trans.

but one has only to look somewhat more closely to discover that there is scarcely another writer in the New Testament who is so careless an historian as he. Like a true Greek, he has paid careful attention to style and to all the formalities of literature; but in regard to his subject matter, in chapter after chapter, he affords gross instances of carelessness, and often of complete confusion in the narrative. This is true both of the Gospel and of the Acts.

And again, p. 123 :—

He certainly believes himself to be an historian (see the prologue); and so he is; but his powers are limited, for he adopts an attitude towards his authorities which is as distinctly uncritical as that which he adopts towards his own experiences, if these admit of a miraculous interpretation.

In the preceding pages I have tried to explain the nature of what is called the Synoptic problem, probing here and there, as it were with the rapier of a *douanier*, the Gospels, in order to sample their contents, and see what they consist of, what claims to credibility they have, what sources their writers used, and how they used them. The examples I have given prove that an evangelist felt himself at liberty to rearrange the traditional matter, and to create backgrounds of incident for any pregnant aphorisms or string of aphorisms that had come down to him isolated and detached. The same sayings are framed by Matthew and Luke in utterly different contexts of action, place, and time; and in such cases one at least of the contexts, and probably both, must be the arbitrary creation of the writer or writers. Luke in especial can be convicted of fabricating not only incidents, but also words uttered in connection with them. In thus concocting speeches for his hero he violated no canon of ancient historical art, since Thucydides, Tacitus, and other serious chroniclers, did the same. So much may be urged in justification of his method. Mark's Gospel being in its character more narrative than didactic, and a relatively small space being assigned in it to what Jesus said, one would expect him to confine himself to genuine utterances of Jesus; but here again we are disappointed, for in ch. xiii. entire paragraphs of a Jewish apocalypse are placed in the mouth of Jesus which he certainly never uttered; and, could we check Mark, we should probably find this to be no isolated case. As to many of the sayings also which Matthew took from the non-Marcan document which he used in common with Luke, we at first sight feel reasonable doubt whether Jesus ever uttered them, because they presuppose an organised church, so that their attribution to Jesus is an anachronism. The same doubt extends even to so famous an utterance as the Lord's Prayer. For in Mark xi. 25, we read: *"And whensoever ye stand praying, forgive if ye have aught against anyone; that your father also which is in heaven may forgive you your trespasses."* Here Jesus lays down no fixed formula, but only general rules for prayer. As J. Wellhausen remarks, it would appear that Mark knew of the prayer as it was liturgically used in history, but did not venture to attribute it to Jesus as a whole, as do Matthew and Luke. As often, so here, these two evangelists assign different occasions for the communication to the apostles of this prayer; for Matthew (vi. 9) introduces it in the Sermon on the Mount, whereas Luke assigns it to a later period in the ministry, after the appointment of the seventy, in the following words: *"And it came to pass, as he was praying in a certain place, that when he ceased, one of his disciples said unto him, Lord, teach us to pray, even as John also taught his disciples,"* etc.

This exordium was made up by Luke *ad hoc*, in accordance with his literary method. But we must not accuse him of bad faith because he thus designs suitable situations for the utterances of Jesus, nor because he freely cuts and carves, and even travesties, the text of Mark. For we must remember that the latter probably came to him merely as an anonymous document in a single stray copy. "*Many*," he says in the preface to his Gospel, "*have undertaken to draw up a narrative concerning those matters which have been fulfilled among us.*" Mark's Gospel was just one of these many attempts. No canon as yet existed, and no one form of gospel had more prestige than another. The modern believer has been taught to invest the four Gospels with a certain sacrosanctity, and to speak of "gospel truth" as if truth lay here enshrined as nowhere else. But Luke saw in his copy of Mark just an odd document to be used up as suited his literary purpose, and then thrown aside. Mark's name may or may not have been attached to it. Even if it was, it was merely the name of one who had for a time attached himself to Paul and then forsaken him. The conception entertained of Jesus in the circle of believers to which Luke belonged had developed, perhaps under the influence of Paul's *a priori* notions, since Mark wrote; and Luke was bound to adapt his text to later conceptions of whose superior validity and truth he would not be likely to entertain a doubt. The same remarks apply to Matthew's Gospel, and yet more to the one ascribed to John. The writer of this last does not even try to represent Jesus as Jewish Messiah; his primitive *rôle* and vocation are forgotten, and he is become the incarnate Reason of God, mixing out of extreme condescension with mankind. To the second great document used by Matthew and Luke, and called by modern scholars the non-Marcan source or Q (*Quelle*), we must now turn.

Chapter VII.

THE NON-MARCAN DOCUMENT

We have seen that Luke and Matthew used, in addition to Mark's Gospel, which has survived, another source, mainly composed of sayings of Jesus, which has not. To this source scholars usually refer as the non-Marcan source, or as Q. In order to form a sound judgment about it we need to reconstruct it and set it out by itself; and several scholars have undertaken this task, and vary little from one another in their results. Matthew appears to have copied it out more faithfully than Luke, so far as regards its original style and phraseology, though he has inserted in it passages which reflect a more developed stage of church organisation than suits the first Messianic movement. The text as reproduced by Luke, on the other hand, is redolent of his peculiar style and idiom, showing that he recast it and threw it into his own language. It is improbable that it was originally penned in Luke's very characteristic language. On the other hand, as it stands in Matthew, it exhibits no special conformity with the general style and manner of writing of that evangelist, and almost wholly lacks his impress.

In the following pages I follow Professor Harnack's reconstruction of this source. The order in which the sections follow one another is that of Luke, who in this respect can be shown to have been more conservative than Matthew. Brackets enclose passages as to which there is a doubt whether they should be included in it.

§ 1.

(Mt iii. 5, 7-12 ; Lc iii. 3, 7-9, 16, 17.)

All the region round about Jordan......John saw many (*or* the multitudes)......coming to baptism, and said to them, Offspring of vipers, who warned you to flee from the impending wrath? Produce therefore fruit worthy of repentance. And think (? begin) not to say in yourselves, We have as father Abraham. For I tell you, that God is able out of these stones to raise up children to Abraham. And already the axe is laid at the root of the trees. Every tree then not producing good fruit is cut down and thrown into the fire. I indeed baptise you in water unto repentance; but he that comes after me is stronger than I, whose shoes I am not worthy to carry. He shall baptise you in [spirit holy and] fire, whose winnowing fan is in his hand, and he shall purge out his threshing-floor, and shall gather his grain into his barn ; but the chaff he will burn up in fire unquenchable.

§ 2.

(Mt iv. 1-11 ; Lc iv. 1-13.)

Jesus was led up into the desert by the Spirit to be tempted by the devil ; and, having fasted forty days and forty nights, he afterwards hungered. And the tempter said to him, An thou art Son of God, bid these stones to become bread. And he answered, It is written, Not upon bread alone shall man live. So he taketh him with him to Jerusalem, and he stood him on the pinnacle of the temple ; and saith he to

THE NON-MARCAN DOCUMENT 109

him, An thou art Son of God, throw thyself down; for it is written that he will give his angels charge concerning thee, and on their hands they shall bear thee up, lest ever thou dash against a stone thy foot. Jesus said to him, Likewise is it written, Thou shalt not tempt the Lord thy God. Again he taketh him with him into a mountain exceedingly high, and shows him all the kingdoms of the world and their glory. And he said to him, All this I will give thee, if thou wilt fall down and worship me. And Jesus says to him: It is written, The Lord thy God shalt thou worship, and him alone shalt thou serve. And the devil leaveth him.

§ 3.

(Mt v. 1–4, 6, 11, 12; Lc vi. 17, 20–23.)

......Multitudes......he taught the disciples, saying ......Blessed are the poor, for theirs is the kingdom of God.

Blessed are the sorrowers, for they shall be comforted.

Blessed are the hungry, for they shall be filled.

Blessed are ye, whenever they revile and persecute you, and say all that is evil against you falsely.

Rejoice and exult, because your reward is great in heaven; for even so they persecuted the prophets who were before you.

§ 4.

(Mt v. 39, 40; Lc vi. 29.)

Whoever smites thee on thy [right] cheek, turn to him also the other. And to one who would go to law with thee and take thy shirt, give up to him also thy coat.

§ 5.
(Mt v. 42; Lc vi. 30.)

To one who asks of thee, give; and from one who would borrow of thee, turn not away.

§ 6.
(Mt v. 44–48; Lc vi. 27, 28, 35b, 32, 33, 36.)

I say to you, Love your enemies and pray for them that persecute you, in order that ye may become sons of your father, for he causes his sun to rise upon the wicked and the good [and his rain to fall on just and unjust]. For if ye love those who love you, what reward have ye? Do not the tax-farmers do this very thing? And if ye love your brethren alone, what that is extraordinary do ye do? Do not the Gentiles also do as much? Ye shall therefore be merciful as your father is merciful.

§ 7.
(Mt vii. 12; Lc vi. 31.)

All things whatsoever ye desire that men should do unto you, even so do ye unto them.

§ 8.
(Mt vii. 1–5; Lc vi. 37, 38, 41, 42.)

Judge not, that ye be not judged; for with whatsoever judgment ye judge, shall ye be judged; and with that measure wherewith ye measure, shall it be measured unto you. And why markest thou the mote in thy brother's eye, but perceivest not the beam in thine own eye? or how shalt thou say to thy brother, Let me cast the mote out of thine eye, while the beam is in thine own eye? Hypocrite, first cast the beam out of thine own eye, and then shalt thou see clearly how to cast the mote out of thy brother's eye.

§ 9.
(Mt xv. 14 ; Lc vi. 39.)

If a blind man lead a blind, they will both fall into a ditch.

§ 10.
(Mt x. 24–25 ; Lc vi. 40.)

A disciple is not above his teacher, nor a servant above his master. Let it suffice for the disciple to be as his teacher, and for the servant to be as his master.

§ 11.
(Mt vii. 16–18, xii. 33 ; Lc vi. 43, 44.)

By its fruit the tree is known. They surely do not gather grapes off thorns or figs off thistles? Even so, every good tree produces good fruit, but the rotten tree produces bad fruit. A good tree cannot bear bad fruit, nor a rotten tree produce good fruit.

§ 12.
(Mt vii. 21, 24–27 ; Lc vi. 46–49.)

Not everyone who saith to me, Lord, Lord, shall enter the kingdom of God, but he who doeth the will of my father. Everyone then that listens to these words and doeth them shall be likened to a man who builded his house on the rock. And the rain came down and the rivers came, and the winds blew, and fell upon that house, and it fell not ; for it was founded on the rock. And everyone who listens to these my words, but doeth them not, shall be likened to a man who builded his house on the sand. And the rain came down, and the rivers came, and the winds blew, and smote upon that house, and it fell, and great was the fall thereof.

§ 13.

(Mt vii. 28, viii. 5–10; Lc vii. 1–10.)

He entered Capernaum, and there approached him a centurion, calling on him and saying, Master, my child lies at home struck down by paralysis, suffering dreadfully. He said to him, I will come and heal him. But the centurion answered and said, Lord, I am not worthy that you should enter under my roof; but only say a word, and my child will be healed. For I am a man in authority, having under me soldiers; and I say to this one, Go, and he goeth, and to another, Come, and he cometh; and to my servant, Do this, and he doeth it. But Jesus heard and wondered, and said to them who followed, Verily, I tell you, not even in Israel have I found so much faith. [And Jesus said to the centurion, Go. As thou hast believed be it unto thee. And the child was healed in that hour.]

§ 14.

(Mt xi. 2–11; Lc vii. 18–28.)

But John, hearing in the prison the works of Christ, sent by his disciples and said to him, Art thou he that is to come, or must we expect another? And he answered and said to them, Go ye, and report to John what ye hear and see. The blind see anew and the lame walk, lepers are cleansed and deaf hear, and dead men are raised and poor receive good tidings. And blessed is he who is not scandalised in me. But as they walked along he began to talk to the multitudes about John: What went ye out into the wilderness to

see? A reed shaken by the wind? But what went
ye out to see? A man clothed in soft raiment? Lo,
they who wear soft raiment are in the houses of kings.
Then why went ye out? To see a prophet? Nay, I
tell you, one even greater than a prophet. For he it
is of whom it is written, Lo, I send my angel before
thy face, who shall prepare thy path before thee.
Verily, I tell you that among those born of women
there hath been raised up none greater than John
the Baptist; yet the least in the kingdom of God is
greater than he.

§ 15.

(Mt xi. 16–19; Lc vii. 31–35.)

To what shall I liken this generation, and what is
it like? It is like to children sitting in the public
square, which address the others and say: We have
piped to you, and ye danced not. We sang dirges,
and ye mourned not. For John came neither eating
nor drinking, and they say, He hath a devil. The
Son of Man came eating and drinking, and they say,
Behold a man, a glutton and a wine-bibber, friend of
publicans and sinners. And wisdom is justified of
her children.

§ 16.

(Mt x. 7; Lc ix. 2, x. 9, 11.)

Go ye and proclaim, saying that the kingdom of
God is at hand.

§ 17.

(Mt viii. 19–22; Lc ix. 57–60.)

One said to him, I will follow thee whithersoever
thou goest. And Jesus answered him: The foxes
have burrows and the birds of heaven nests; but the
Son of Man hath not where to lay his head. But

another one said to him: Permit me first to go away and bury my father. But he answered him: Follow me, and let the dead bury their dead.

§ 18.
(Mt ix. 37, 38; Lc x. 2.)

He saith to his disciples: The harvest is abundant, but the workers few. Beseech, then, the lord of the harvest to send forth workers for his harvest.

§ 19.
(Mt x. 16a; Lc x. 3.)

Behold, I send you forth as sheep amidst wolves.

§ 20.
(Mt x. 12, 13; Lc x. 5, 6.)

But when ye enter into the house, give it greeting. And if the house be worthy, let your peace descend upon it. But if it be not worthy, let your peace return unto you. [Carry not a purse, nor wallet, nor shoes, and on the way salute no one.]

§ 21.
(Mt x. 10b; Lc x. 7b.)

[Remain in the house eating and drinking what they provide.] For the worker is worthy of his food.

§ 22.
(Mt x. 15; Lc x. 12.)

Verily, I tell you, it shall be more tolerable for the land of Sodom and Gomorrah in that day (*or* in the day of judgment) than for that city.

(In Lc x. 8–11 the above is preceded by the following: Into whatever city ye enter and they welcome you, eat ye what is set before you, and say to them, The kingdom of God is at hand. But into whatever city ye enter and they receive you not, go ye out into the streets thereof and say, Even the dust which cleaves unto us from your city on our feet we wipe off on you.)

§ 23.

(Mt xi. 21–23; Lc x. 13–15.)

Woe to thee, Chorazin; woe to thee, Bethsaida. For had the works of power which have been wrought in you been wrought in Tyre and Sidon, they would long ago have repented in sackcloth and ashes. But I tell you, it shall be more tolerable for Tyre and Sidon in the day of judgment than for you. And thou, Capernaum, instead of being exalted to heaven, shalt go down unto hell.

§ 24.

(Mt x. 40; Lc x. 16.)

[He that welcomes you, welcomes me; and he that welcomes me, welcomes him that sent me.]

§ 25.

(Mt xi. 25–27; Lc x. 21–22.)

In that season he said: I give thee thanks, Father, Lord of heaven and earth, that thou hast hidden these things from the wise and clever, and hast revealed them to infants. Yea, O Father, for so it was thy good will, before thee. All things have been made over to me by the father, and no one hath known [the son except the father, nor] the father [hath anyone known] except the son and to whomsoever the son wills to reveal.

§ 26.
(Mt xiii. 16, 17; Lc x. 23b, 24.)

Blessed are your eyes, because they see, and your ears, because they hear. For verily I say to you, that many prophets and kings desired to see what ye see, and saw not, and to hear what you hear, and heard not.

§ 27.
(Mt vi. 9–13; Lc xi. 2–4.)

Father, give us this day our daily bread, and forgive us our debts, even as we have forgiven our debtors, and lead us not into temptation.

§ 28.
(Mt vii. 7–11; Lc xi. 9–13.)

Ask, and it shall be given to you; seek, and ye shall find; knock, and it shall be opened to you. For everyone who asks receiveth; and who seeks finds; and to the knocker it shall be opened. Or is there any one of you, of whom his son shall ask for bread, he will surely not give him a stone? Or if he ask for a fish, he will surely not tender him a viper? If, then, ye, being sinners, know how to give good gifts to your children, how much more shall your father from heaven give good things to them that ask him?

§ 29.
(Mt xii. 22, 23, 25, 27, 28, 30, 43–45; Lc xi. 14, 17, 19, 23–36.)

He healed one possessed by a devil, dumb, so that the dumb one spake, and all the multitudes were astonished.......Every kingdom divided against itself is made desolate.......And if I through Beelzebul cast out devils, through whom do your own sons cast them out? Therefore shall they be your judges. But if I by spirit of God cast out demons, then indeed hath the kingdom of God hastened to come upon you....... Unless a man is with me, he is against me; and he who gathers not in with me, scatters.......Whensoever the unclean spirit quits a man, he passes through dry places seeking rest, and finds none. Then he says, I will return into the house whence I went forth. And he goes, and finds it vacant and swept and adorned. Then he goes and takes with him seven spirits more evil than himself, and they enter and dwell there. And the last state of that man is worse than the first.

§ 30.

(Mt xii. 38, 39, 41, 42; Lc xi. 16, 29–32.)

They said, We wish to see a sign wrought by thee. But he said, An evil and adulterous generation seeks for a sign, and sign shall not be given to it, except the sign of Jonah. For as Jonah was a sign to the Ninevites, so shall be the Son of Man to this generation. The men of Nineveh shall rise up in the judgment with this generation, and shall condemn it; for they repented at the preaching of Jonah, and behold more than Jonah is here. The Queen of the South shall rise up in judgment with this generation and condemn it, for she came from the ends of the earth to listen to the wisdom of Solomon, and behold more than Solomon is here.

§ 31.

(Mt v. 15; Lc xi. 33.)

They light not a lamp and set it under the bushel, but on the candlestick, and it lights all who are in the house.

§ 32.
(Mt vi. 22, 23 ; Lc xi. 34, 35.)

The light of the body is thine eye ; if, then, thine eye be simple, thine whole body will be full of light. But if thine eye be wicked, thy whole body will be dark. If, then, the light within thee is darkness, how great the darkness !

§ 33.
(Mt xxiii. 4, 13, 23, 25, 27, 29, 30–32, 34–36 ;
Lc xi. 46, 52, 42, 39, 44, 47–51.)

They bind up heavy burdens, and lay them on the shoulders of men ; but they themselves would not move them with their little finger.

Woe to you Pharisees, because ye shut up the kingdom of God before men's faces. For ye enter not yourselves, nor permit them to enter who would do so.

Woe to you Pharisees, for ye tithe mint and anise and cummin ; but have left undone the weightier parts of the law, judgment and mercy.

Now, ye Pharisees, ye cleanse the outside of the cup and platter, but within they are full of robbery and licence.

Woe to you, for ye are like graves unseen, and men who walk over them recognise them not.

[Woe to you Pharisees, for ye are to be likened to whitewashed graves, which outside appear beautiful, but within are full of dead bones and all uncleanness.]

Woe to you, because ye build the tombs of the prophets and say : Had we been in the days of our fathers, we would not have been sharers with them in the blood of the prophets. So that ye bear witness that ye are sons of them that slew the prophets. And ye fill up the measure of your fathers.

Therefore the Wisdom of God said: I send unto you prophets and wise men and scribes. Some of them ye will slay and persecute, that there may come on you all the blood shed on earth, from that of Abel until that of Zacharias, whom ye slew between the shrine and the altar. Verily I say to you, All these things shall come on this generation.

§ 34A.
(Mt x. 26-33; Lc xii. 2-9.)

Nothing is hidden which shall not be revealed, or secret which shall not be known. What I speak to you in darkness, do ye speak in the light; and what ye hear in a whisper, proclaim ye on the housetops. And fear ye not them that slay the body, but have no power to slay the soul. But fear rather him that is able to destroy soul and body in Gehenna. Are not two (or five) sparrows sold for one (or two) pennies? And one of them shall not fall to the ground without God's will. And of your heads the very hairs are numbered. Fear not then. Ye are of far more account than sparrows. Everyone then who shall make confession of me before men shall the son of man (or shall I) also make confession of before the angels of God. But whosoever denies me before men, I also will deny him before the angels of God.

§ 34B.
(Mt xii. 32; Lc xii. 10.)

And who ever speaketh ill of the son of man, it shall be forgiven him; but who ever speaketh ill of the holy spirit, it shall not be forgiven him.

§ 35.

(Mt vi. 25–33 ; Lc xii. 22–31.)

Therefore I say unto you, feel no concern for your life, what ye shall eat, nor for your body, what ye shall put on. Is not the life more than food, and the body than raiment? Look at the crows (*or* the birds of heaven), how they sow not nor reap nor gather into barns, yet God feedeth them. Are ye not of more account than they? And who of you by fussing can add to his stature one cubit? And about raiment why fuss thee? Mark the lilies how they grow. They labour not, nor do they spin. Yet I say to you, not even Solomon in all his glory was clad as one of these. But if God so dresses the weed which is today in the field and to-morrow is cast into a furnace, how much more you, O ye of little faith? Therefore ye shall not worry and say : What shall we eat? or what shall we drink? or what shall we wear? For all these things are in quest for the Gentiles. For your father knows that ye are in need of all these. But seek ye his kingdom, and all these things shall be added to you.

§ 36.

(Mt vi. 19–21 ; Lc xii. 33, 34.)

Treasure not up for yourselves treasures on earth, where the moth and the rust deform, and where thieves break through and steal. But treasure up for yourselves treasures in heaven, where neither moth nor rust deform, and where thieves neither break through nor steal. For wherever your treasure is, there will be also your heart.

§ 37.

(Mt xxiv. 43–51; Lc xii. 39–46.)

But this know ye, that if the householder knew in what hour the thief cometh, he would keep awake and not allow his house to be broken into. [Therefore do ye be ready, because the son of man comes in an hour when ye expect him not.] Who, then, is the faithful servant and thoughtful, whom the master set over his household to give its members food in season? Blessed is that servant whom the master shall find so doing when he comes. Verily I tell you that he will set him over all that belongs to him. But if that servant say in his heart: My master delays, and begins to beat his fellow-servants, and eats and drinks with drunkards, the master of that servant shall come in a day when he expects him not and in an hour of which he is not aware, and shall cut him in two and set his portion together with the hypocrites.

§ 38.

(Mt x. 34, 35, 36; Lc xii. 51, 53.)

Think ye that I came to shed peace upon the land? I came not to shed peace, but a sword. For I came to part asunder a man against his father and a daughter against her mother, and a daughter-in-law against her mother-in-law. And a man's foes are those of his own household.

§ 39.

(Mt v. 25, 26; Lc xii. 58, 59.)

Be reconciled with thine adversary quickly, whilst thou art still with him in the street; lest the adversary deliver thee to the judge, and the judge to the officer, and thou be cast into prison. Verily, I tell you, thou shalt not depart thence, until thou hast paid the last farthing.

§ 40.

(Mt xiii. 31-33 ; Lc xiii. 18-21.)

And again he said : To what shall I liken the kingdom of God ? It is like leaven which a woman took and hid in three measures of meal, until the whole was leavened.

(The above was probably preceded by the following : Unto what is the kingdom of God like, and to what shall I liken it ? It is like a grain of mustard seed, which a man took and sowed in his field ; and it grew and became a tree, and the birds of heaven nest in its branches.)

§ 41.

(Mt vii. 13, 14 ; Lc xiii. 24.)

Enter ye through the narrow gate. For wide [is the gate] and broad the road, which leads to ruin, and many are they that pass in along it. For narrow is the gate and worn the road which leads unto life, and few are they who find it.

§ 42.

(Mt viii. 11, 12 ; Lc xiii. 28, 29.)

I tell you that from East and West they shall come, and lie down with Abraham and Isaac and Jacob in the kingdom of God ; but the children of the kingdom shall be cast out (*or* go forth). There shall be wailing and gnashing of teeth.

§ 43.

(Mt xxiii. 37-39 ; Lc xiii. 34, 35.)

Jerusalem, Jerusalem, thou that killest the prophets and stonest them that have been sent unto thee!

How many times have I wished to gather together thy children, as a bird gathers her nestlings under her wings, and ye would not have it. Behold, your house is abandoned unto you desolate. For I tell you, ye shall not see me henceforth until [he come when] you shall say: Blessed he who cometh in the name of the Lord.

§ 44.
(Mt xxiii. 12; Lc xiv. 11.)

Whosoever shall lift himself up shall be abased, and whosoever shall abase himself shall be lifted up.

§ 45.
(Mt x. 37; Lc xiv. 26.)

[He who loves father or mother more than me is not worthy of me; and he who loves son or daughter more than me is not worthy of me.]

§ 46.
(Mt x. 38; Lc xiv. 27.)

He that takes not up his cross and follows me is not worthy of me.

§ 47.
(Mt v. 13; Lc xiv. 34, 35.)

Ye are the salt [of the earth]; but if the salt be spoiled, wherewith shall it be salted? It is useful for nothing any more, except to be cast outside and trodden under foot by men.

§ 48.
(Mt xviii. 12, 13; Lc xv. 4–7.)

What think ye? If a man should have a hundred sheep, and one of them lose its way, would he not leave the ninety-nine on the mountains, and go and seek the lost one? And if so be it he find it, I say unto you that he rejoiceth over it more than over the ninety-nine that lost not their way.

§ 49.
(Mt vi. 24 ; Lc xvi. 13.)

No one can serve two masters. For either he will hate the one and love the other, or he will adhere to the one and despise the other. Ye cannot serve God and mammon.

§ 50.
(Mt xi. 12, 13 ; Lc xvi. 16.)

The prophets and the law lasted until John. From then till now the kingdom of God is being wrested by force, and men of violence snatch at it.

§ 51.
(Mt v. 18 ; Lc xvi. 17.)

Verily I tell you, until heaven and earth pass away not one jot or tittle shall pass away of the law.

§ 52.
(Mt v. 32 ; Lc xvi. 18.)

I tell you, everyone who divorces his wife causes her to commit adultery; and whoever shall marry a divorced woman commits adultery.

§ 53.
(Mt xviii. 7 ; Lc xvii. 1.)

It must be that scandals come, but woe to the man through whom the scandal comes.

§ 54.

(Mt xviii. 15, 21, 22; Lc xvii. 3, 4.)

If thy brother sin, rebuke him; if he listen to thee, thou hast won thy brother to thy gain.......How often shall my brother sin against me and I forgive him? Until seven times? Jesus said to him: I tell thee, not until seven times, but until seventy times seven.

§ 55.

(Mt xvii. 20b; Lc xvii. 6.)

If ye have faith as a grain of mustard, ye shall say to this mountain, Get thee hence, and it shall be removed.

§ 56.

(Mt xxiv. 26, 27, 28, 37–41; Lc xvii. 23, 24, 37, 26, 27, 34, 35.)

If, then, they say to you, Lo, he is in the wilderness, go ye not out. Lo, in the store-rooms, believe them not. For as the lightning quits the east and flashes across to the west, so shall be the coming (*parusia*—i.e., presence) of the Son of Man. Wheresoever is the corpse, there shall the eagles be gathered together.

As were the days of Noah, so shall be the coming of the Son of Man. For as they were, in those days which preceded the flood, eating and drinking, marrying and giving in marriage, until the day when Noah entered the ark, and as they knew not until the flood came and swept them all away, so shall be the coming of the Son of Man. There shall be two in the field, one is taken and the other left; two women grinding in the mill, the one is taken and the other left.

§ 57.
(Mt x. 39; Lc xvii. 33.)

He that finds his life shall lose it, and he that loses his life shall find it.

§ 58.
(Mt xxv. 29; Lc xix. 26.)

To everyone who has shall be given, and in abundance; but from him who has not, even what he has shall be taken from him.

§ 59.
(Mt xix. 28; Lc xxii. 28, 30.)

Ye who have followed me shall sit upon twelve thrones, judging the twelve tribes of Israel.

Chapter VIII.

THE NON-MARCAN DOCUMENT—*(Continued)*

Such, or nearly such, was the second document, which, together with Mark's Gospel, drifted into the hands of the first and third evangelists. It must have comprised other incidents and sayings found in one or the other of these, but not given in the above reconstruction, which necessarily takes account only of what stands in both of them. It remains to ask: What is the age of this document? What its origin? What is the probability that its contents really reflect the life and teaching of Jesus, as Xenophon's *Memorabilia* reflect the life and teaching of Socrates, or the pages of Boswell the conversations of Dr. Johnson?

Let us begin by enumerating those traits of the document which encourage us to believe that it must be very old, and almost a contemporary record.

(1) Firstly, then, there is no mention of the death and resurrection of Jesus. We have seen how Paul insists on the importance of these—how his mind is filled with them, even to the neglect of the real life and teaching of Jesus. In the same spirit as Paul, Mark, the earliest of the evangelists, relates how, from the moment of Peter's recognition of him as the Messiah, Jesus "*began to teach that the Son of Man must suffer many things, and be rejected by the elders and chief priests and scribes, and be slain, and after three days rise again.*"

From this point on of Mark's Gospel, this is the main theme of Jesus' discourses—his gospel proper; and about the last fourth of Mark's Gospel is given up to the incidents of the death and resurrection. The same is true of the other three Gospels, and the lately-recovered fragment of the so-called Gospel of Peter pictures these events with no less detail than the canonical sources. Matthew's Gospel in particular exemplifies how much the minds of Christians were pre-occupied towards the end of the first century with the death and resurrection. In the non-Marcan source (see above, p. 117, § 30), here reproduced more faithfully by Luke than by Matthew, stood the saying that, although that evil and adulterous generation sought a sign, they yet should be given none except that of Jonah. As Jonah was a sign to the Ninevites, so was the son of man to the later generation. In other words, Jesus was a sort of modern Jonah, whose advent heralded destruction to the Jews unless they repented, even as the Ninevites of old had repented at the preaching of the older prophet.

In all this there is no reference to the death and resurrection of Jesus. But Matthew, with passages ringing in his ears like the one from Mark which has just been cited, saw in this saying about Jonah an occasion for putting into the lips of Jesus a prophecy of his death and resurrection after three days. Had not Jonah been swallowed by a whale, and, after three days' confinement in its entrails, vomited up afresh into the light of heaven? Here was a chance for this evangelist, who excels all the others in the art of discovering in the Jewish scriptures foretypes and prophecies of Christ. Accordingly, he re-writes his source as follows: "*Then certain of the scribes and*

Pharisees answered him, saying, Master, we would see a sign from thee. But he answered and said unto them, An evil and adulterous generation seeketh after a sign; and there shall no sign be given to it except the sign of Jonah the prophet: for as Jonah was three days and three nights in the belly of the whale, so shall the Son of Man be three days and three nights in the heart of the earth. The men of Nineveh shall stand up in judgment with this generation; for they repented at the preaching of Jonah; and behold, a greater than Jonah is here."

In thus rewriting his source Matthew makes nonsense of it, for it was the preaching of Jonah which led the men of Nineveh—however much against his will—to repent, and not the circumstance, unknown to them, that on a former voyage he had met with such an odd mishap. In full accordance with this general absence of reference to his death is Jesus's answer (§ 17) to the man who said: "*I will follow thee whithersoever thou goest.*" Jesus does not answer him, "I go to meet my death," as from such passages as Mark viii. 30–32, Mark x. 32–34, we should expect him to do, but merely thus: "*The foxes have burrows and the birds of heaven their nests, but the son of man hath not where to lay his head.*" No hint here of death being the guerdon of discipleship. At the worst, a life of homeless wandering is in store for those who follow him, as it is already the life which he has made his own.

There is, however, one saying in this document which favours the view that its author knew of the crucifixion. It is in § 46: "*He that takes not up his cross and follows me is not worthy of me.*" That this saying was an integral part of the source, as Matthew and Luke inherited it, we cannot doubt. That it was an old saying is also to be inferred from the fact that Mark viii. 34 records it independently as follows: "*If anyone wishes to come after me, let him deny himself, and take up his cross, and follow me.*"

Was this saying put into the lips of Jesus, *ex post facto*, after the event, so as to involve a *hysteron proteron*? Or can we let it stand, and interpret it apart from the crucifixion? There are grounds to justify the latter course. Firstly, it is certain, as M. Salomon Reinach has pointed out, that crucifixion was long antecedently to Jesus regarded as the typical death which the just man must expect at the hands of malefactors and oppressors. It is so represented in an eloquent passage of Plato, in which the Christians later on discerned a pagan prophecy of Christ. Jesus, of course, did not read Plato, but the idea may very well have been current in the Grecised parts of Galilee, and it seems to be glanced at in the Hebrew psalm xxii. 16, with which, of course, Jesus was familiar: "*The assembly of evil-doers have inclosed me; they pierced my hands and my feet.*"

Secondly, in the very lifetime of Jesus, Philo, his Alexandrine compatriot, constantly refers to death on the cross—and he had witnessed hundreds of his compatriots die in this way—as if it symbolised, to his mind, the extreme of disgrace and humiliation. Thus, in his treatise on the posterity of Cain (§ 17), he remarks that those who are too much attached to the body and to material outward goods have, as it were, hung themselves on lifeless objects, and, like persons crucified (he uses Plato's word, *anaskolopizô*), are nailed until death to perishable matter. In another treatise (*On Dreams*, ii. § 31) the tale of Pharaoh's hanging his cook suggests the same thought again. Like the crucified, the understanding of a selfish and sensual man is nailed to the tree of poverty-stricken ignorance. This use made of the idea is, it is true, quite different from that of the gospel, where not the self-indulgent, but the ascetic, undergoes crucifixion; but they show that allegorists were prone to use it one way or the other. In the Testaments of the Patriarchs (Test. of Levi) it is predicted that the divine Messiah is to be crucified *(anaskolopizô)*, but it is not certain that this is not a Christian interpolation in an old Jewish document. It is not impossible, therefore, that we should find such a reference even among genuine sayings of Jesus, and it is far from being the only point of contact between the Gospels and the works of Philo, as we shall see later on.

On the other hand, the saying is likely enough to have been slipped into the collection some time before it fell into the hands of Matthew and Luke. It hardly formed part of it originally. In any case, this saying, by its very uniqueness, does but render all the more remarkable the absence of references to an episode which already, in Paul, and soon in the minds of Christians in general, overshadows every other aspect of the master's life and activity.

(2) The horizon of Jesus, in these sayings, is wholly Jewish and Palestinian—one might, except for § 43, say Galilean; and even the apostrophe to Jerusalem in the latter passage is so general in character that we could not, from it alone, and apart from the fuller Gospels, infer that the preaching begun in Galilee had been continued in Jerusalem. The only other places mentioned—Chorazin, Bethsaida, Capernaum—are all in Northern Palestine.

THE NON-MARCAN DOCUMENT

(3) There are touches, asides, hints, presuppositions, in these addresses which can only belong to the earliest age, because they militate so sharply against the beliefs and prejudices of any later time. Contrast, for example, what is said of John the Baptist in § 14 with the asseverations of the evangelists. Thus, Matthew is careful to explain to his readers that John the Baptist recognised Jesus as the Messiah so soon as he came to be baptised. "*But John would have hindered him, saying, I have need to be baptised by thee, and comest thou to me?*"

Again, in the Gospel of the Ebionites, a very early document, John is made to ask, "*Who art thou, Lord?*" and a voice answers from heaven: "*This is my beloved son, in whom I am well pleased. And forthwith John fell down before him and said, I beseech thee, Lord, do thou baptise me.*"

It is the evident intention of Mark and Luke, in their narratives of the baptism, that their readers should understand John to have acclaimed Jesus as the Messiah from the first. The Fourth Gospel is still more explicit, for in it we read (i. 29) that John, seeing Jesus coming unto him, said: "*Behold the Lamb of God which taketh away the sin of the world;......he that sent me to baptise with water said unto me, Upon whomsoever thou shalt see the Spirit descending, and abiding upon him, the same is he that baptiseth with the holy spirit. And I have seen, and borne witness that this is the Son of God.*"

This, then, is the form in which the legend was fixed well before the end of the first century. It could not be admitted that John felt even a moment's hesitation in recognising Jesus as the Messiah. How different is the record of this non-Marcan source!

According to it, John, hearing in his prison of the works of Christ, "*sent by his disciples and said to him, Art thou he that should come, or are we to expect another?*" Such hesitation utterly contradicts the legend that John recognised Jesus in the Jordan, and must belong to an older and much more credible tradition.

Again, in § 28 Jesus addresses his disciples thus: "*If you, wicked as you are,*" etc. In none but an early document could such an epithet as "wicked" be applied to the immediate companions of Jesus. Their reputation for holiness was well established long before the first century was out.

(4) In this document there are recorded no stupendous miracles such as meet us everywhere in Mark; and the Messiahship of Jesus is based as much on his teaching as on his works of power. "*Go and report to John what ye do hear and see,*" he says to the disciples sent by the Baptist to inquire who he was. He is made (in § 23) to appeal to the works of power which he had wrought, but which the inhabitants of Chorazin and Bethsaida had found so singularly unconvincing. These works are enumerated (in § 14) to the disciples of John, and they are almost exclusively works of faith-healing such as figure in authentic histories of religious enthusiasm in every age and clime. The clause, "the dead are raised," may be regarded as a bit of rhetorical exaggeration. The only cures narrated or referred to in detail are those of the blind demoniac, in § 29, and of the paralytic child, in § 13. In the former of these two sections it is frankly acknowledged that the Jews and enemies of Jesus were in the habit of effecting the same sort of cures,

as, indeed, we learn from the historian Josephus; and the curious story of the expelled demon returning with seven demons worse than himself is an interesting admission that Jesus's exorcisms were not always permanently successful.

The obvious aim of the writer in telling the story of the centurion's child (§ 13) is not to narrate a startling miracle, but to provide a background for the saying, "*Verily I say unto you, not even in Israel have I found so much faith.*" The concluding clause of this section, attesting a cure at a distance, seems to be Matthew's way of rounding off the story; Luke's ending also, which has nothing in common with Matthew, is probably an addition of his own. Their common source seems to have stopped short with the deliverance of the apophthegm.

(5) The writer, or compiler, of this document himself entertains no doubt but that Jesus became the Messiah at his baptism. He tells the story of John, and he tells the story of the temptation. He almost certainly related the baptism of Jesus as well, though Matthew and Luke are content to transcribe Mark's account of it. He wishes his readers to bear in mind all through that the person whose teaching he reproduces was he who had, in the Jordan, been spiritually anointed, and promoted to be Son of God and Messiah. But, as Harnack remarks, if we think away §§ 1 and 2, Jesus addresses us in most of these sayings simply as a teacher, as a prophet, or as one greater than a prophet, as the last and final emissary of God. He nowhere says, "I am the Messiah." His claims are rather of the same order as those which Mohammed made on his followers. He believes himself to be the possessor of a new, unique, and final revelation of the

Father's nature. He calls his countrymen to repentance, and the Sermon on the Mount and the rest of the moral precepts figure forth the temper and conduct of repentant souls. It is only towards the close of the document that Jesus presents himself as a Messiah, and then not as a present Messiah, but as a future one. Except for the first two sections, we might gather that it was only towards the close of his career that the self-confidence of Jesus ripened into the conviction that he would come again as king and judge. Thus he says, in § 43 : "*Ye shall not see me again, until ye say, Blessed is he that cometh in the name* [*i.e.*, power and personality] *of the Lord.*" So in § 56 he compares his future advent to the deluge that none foresaw except Noah and his faithful ones. And how singularly naïve and Jewish is his conception of the Kingdom of God which his second advent shall inaugurate: "*Ye who have followed me......shall sit upon twelve thrones and judge the twelve tribes of Israel.*" The faithful, again, in § 42, are to come from east and west and to lie down at a banquet with Abraham and Isaac and Jacob in the kingdom of God. The sons of the kingdom—*i.e.*, Jews by birth—are, indeed, to be cast out; but that does not mean that the guests admitted are not Jews by faith. Proselytes certainly are meant who have adopted the law, for in § 51 we learn that, as long as heaven and earth last, not a jot or tittle of the law is to be allowed to lapse.

(6) The precepts in this document are addressed to the immediate disciples of Jesus, and have no reference to organisation and church discipline. This is in itself a sign that they belong to an age anterior to that organised Church of Jerusalem of which we already get glimpses in the Epistles of Paul, especially in the

Epistle to the Galatians, which is probably the earliest of them.

(7) Critics, such as Wellhausen and Nestle, agree that this non-Marcan source is a translation of an Aramaic document. Semitic terms and idioms show through the Greek dress in every sentence. Now, Papias, who flourished about 130 A.D., relates that Matthew, one of the twelve apostles, arranged or composed the *Logia*, or sayings, in the Hebrew (*i.e.*, Aramaic) dialect, and that these were subsequently translated (into Greek) by sundry persons as each of them best was able.

On such a point we cannot hope to reach more than probability; but the probability certainly is that Q is the collection of sayings thus put together. The existing "Gospel according to Matthew" is obviously not the work of that apostle; for, firstly, it is written in Greek, and not in Hebrew or Aramaic; and, secondly, one who was an apostle and eye-witness of the ministry of Jesus would not have gone, on the one hand, to Mark, who was neither, for his knowledge of the facts and his arrangement of them; or, on the other, to a Greek document like Q for the teaching of his master. He would have known first hand the incidents of Jesus's life, and in what sequence they occurred, and also how and what Jesus taught. The so-called Gospel of Matthew, therefore, is the work of an unknown writer, possibly of a Jewish Christian in Palestine, who handles in the main the same materials as Luke. It was probably compiled between 80 and 100 A.D., but underwent several redactions before it reached the form in which we have it in the earliest manuscripts and versions.

What, then, is the chance that Jesus of Nazareth

really uttered these sayings collected in Q and arranged, it would seem, under various heads? Most of them, if not all, have, if we may use the expression, a common *cachet*. Homely enough they are, and yet the same *ethos* and character pervades them, as if they were all or mostly the utterances of one man. If we had the poems of Burns scattered anonymously throughout an anthology, and mixed up in it with poems by a score of other writers, we could nevertheless pick most of them out and collect them together as the work of a single master hand. In like manner a common genius pervades most of these utterances; and since we find them all in a single collection and professing to be all from a common mint, it seems hypercritical, not to say absurd, to regard them as a collection of sayings uttered by several persons. But if they were uttered by some one person, then why not by Jesus? It is well known, and the Talmuds survive to attest it, that the Jews, before and after and during the age of Jesus, were in the habit of collecting and preserving notable sayings and decisions of their rabbis. Whether they were written down on the spot we do not know; but that was not impossible in an age when both art of writing and materials were as common nearly as they are to-day. No one, so far as I know, has ever suggested that the sayings ascribed in the Mishnah to Hillel, Gamaliel, Eliezer, and other rabbis, could never have been uttered by them. We can trace back the record of Jesus's sayings many generations nearer to his age than we can those of Hillel. Why, then, deny that in the main Q may reflect the real teaching of Jesus? It is indeed probable that in the process of translation into Greek from so dissimilar an idiom as the Semitic they may have been more or less recast and modified; and also that the Greek version, before it reached the form in which we have it, may have been a good deal retouched and adjusted to the new conceptions of Jesus which were growing up, especially among the Pauline converts. Yet the most searching criticism can detect few traces of repainting, little colour which we can be sure is secondary.

Chapter IX.

THE TRUE JESUS

We can write a life of Julius Cæsar or of Cicero, because we have in the first line letters, commentaries, and other authentic documents written by them and their friends; in the second, lives written by Plutarch and others who had in their hands monuments of them, now lost; and in the third, masses of contemporary coins and inscriptions. Contrast with this wealth of sources the scanty material which remains, after the examination of the preceding chapters, for a portrait of Jesus of Nazareth. So slender is it, indeed, that it seems not absurd to some critics to-day to deny that he ever lived. The truth is that the Church, by fencing round this corner of history, by refusing to apply within it the canons by which in other fields truth is discerned from falsehood, by beatifying credulous ignorance and anathematising scholarship and common sense, has surrounded the whole with such a nimbus of improbability that any clever schoolboy of the twentieth century is inclined to dismiss the entire New Testament as a forgery and concoction of the priest. A child of my own, at the age of twelve, was set to do as his Sunday task a map of the missionary travels of Paul, and, having completed it, brought it to me for my approval before he showed it up to his master. When I had approved it, he said to me, in his most confidential tone: "Father, did St. Paul ever really exist?" It was evident what was in his mind. Jesus was not a historical personage like Pericles or Julius Cæsar; for who save a mythical hero walks on the water, chides wind and storm into silence, and feeds thousands at once upon nothing at all? Jesus had in this child's mind—and very justly too, considering the general character of what is called religious instruction—taken his place alongside of Heracles and Dionysus. But Paul seemed to him to be more in touch with reality. Had he not been shipwrecked and imprisoned, and faced other perils of land and sea? Clearly he was the only quasi-historical personage left in the divinity lessons. If he can be eliminated, the schoolboy can relegate to mythology the whole subject-matter of these lessons. Such is the nemesis of creeds and orthodoxy.

We cannot, then, aspire to write a life of Jesus. Even a Renan failed, and from the hands of a Farrar we merely get under this rubric a farrago of falsehood, absurdity, and charlatanry. At the best, perhaps, we can only hope to see Jesus, as it were, through the mist, ever thickening, of the opinions which the second and third generations of his followers formed of him. Between ourselves and him intervenes— earliest of our sources in point of time—Paul, with his apocalyptic preconceptions of what a Messiah had to be, with his turbid, swirling flood of obscure fancies, his epileptic ecstasy and private revelations. Next after him in order of time we have the non-Marcan document, in which, as we have seen, we have almost certainly echoes, perhaps more than echoes, of his teaching. Nearly contemporary with this must be the saner parts of Mark's Gospel, for the greater part of that Gospel is the work of someone who was by instinct and predilection a miracle-monger. Finally, we have the Fourth Gospel, hardly less fabulous than the apocryphal rigmaroles of the second and third century.

Discounting all that is doubtful, what have we left? I think we may take it as true that some time about the beginning of our era there was born in Nazareth, of parents whose names were Joseph and Mary, a child who was duly circumcised and named Jesus. He was not their only child, for Mark introduces his fellow-townsmen as saying: *"Is not this the carpenter, the son of Mary, and brother of James and Joses and Judas and Simon? And are not his sisters here with us?"*

How much younger he was than John the Baptist, under whose influence he fell on reaching manhood, we do not know. Luke's story that he was but six months younger is clearly impossible. It was a sore point with the first generation of Christians that the disciples of John did not merge themselves in the following of Jesus, but remained distinct, as is recorded in Acts. It was one way of controverting them to pretend that their master John, when he baptised Jesus by way of preparing him for membership in the impending messianic kingdom, also acclaimed him as the promised Messiah. This fiction is in Luke's narrative crowned by another—namely, by the story which brings together their two mothers before their births, in order that John, a fœtus of six months, might leap in his mother's womb when she saluted Mary, who had conceived the day before! A more reliable tradition, and anyhow one which cannot be reconciled with Luke's story, is that which survives in many early representations on stone or in ivory of Jesus's baptism. In these he stands knee-deep in the water, a beardless stripling, while John, a bearded man of greater height and age, pours water over his head, or, setting his hand thereon, actually ordains him.

It would seem, then, as if a certain interval of time must have separated John and Jesus in the plenitude of their activities; and § 50 of the non-Marcan document, though obscure, yet favours such a view. For in this passage Jesus uses these words, or similar: "*From the days of John the Baptist until now the kingdom of heaven is taken by force, and men of violence snatch at it.*" We infer that sundry patriots, carried away by John's proclamation of the impending great event which was, among other things, to bring liberation from the Gentile yoke, had tried to hurry it on by active rebellion against the Roman Government. The lesson of their failure was not lost on Jesus, who, like Philo, believed that moral regeneration, repentance, non-resistance, justice and mercy, and in general a faithful observance of the laws of Jehovah, could alone bring it about. However we explain these words, they anyhow militate against the later view, which foreshortened the past and made John and Jesus full contemporaries of one another. There are no limits in Q of time-transition and order of events in the life of Jesus. If he really uttered these words— and he probably did, since they are so repugnant to later tradition—he must have uttered them late in his career.

That Jesus was a successful exorcist we need not doubt, nor that he worked innumerable faith-cures. Josephus describes how a famous rabbi named Eliezer drew a demon out of an afflicted man through his nostrils, and how in issuing forth it tipped over a basin of water set to receive it—all this in presence of himself and of the Roman emperor. A generation later than Jesus, Apollonius of Tyana was casting out demons in Syria wherever he went. These demons talked just as they do in Mark's narrative, and the stories of Apollonius, which are probably from the pen of his Syro-Greek disciple, Damis, read like pages out of Mark or Matthew. From the first the exorcists had a recognised position in the Church; and in the less advanced parts of Christendom the priests are still called upon to drive out by their adjurations the demons of madness and disease. The same expulsions can be daily observed in India, China, Japan, Africa—in fact, all round the globe.

Everywhere, in primitive communities, certain individuals are reputed to possess a peculiar power over demons, and in West Africa a leading medicine-man is occasionally murdered by some rival anxious to possess himself of this power for his own use and profit. Accordingly, Mark relates how, when Jesus had expelled a noisy evil spirit, the crowd exclaimed, "*With authority* [or power] *he commands even the unclean spirits, and they obey him.*" Elsewhere Mark notes that the people found this great difference between Jesus on the one hand, and the scribes and pharisees on the other—namely, that he taught as one having *authority* or power over the spirits. It is beyond a doubt that Jesus regarded fever, epilepsy, madness, deafness, blindness, rheumatism, and all the other weaknesses to which flesh is heir, as the direct work of evil spirits. The storm-wind which churned the sea or inland lake into fury is equally an evil sprite in the Gospel story. In the Vedic poems it is the same; and, indeed, we have here a commonplace of all folklore.

Jesus also regarded himself as gifted with the special power to control evil spirits; the African medicine-man is credited with the same by the cowering tribesmen. It is recorded that on one occasion a hysterical woman, who suffered from a flux of blood, touched the hem of Jesus's raiment, and was healed, whereon Jesus felt that power had gone out of him. In the same way napkins or wrappers, taken from the body of Paul, were found to heal sufferers among his hearers, who applied them to themselves. The annals of superstition supply a thousand parallels to these stories. The application by Jesus of his spittle to the ears or eyes of the blind or deaf can be similarly paralleled. We know from the *Natural History* of the elder Pliny, a Latin author of the first century, that the spittle of the medicine-man was a sovereign remedy all round the Mediterranean. The history of Tacitus (bk. iv., ch. 81) supplies a striking parallel to the stories told of Jesus. It deserves to be cited at length from Church and Brodribb's excellent translation:—

> In the months during which Vespasian was waiting at Alexandria for the periodical return of the summer gales and settled weather at sea, many wonders occurred, which seemed to point him out as the object of the favour of heaven and of the partiality of the gods. One of the common people of Alexandria, well known for his blindness, threw himself at the emperor's knees, and implored him, with groans, to heal his infirmity. This he did by the advice of the god Serapis, whom this nation, devoted as it is to superstitions, worships more than any other divinity. He begged Vespasian that

he would deign to moisten his cheeks and eye-balls with his spittle. Another with a diseased hand, at the counsel of the same god, prayed that the limb might feel the print of a Cæsar's foot. At first Vespasian ridiculed and repulsed them. They persisted; and he, though on the one hand he feared the scandal of a fruitless attempt, yet, on the other, was induced, by the entreaties of the men and by the language of his flatterers, to hope for success. At last he ordered that the opinion of physicians should be taken as to whether such blindness and infirmity were within the reach of human skill. They discussed the matter from different points of view. "In the one case," they said, "the faculty of sight was not wholly destroyed, and might return, if the obstacles were removed; in the other case the limb which had fallen into a diseased condition might be restored if a healing influence were applied: such, perhaps, might be the pleasure of the gods, and the emperor might be chosen to be the minister of the divine will; at any rate, all the glory of a successful remedy would be Cæsar's, while the ridicule of failure would fall on the sufferers." And so Vespasian, supposing that all things were possible to his good fortune, and that nothing was any longer past belief, with a joyful countenance, amid the intense expectation of the multitude of bystanders, accomplished what was required. The hand was instantly restored to its use, and the light of day again shone upon the blind. Persons actually present attest both facts, even now, when nothing is to be gained by falsehood.

We see that the atmosphere of Alexandria, in the first century, in no way differed from that of Galilee; there Serapis had long filled in men's minds the place which Jesus presently filled in the minds of Christians.

And Vespasian might have used to those he healed the words constantly addressed by Jesus to those whom he healed: "*Thy faith hath made thee whole.*" The imperial cures which Tacitus here relates, on the testimony of men who witnessed them, who were still alive in his day, and who had nothing to gain by flattering Vespasian now that another dynasty occupied the throne, resemble the faith-healings common at Lourdes, and not unheard of in English Methodist circles. That the cures effected by Jesus were often due to what, in scientific phrase, we to-day term auto-suggestion is certain from the naïve admission made in Mark's Gospel that, in his own country, where they knew him and his kinsfolk too well to acclaim him at once as a prophet, "*he could do no mighty work, because of their unbelief.*" The most he could effect in the midst of these critical surroundings was to "*lay his hands on a few sick folk and heal them*" (Mark vi. 6).

There is no reason to doubt that Jesus effected many cures of this kind beyond those which Mark records. When he had succeeded in effecting a few such cures, all would forget the failures; and his fame as a healer would gather volume like a snowball, and precede him wherever he went. We cannot doubt that Mark's description of his triumphal career, though gathered long after the event from the lips of the country folk among whom his fame lingered, is substantially correct. It is as follows (Mark vi. 53–56) :—"*And when they* (Jesus and his disciples) *had crossed over to the land, they came unto Gennesaret, and moored to the shore. And when they were come out of the boat, straightway the people recognised him, and ran round about that whole region, and began to carry about on their beds those that were sick, wherever they heard he was. And wheresoever he entered, into villages or into cities, or into the country, they laid the sick in the public places, and besought him that they might touch if it were but the border of his garment: and as many as touched him were made whole.''*

And, similarly, in chap. iii. 10 we read that "*he had healed many, insomuch that as many as had plagues pressed upon him that they might touch him.*" Jesus would have been more than human if he had not come to believe that he really possessed in his organism some peculiar power capable of counteracting disease; and, accordingly, Mark relates, as we noted above, how he turned round, when a woman had touched his garments and been healed, and asked, "*Who touched my garments?*" because "*he perceived in himself that the power proceeding from him had gone forth.*" This, of course, is a touch of exaggeration on the part of the story-teller, but it nevertheless exhibits to us the sort of belief which accompanied faith-healing, and still accompanies it. The power of healing, which among the peasants of Galilee marked out a man as the Messiah, is comparable to the mysterious power which in our own generation is vested in the Mikado of Japan, who, in the belief of his humbler subjects, can barely nod his head without shaking the entire land. The chieftains of primitive peoples are all endowed with similar magic powers, which render them so dangerous that their names, persons, head, hair, and even nail-parings, are taboo—that is, sacrosanct and dangerous. Mr. J. G. Frazer, in his *Golden Bough*, gives examples of chiefs and princes held to be so holy or taboo that a servitor walks behind them with a spittoon reserved specially for the royal spittle, for this even is endowed with such mysterious power as to be dangerous to any whom it may touch. The spittle of a Roman emperor or of a Jewish Messiah was equally pregnant with miraculous power. Mohammed also was "so highly respected by his companions that, whenever he made the ablution, in order to say his prayers, they ran and catched the water that he had used; and, whenever he spit, they immediately licked it up, and gathered up every hair that fell from him with great superstition" (Sale's *Coran*, ed. 1801, i., p. 69).

This mysterious power, as it was chiefly revealed in the expulsion of evil spirits or demons, was itself interpreted to be a spirit, though a holy or clean one. Mark preserves to us the outlines of an early dispute, in which Jesus's own mother and brethren took part, as touching the quality of the spirit within Jesus which enabled him to cast out demons. The scribes from Jerusalem, we read, said, "*He hath Beelzebub*," and "*By the prince of the devils he casteth out the devils.*" No prophet can allow the quality of the spirit which moves him to be called in question; and Jesus answers the accusation in a twofold manner. First he points out that Satan would not turn upon Satan, as his accusers assumed; and in the second place he declares that "*all their sins shall be forgiven to men, and also all their blasphemies; but whoso shall blaspheme against the holy spirit hath never forgiveness, but is guilty of an eternal sin.*" Mohammed, as we said above, defended himself much in the same manner and with equal vigour against those who said of him, "He hath an unclean spirit."

We have seen that in Mark's Gospel there was no immediate recognition of Jesus by his disciples as the

Messiah. Their recognition of him was slow and gradual and tardy, and even to the end they seem to have expected him, like a second David, merely to expel the unclean Roman from their holy soil by a sudden display of supernatural force. How soon the conviction formed itself in Jesus's own mind that he was the "*man sent from God*" we do not know. Both our documents, Mark and Q, assume that he knew himself to be such from the first; but that is improbable. It is more likely that it was his success as a healer, his evident control of evil spirits, the plaudits of the crowd, and, above all, his own followers' recognition of his supernatural *rôle*, that forced this conviction upon him towards the close of his career. There must have been an inner development of his mind and aspirations, although our earliest documents have lost all memory of it.

And, even if Jesus at the end admitted the Messiahship thrust upon himself by his enthusiastic followers, it is not clear that he admitted it except in a potential sense. He was not the present Messiah, for the moral regeneration of his countrymen was only begun. Perhaps they were right in hailing him as a prophet, as a greater than John. But the Messiah, when he came, was to come from heaven as king and judge, baptising with fire; whereas John only baptised unto repentance with water. Now, Pilate and the priests left to Jesus no room during this life to play so stupendous a part. To carry it out he was bound to come again in glory from heaven. Little is certain about Jesus; but there is a fair certainty that, late in his career, he imbued his followers with the conviction, which he also entertained himself, that he was destined to return after death and inaugurate a reign of God upon earth.

We have described the vision which floated before the eyes even of a cultivated Jew of Alexandria like Philo—the vision of a time when the repentance and moral regeneration of the Jews would soften the hearts of the oppressors, and move them to let their captives go free. When that time arrived a supernatural presence, visible only to the faithful, would lead the liberated Jews of all the earth back into the land of promise and plenty. Jesus seems to have convinced himself and his followers that, as he was already an agent and vehicle of the divine will, so he was destined to come again, a supernatural presence, amid the clouds of heaven. That his followers, both in Galilee and in Jerusalem, were penetrated with this conviction led to great results. It was the main psychological factor in the visions they had of him after his death.

In Acts i. 6 it is recorded that they expected him to come again at once, "*and restore the kingdom to Israel.*" He did not come, and has not come yet; and, after nearly twenty centuries of waiting, Christian belief in the second coming is grown faint and tenuous. At the same time, the future kingdom has been spiritualised; and the millennial corn and vine, with their phenomenal output of bread and wine, no longer float before the imaginations of the pious, as they did before the minds of the early generations of believers. Filled with such dreams of the future, Jesus's immediate followers could not but have confirmatory visions of him who was to come again. Like Stephen, they saw him up in heaven, where he was reposing on a throne at the right hand of a God who has a left and right, only waiting until his followers on earth had got things ready for his second advent.

The hymns of that first age, as we know from Paul and from the Book of Revelation of John (a work of 92–93 A.D.), bore the refrain *Maranatha*, the Aramaic equivalent of "May the Lord come." It was this belief that the Christ was waiting up in heaven for the season to fulfil itself of his second advent in glory that generated the tales of his resurrection out of the tomb and ascension into heaven after forty days—the statutory and conventional period fixed among the Jews for all unlikely and legendary episodes.

CHAPTER X.

JESUS'S MORAL TEACHING

In these and many other respects Jesus was the child of his age, sharing its superstitions and prejudices. Much has been written of the universality of his teaching, as if he, alone of ancient teachers, had revealed an ideal whole of precept and practice applicable to all ages and races. It may be doubted whether its universality is as real as it seems. No State, ancient or modern, has ever tried to regulate its dealings with other States on the principle of turning the other cheek to the smiter; and it would not be just to others to do so in private or municipal life. The object of law and police, and, in a word, of all government, is so to safeguard the person and liberty of the individual that he may make the best of himself and his faculties. If we allow the bully and the thief to insult and rob us and ours with impunity, we encourage him to do the same to others, and betray a sad want of public spirit, even if we do not, by our cowardice, make ourselves his accomplices in evildoing. It has been argued that Jesus, when he uttered this precept, meant no more than that, in defending ourselves, we ought not to be actuated by any vindictive feeling, nor nourish any grudge against our oppressors. Those who thus gloss the precepts of Jesus are specially they who hold that he was God incarnate, omniscient, and morally infallible. It is a pity they do not ask themselves why, in that case, he was not more explicit.

The next precept in the collection (§ 5), "To him that asks of thee give, and from him that would borrow of thee turn not away," has been similarly glossed by the orthodox, and interpreted to mean simply that in our commercial dealings we ought to be inspired by generosity, and avoid meanness. If this be all, it must be confessed that Aristotle and other ancient teachers said the same thing quite as well. Certain it is that, applied unconditionally, such a precept leads to indiscriminate charity, so that its practice would do more harm than good. I have known ladies who, by giving to all who asked and lending to everyone without any thought of taking security, wasted their fortunes in a few years, and then became a burden on their friends and relations.

Much of the seeming universality of the moral teaching of Jesus is perhaps due to two reasons: firstly to the fact that the Jews in his day had no State, but were governed by aliens, who had no sympathy with their religious and political notions. The Roman garrison just held them down by force, and taxed them. The Jewish polity proper had long ceased to exist, and consequently Jesus ignored it; but for that very reason the citizens and administrators of a free, self-governing State, like our own, will find in a study of the political and ethical treatises of Plato and Aristotle more of value, more to widen their outlook, more of insight and sagacity, than in the gospel. And this fact the Catholic Church has amply recognised for a thousand years. We owe the fixed categories of moral judgment more to the Greek philosophers than to Christ. And, secondly, much of the teaching of the gospel was uttered in view of an impending catastrophe and liquidation of this world's affairs, out of which, at a wave of the divine wand, a new and blessed condition was to emerge, just as the phœnix arises, renewed and immortal, out of its own ashes. Jesus felt himself to be the harbinger of a new and divine constitution—we cannot say of the world, for his horizon was rather limited to his own land; and this new society was not to grow slowly and organically out of existing circumstances, but was to be suddenly imposed by divine power and interference. Hence the precepts to follow him; to forsake parents, wife, children, and home; even to neglect the most sacred of all ancient duties—that of burying one's own father. We shall point out later on what ravages upon civil society were afterwards committed by men and women whose heads were turned by these dreams of a millennium.

In Philo, it is true, we read, in a hundred passages, similar exhortations to abandon home and kindred, as Abraham had done, in order to be free to worship the one God. But he always has in view the case of proselytes. In a pagan home every meal was an act of communion with demons, whose idols confronted the eyes of all who entered. No animal was killed without its blood and flesh being consecrated to one or another of the gods whom the proselyte was taught to regard as impure demons. Every day of the week had its presiding demon, every village and city had arch-devils for patrons and protectors, had holidays and feast-days, when the legends of these demons were recited and rehearsed in public pantomimes and dances. At every street-corner was an idol, often obscenely devised, to which the pious were expected to render homage when they passed. Births, deaths, and marriages then, as now, were surrounded with a hundred superstitious observances. Lastly, the gods were for ever being carried in public procession; and woe to those who flouted them. The Jewish proselyte, like the later Christian convert, was set down as an atheist, as a man without gods, who denied all that was true and violated all that was sacred. His presence was an insult to heaven, and was likely to provoke the wrath of heaven against the community that tolerated him, to bring down hail that ruined the harvest, to cause drought and famine, disease—even defeat at the hands of the national enemy. It was in view of such popular prejudices, which were directed against philosophers and Epicureans, as well as against Jewish converts, that the emperor Tiberius uttered the famous aphorism reported by Tacitus: *Deorum injuriæ diis curæ*—"Let injuries to the gods be the gods' own concern." All this being so, it needs little imagination to realise the obloquy to which a Jewish convert exposed himself. He cut himself off from intercourse with his family and its religious rites. He could not retain or undertake public offices and duties, because these entailed acts of public sacrifice and religion. Often he could not inherit, because in ancient society inheritance depended on the due funeral rites being performed, and on homage being offered to unseen powers which his new religion taught him were unclean and malign. Thus the convert's position resembled that of an isolated Mohammedan among Hindoos, or of a similarly isolated Jew or Protestant in Spain or Southern Italy. The member of a pagan family who became a Jew must have done so at the cost of much personal sacrifice;

and not the least of his sufferings must have lain in the forfeiture of the affections of parents and brothers and sisters, perhaps even of those of wife and children. Early Christian canonists even ruled that conversion annulled an existing marriage. On these aspects of ancient proselytism Philo, the Greek Jew of Alexandria, incessantly dwells; and he often exhorts those who were Jews by birth not to be supercilious and cold towards the polytheists who, at such cost, had come over to the worship of the true God, but rather by becoming, as it were, parents and brothers and sisters to them, to make up for the losses they had sustained. The shoots thus grafted, so he warns his countrymen, often bear better fruit, and more acceptable to heaven, than the parent stock and stem. A good proselyte, in the sight of God, is better than a born Jew who is cruel and evil. For long before Jesus was born the Jews had disseminated over the Gentile world their monotheism and their customs, especially that of the sabbath rest. Witness the following passage of Philo, in his *Life of Moses*, ch. 4 :—

Nearly everywhere, from East to West, there is no country, race, or city, which does not reject, as alien, the institutions of strangers—does not imagine that the best way of encouraging a faithful acceptance of its own customs is to heap dishonour on those of others. How differently the case stands with regard to our own (*i.e.*, Jewish) institutions and beliefs! For these supply a motive and something to rally around to barbarians (*i.e.*, non-Greeks), to Greeks, to inhabitants both of mainland and of islands, to races of East as of West, of Europe, of Asia—of the whole inhabited world, from end to end of the earth. For who is there that does not respect to the uttermost that holy seventh day which brings release from toil and leisure to

himself as to his neighbours; not to free men alone,
but to serfs also—nay, even to the beasts of burden?

That this was no idle boast on the part of Philo is
clear to anyone who considers that all round the
Mediterranean, to this day, the seventh day of the
week bears the Jewish name of sabbath. The other
days often retain their old pagan names, but Saturday
is ever the sabbath, lightly disguised as *Sabbato*,
Sabbado, *Samedi*, *Shabath*, etc. To the influence of
Jews and their proselytes alone can we ascribe this
adoption of the Jewish word. Old Greek and Latin
writers equally testify to the widespread observance
of the sabbath, especially in ancient Rome. There was
nothing distinctively Christian in it. On the contrary,
the Christians, in order to spite the Jews, very soon
began to violate the sabbath; and in time substituted
their Sunday for it as the day for holding the *synaxis*
or *ecclesia* (church or assembly), at which the Jewish
and later on the Christian Scriptures were read, and
prayer and praise offered. Efforts were made in the
Church sporadically, from the fourth century on, to
suspend work on Sundays, but these never succeeded;
and in Southern Europe there is no day of the week
on which man and brute are harder tasked. Had the
leaders of early Christian opinion been inspired by
feelings of humanity, and not by mere theological
hatred, they would have encouraged instead of dis-
couraging the Jewish day of rest. They destroyed
the thing, though they could not destroy the name.
At the beginning of the twentieth century the popular
Governments of France and Italy, which both equally
lie under the ban of the Church, are seeking to
enforce by legislation a day of rest for man and beast.
But for the cantankerous opposition of the Church,

the result aimed at in such legislation might have been secured eighteen centuries ago.

Philo often dwells on the trials to which Jewish converts exposed themselves by their desertion of the old cults. Thus in his tract on *Justice*, § 6, he ranks them with orphans and widows. "The proselyte," he writes,

> has turned his own kinsmen, who alone were his natural allies and champions, into truceless enemies by his repudiation of mythical fictions and polytheism and his adhesion to the truth; casting away all that his parents and grandparents and ancestors and all his kith and kin did homage to, he has set forth on a noble pilgrimage to a new land.

And in his book *About Philanthropy*, § 12, he writes:—

> The strangers who come to us (*i.e.*, proselytes) must be held worthy of every privilege, because they have abandoned blood-kinship, fatherland, customs, the holy shrines of their gods, high positions and honours; and like colonists have nobly abandoned their homes, leaving behind myths and fictions in order to win the truth's clearness of vision and embrace the worship of the one really existent God. Hence the divine law bids us love the proselytes, not only as friends and kinsmen, but as ourselves; sharing so far as possible in common with them in body and soul; in spirit we must have the same sorrows and joys, so that our society resemble one organism with divers members joined and knit together in a natural harmony.

And in his description of the *Therapeutæ* or "worshippers" of God, a society of ascetic Jews and proselytes, male and female, which had its headquarters near Alexandria, but ramified all round the

Mediterranean, Philo uses these words, specially applicable to those who had joined it as converts to Judaism :—

> Their longing for the immortal and blessed life leads them to esteem this mortal existence as already at an end, and they abandon their property to sons or daughters, or to other kinsfolk, of free will bestowing it on them; and, if they have no kinsfolk, then on their companions and friends.......But once they have divested themselves of their goods they are rid of all snares and entanglements, and they flee without a backward glance, abandoning brothers, children, wives, parents, wide circles of kinsmen, intimate friendships, the fatherlands in which they were bred and born.

The spread of Christianity among the Gentiles, so far as it involved rejection of paganism and all the network of ties, duties, and relationships which went therewith, was one in character with Jewish proselytism, and, in fact, little else than an extension thereof. Philo boasted that the Jews were destined to be teachers of true religion to the entire world; and the Christian missionaries in some ways carried on his work; for, as against the old cults of gods and goddesses, the monotheism taken over from the Jews presented itself as a simple monistic creed, and in relation to the times was the most radically sceptical and rationalist movement of the intelligence that Europe has ever witnessed. Such a movement, indeed, had already begun among the cultivated Greeks and Romans, and expressed itself in those writings of the Greek thinkers from which Jewish and Christian apologists and missionaries borrowed their most effective weapons against the pagan religion. But Greek scepticism was philosophical, aristocratic, and confined to the few; whereas the monotheistic propaganda, like the anti-clericalism of modern Catholic countries, was addressed to the masses.

Now we could understand such passages as Matthew x. 34–37[1] or Luke xviii. 29, were they from the lips of a Jewish missionary urging his faith on Gentiles, and warning them of the sacrifice they must make of old ties. And, accordingly, some critics have argued that such exhortations were not uttered by Christ, but rather reflect the persecutions to which Gentile converts of the new religion—the Atheists of the old world—were exposed at the hands of pagan kinsfolk and authorities. But there are insuperable difficulties in this view; not the least of which is the fact that they are embedded in, and inextricable from, a larger document of which the horizon is confined to Galilee and Judæa. Nowhere, indeed, in these passages is there a hint of polytheism and idolatry. Jewish monotheism is everywhere taken for granted, and presupposed as the religious background alike of teacher and of taught. Their context and intrinsic character relegate them, therefore, to the first age,

[1] "Think not that I came to send peace on the earth: I came not to send peace, but a sword. For I came to set a man at variance with his father, and the daughter against her mother, and the daughter-in-law against her mother-in-law: and a man's foes shall be they of his own household. He that loveth father and mother more than me is not worthy of me; and he that loveth son or daughter more than me is not worthy of me" (Matthew x. 34–37).

"There is no man that hath left house or wife or parents or children for the sake of the kingdom of God who shall not receive many times more in this age, and in the age to come eternal life" (Luke xviii. 29).

"If any man cometh unto me, and hateth not his own father and mother, and wife, and children, and brethren, and sisters, yea, and his own life also, he cannot be my disciple" (Luke xiv. 26).

JESUS'S MORAL TEACHING

when the message was confined to *the lost sheep of the house of Israel;* when as yet there was no talk of admitting even Samaritans into the kingdom, much less uncircumcised Gentiles. There is, consequently, no alternative but to suppose that the pursuit of the Messianic Kingdom, as Jesus already proclaimed it, entailed enormous personal sacrifices. It is at once obvious that it was politically dangerous, and a menace to more than one very powerful vested interest. The members of the Herodian dynasty, for example, would not be likely to welcome with open arms the heralds of a cataclysm which would sweep them away. The Roman authorities would equally take umbrage at a movement which to them was indistinguishable from projects for their violent and instant expulsion. According to Luke xix. 11, the disciples, as they accompanied Jesus to Jerusalem for the Passover, *supposed that the kingdom of God was immediately to appear.* Far from expecting their master to be condemned to death and crucified, they had *hoped* up to the last *that it was he which should redeem Israel* (Luke xxiv. 21), and (Acts i. 6) *restore the kingdom to Israel.* Such passages attest a strong patriotic element in the following of Jesus; and the tradition they embody is all the more reliable because the real course of events so signally falsified these early hopes and expectations. The early disciples believed that Jesus was destined, somehow or other, they knew not how, to get rid of the Roman incubus. He believed the same, but opposed and condemned the frequent *émeutes* of the physical-force party, and thereby earned from them also both hatred and scorn. The priests and sadducees, again, detested him; for, like any other established clergy, they were thoroughly comfortable and contented with their lot. What well-paid priest ever liked a prophet? Lastly, the Pharisees and scribes resented his more humane interpretation of the rule of the sabbath, his denunciations of the rich, his championship of the cause of the poor. He also endangered their monopoly of the teaching and exposition of the Law. In how many other ways he raised up enemies to himself we do not know; but we must ever bear in mind that our ignorance of the social and religious conditions of Judæa in that age is very great, and that the stray gleams we get from more or less contemporary authors —like Philo, Josephus, the evangelists, and Tacitus— throw, after all, about as much light on the subject as two or three rushlights would throw on an entire landscape sunk in night.

Our conclusion, then, is this: Our knowledge of the circumstances under which these sayings were uttered is very imperfect; but the little we do know does not lead us to expect them to be applicable to circumstances of modern life; for our modern conditions, social and political, lay beyond and outside the horizon of him who uttered them. The wonder is that so much of a teaching, framed in view of an imminent collapse of the political and social institutions of Judæa in that age, has nevertheless a value in our own, which rejects Messianic dreams and trusts to slow, patient, and long effort for the amelioration of its ills and diseases. It may be that Jesus of Nazareth sharpened to a point many of his precepts, and imported an almost paradoxical vigour into his utterances, just because he desired to raise a hedge against the most common forms of selfishness; against envy, spite, illiberality, and time-serving timidity; against clinging to the lower forms of well-being at the expense of the higher; against the suppression of truths which seem to menace our comforts and vested interests. For a sublime intransigence breathes through these parables and precepts: a fierce scorn for the rich and selfish, a tender love of the poor and suffering, a contempt for shams and empty conventions, an uncompromising devotion to truth, a true humility. There is about them a ring of real manliness; and that is why the document which records them has proved itself, in every age, a text-book of martyrdom, extorting for itself the homage, however hypocritical, even of clerics and oppressors.

CHAPTER XI.

THE BAPTISM OF JESUS

IT has been pointed out in the preceding pages that, thanks to the preservation of several parallel forms of the evangelical tradition, we are able to trace the successive stages or steps by which genuine personal traits and memories of Jesus were amplified, idealised, interpreted, transformed, and falsified—for there is no other word that fits the facts. The story of his baptism by John is a good example of such re-moulding. Mark's account is the simplest and shortest. According to it, John is in the wild region which borders the head of the Dead Sea, a region unfruitful because the soil is so saturated with chemical salts. He exhorts his countrymen to repent and to reform their lives, because the promised kingdom is at hand and a Messiah about to appear who will, in his *rôle* as judge, drive out all bad Jews, but gather the good ones into a realm of lasting joy and peace. We know nothing of the earlier history of Jesus, nor what prompted him to leave his home at Nazareth and betake himself to the far-off cleft of the Jordan valley where John was conducting his mission. It is not rash, however, to suppose that he shared the widespread Messianic longings of that age, that he too believed the great catastrophe to be at hand, and for that reason sought the traditionally sacred waters of the Jordan in order to seal and symbolise outwardly,

THE BAPTISM OF JESUS

by a ceremonial bath in the holy tide, that purification from sin of which repentance and remorse were the initial stage. He doubtless at that time believed, like other Jews, that the taint of sin was in some way or other akin to a physical stain, and that actual washing in a traditionally sacred river helped to efface it. Whether he continued to believe in the moral efficacy of material ablutions is doubtful, for in his teaching he never,[1] so far as our record extends, insisted on baptism. At the very moment in which, after plunging himself in the Jordan's stream, *he ascended out of the water, he saw*, writes Mark, *the heavens cloven asunder and the Spirit like a dove descending into* (or *upon*) *himself*. Some ancient texts of Mark add here, *and abiding in him*. Forthwith, the record continues, *a voice from heaven, Thou art my son beloved above others; in thee am I well pleased*.

This narrative does not imply that anyone saw the vision or heard the voice except Jesus himself, and therefore it in no way conflicts with well-known facts of sudden conversion and of religious psychology in general. We are, in general, ignorant of what forces ultimately control and generate our internal experiences and moral development. To appeal to cerebral processes and to heredity simply pushes the problem further back; to appeal to the contact and society of others is to explain nothing, for the same problem arises in the case of each of them. One thing is

---

[1] The only text in which he enjoins baptism is Matthew xxviii. 19: "baptising them into the name of Father, Son and Holy Spirit." But there is the very ancient and weighty evidence of Eusebius the historian that these words are an interpolation, and that instead of them the words *in my name*, and no more, originally stood in the text. The last twelve verses of Mark are notoriously a later addition to that Gospel.

certain—namely, that nothing is more common in certain exalted and abnormal temperaments than the hearing of sudden internal calls and voices. It would seem as if ideals we have long brooded over, intense aspirations which have long preoccupied us, could suddenly, if an occasion presents itself, gather force and transform themselves into, as it were, a higher personality and constitute another being within us— could so address and speak to us, even confront us face to face. Some of us, moreover, seem to possess a second personality not traceable in our conscious life, nor connected with it by the tie of memory, but capable, under certain abnormal mental conditions, akin to but not identical with the morbid state of madness—whatever madness means—of taking possession of our organism. The excitement natural to the occasion of his baptism may well have induced in Jesus's case such a mental crisis and paroxysm. He suddenly became aware in himself that he was the chosen Messiah. His own age, almost his own contemporary society, supply the elements of his vision, and we need not seek them beyond. The holy spirit to his excited imagination appeared as a dove. Why? Because in Syria and Palestine in that age the dove was a sacred bird, never molested or killed, being protected by ancient and widespread religious taboos. Philo, in his dreamy allegorical way, seeks to account for the bird's sacrosanctity. As the best of animals, he says, the lamb is a symbol of the purification of what is best in us—namely, our mind and intelligence; so also birds, light and winged, symbolise the word or *logos*, which moves more swiftly than an arrow and penetrates everywhere; and because *logos* or spoken word is twofold, false or true, it is symbolised by a

THE BAPTISM OF JESUS 167

yoke of turtle-doves or of pigeons.[1] If it be objected that Philo here speaks of *logos*, whereas it was a *spirit* that entered Jesus, it is enough to answer that the teachers of the early Church did not distinguish between *logos* and spirit, and that in the earliest liturgies[2] the *logos*, and not the spirit, is represented as having on this occasion descended and entered Jesus. In several other passages[3] Philo declares the divine wisdom and spirit to be "symbolically called a turtle-dove" because that wisdom loves solitude. In rabbinic tradition, equally, the Spirit of God brooded upon the face of the waters (Genesis i. 1) *like a dove;* and it is the dove in the legend of the Flood which returns to Noah in the ark bearing good news in the form of an olive-leaf plucked off. The idea of a soul entering or quitting the body in the form of a bird is widespread. In the Odyssey, xi. 222, the soul of a hero flutters up like a bird and flies off; and in Celtic myths the good souls appear as white birds, and especially as white doves. The idea meets us everywhere in myths old and new. The other element in the vision, the voice from heaven, is still commoner in Jewish tradition, and in the earliest Talmuds we have frequent references to the *Bath Kol*, as it was called. Thus, in the Babylonian Talmud (Sanhedr., fol. xi. 1), we read how when Hillel, a rabbi and older contemporary of Jesus, was walking in Jericho, the *Bath Kol* bore witness that he was one who for his righteousness merited that the Holy Spirit should dwell within him. The *Bath Kol* once rendered in

---

[1] *De mutatione Nominum*, ch. 42.
[2] *E.g.*, of Serapion of Thmuis, *circa* A.D. 330.
[3] *Quis rerum Divinarum heres?* "Who is the heir of divine things?" chs. 25 and 48, and Philo, ed. Mangey, i. 506.

Jabneh the same testimony in favour of the child Samuel.

The story of Hillel is an exact parallel to that of Jesus, and has somewhat embarrassed orthodox divines, bound by their prejudices to regard everything related of Jesus in the Gospels as unique. Thus the learned English Hebraist of the seventeenth century, Bishop Lightfoote, in his commentary on Matthew, adduces the passage about Hillel above cited, and then adds these quaint remarks :—

> I cannot but suspect that we have here either fables, or that these voices from heaven were by magic arts contrived to do honour to the rabbis...... You may, my reader, safely suppose, in the case of a race so contented to be deceived as the Jews, that these voices, which they believed to be from heaven and called by the name *Bath Kol*, were either formed in the air by the Devil in order to impose on the people, or by the magicians by means of their devilish arts in order to promote their own interests.

Philo, the contemporary of Jesus, attempts a philosophical explanation of the *Bath Kol*, and of the appearance of fire which attends it, in his work on the Ten Oracles (*i.e.*, commandments) :—

> God is not like a man in need of mouth and tongue and larynx, but He seems to me on this occasion (viz., the giving of the law on Sinai) to have worked an august and holy miracle. He bade sound to be created unseen in the air, a perfectly harmonious sound more wonderful than any instruments give forth, not soulless indeed, yet not composed of body and soul together like a living being, but a rational soul, full of clearness and distinctness, which gave a form to the air and distended it and changed it into flame-like

fire, and, like breath through a trumpet, sounded forth such an articulate voice as that those far off, equally with those who were close by, seemed to hear it address them.

In the so-called Testaments of the Patriarchs, a Hebrew apocryph, composed early in the second century B.C. and surviving in a Greek translation, we have (Test. of Levi, ch. xviii.) a Messianic hymn in honour of the Maccabean priest John Hyrcanus (according to the learned editor, Dr. Charles) which may, with other documents and tales of the same kind, have inspired the story of the heavenly voice heard at the baptism of Jesus, as well as other features of the Christian myth—*e.g.*, the Star in the East. It runs as follows in Dr. Charles's version :—

> Then shall the Lord raise up a new priest,
> And to him all the words of the Lord shall be revealed ;
> And he shall execute a righteous judgment upon the earth for a multitude of days.
> And his star shall arise in heaven as of a king,
> Lighting up the light of Knowledge as the sun the day,
> And he shall be magnified in the world.
> He shall shine forth as the sun on the earth,
> And shall remove all darkness from under heaven,
> And there shall be peace in all the earth.
> The heavens shall exult in his days,
> And the earth be glad,
> And the clouds shall rejoice ;
> And the knowledge of the Lord shall be poured forth upon the earth, as the water of the seas ;
> And the angels of the glory of the presence of the Lord shall be glad in him.
> The heavens shall be opened,

And from the temple of glory shall come upon him consecration,
With the Father's voice as from Abraham to Isaac.
And the glory of the Most High shall be uttered over him,
And the spirit of understanding and sanctification shall rest upon him [in the water][1]......
And in his priesthood the Gentiles shall be multiplied in knowledge upon the earth,
And enlightened through the grace of the Lord:
In his priesthood shall sin come to an end,
And the lawless shall cease to do evil.
And he shall open the gates of paradise,
And shall remove the threatening sword against Adam.
And he shall give to the saints to eat from the tree of life,
And the spirit of holiness shall be on them.
And Belial shall be bound by him,
And he shall give power to his children to tread on the evil spirits.
And the Lord shall rejoice in his children,
And be well pleased in his beloved ones for ever.

In Mark, then, John the Baptist does not recognise Jesus as the Messiah, and the experience of the Spirit's descent and of the voice belongs to Jesus alone. In Matthew the story grows, for it is assumed that John recognised him, and, as being Jesus's inferior, sought to dissuade him from being baptised by himself, saying, "*I have need to be baptised by thee, and thou comest unto me.*" Matthew also makes the *Bath Kol* speak of Jesus in the third person, and say, "*Yonder man is my son beloved.*" We are thus given to understand that Jesus was proclaimed Messiah to all who were present, and not to himself alone. Lastly, Luke takes

---

[1] The words *in the water* are a Christian addition.

THE BAPTISM OF JESUS

care that his readers should not regard the descent of the dove as a merely subjective experience of Jesus, for he goes out of his way to declare that the Spirit descended in *corporeal* or *material form as a dove*. Thus the vision is externalised, and becomes an objective experience, not of Jesus only, but of *all the people*.

Some early texts of Matthew furnish a fresh wonder, and relate that "*when Jesus was baptised a great light shone around from the water, so that all congregated there were afraid*." Other fresh details were soon added, which, however, did not gain a footing in the canonical tradition. Thus Lactantius, a Latin Father of about 300 A.D., records that the dove was a white one, such as a pure spirit is likely to embody itself in; and, according to another tradition of that age or earlier, the voice came out of a luminous cloud, the waters of Jordan banked themselves up in honour of Jesus, and he walked upon them. In the Gospel of the Hebrews, an Aramaic Gospel used by the Jewish Christians of Palestine, the dove seems to have been omitted, for, according to Jerome, the Latin Father, this document related the descent of the Spirit thus: "But it came to pass, when the Lord had gone up out of the water, the entire stream of the Holy Spirit came down and was at rest upon him, and said to him: My son, in all the prophecies I awaited thee, that thou mightest come and I rest and settle in thee; for thou art my resting-place, thou art my first begotten son, who rulest for ever." The idea that a fire was kindled in the Jordan at the baptism was suggested by many old myths. "The idea," writes Robertson Smith (*Religion of the Semites*, Lecture V., p. 175), "that the godhead consecrates waters by descending into them appears at Aphaca (in Syria) in a peculiar form associated with the astral character, which, at least in later times, was ascribed to the goddess Astarte. It was believed that the goddess on a certain day of the year descended into the river, in the form of a fiery star, from the top of Lebanon." In the old hymns the River Jordan is represented as having been hallowed by the descent on it of the fire of the Spirit, and the immersion in it of the son of God. An enormous dragon also lurked in the water, and was trampled underfoot by Jesus. There was a local myth of a dragon that haunted the waters of the Orontes,[1] and a similar tradition about the Jordan found its way into the early Church hymns sung at the commemoration of Christ's baptism.

It is fairly certain that in the primitive text of Luke the voice from heaven said: "*Thou art my beloved son, this day have I begotten thee*," repeating the words of Psalm ii. 7; and the same reading occurred in the Gospel of the so-called Ebionites, or Christians of Palestine who rejected the legend of the Virgin Birth.[2] The idea conveyed by these words is that Jesus was spiritually re-born or regenerated on this occasion, a new soul, as it were, being engendered in him by the spirit which now entered into him and thenceforth inspired his words and actions. The same idea underlies the older reading of ch. i., verse 13, of the Fourth Gospel, where it is said that Christ, the Word or Reason, the light of the world, was engendered or "*begotten not of blood nor of the will of the flesh nor of the will of man, but of God*"; and in the same Gospel, iii. 3 and 8, Jesus assures Nicodemus that "*unless a man be born from above*" (or *over again*) "*of water and*

---

[1] Robertson Smith, *Religion of the Semites*, Second Edition, Lect. V., p. 171.
[2] See below, p. 180.

THE BAPTISM OF JESUS

spirit, he" cannot enter the kingdom of heaven. Thus formulated, the doctrine of the re-birth of Jesus in baptism was destined to have a long and interesting history. It was believed by zoologists of the ancient world that fish are born of the water without commerce on the part of the parents. Fish were also sacred or *taboo* all over ancient Syria. The early Christians, from fear of persecution or instinctive love of mystery, were prone to conceal under symbols the objects they revered, and the fish was accordingly chosen as a symbol of Jesus Christ. He was the great fish, his followers were little fish; and Tertullian of Carthage begins his defence of baptism with water against those who denied its need and utility with the words: "*We little fishes, following the example of our Fish* [*Ichthun*] *Jesus Christ, are born in the water, nor otherwise than by abiding in the water*"—*i.e.*, in the regenerate state—"*are we in a state of salvation.*" In the old Roman catacombs the sign of the fish meets the eye at every turn. The most striking monument of the kind is in the museum of the Greek monastery of Grotta Ferrata, near Rome. It is a large marble receptacle used for storing the water which has been blessed on January 6th, the feast of the baptism of Christ. It is adorned all round with elaborate sculptures, perhaps of the age of Constantine or earlier. From the summit of an Ionic colonnade human figures jump head foremost into the water below, and are there depicted as swimming in the form of fishes round about a single gigantic fish, who symbolises Christ. On a promontory opposite sit two figures, intended, it would seem, for the apostles whom Jesus made "fishers of men," hauling up some of the fish with line and pulley. Presumably the latter are for transference into the kingdom of heaven. On the opposite side is another large fish alone in the water, over the nose of which a large naked human figure pours out a *canistrum*, or jar of some fluid. This figure may represent John the Baptist presiding over the spiritual anointing of Christ. Tertullian wrote about 200 A.D., while the meaning of the symbolism was still fresh in men's minds. In the third century this interpretation of the baptism of Jesus came to be condemned as heretical in Rome, and was supplanted by the teaching that he was Messiah, son of God, filled plenarily with the holy Spirit from the moment of his conception by the Virgin Mary. It then became necessary to find an orthodox interpretation of the fish symbol; and in the early fourth century the word *Ixthus* was explained as an anagram, as follows: *Iesus Xristos Theou Uios Sôtêr*—*i.e.*, Jesus Christ, of God son, saviour.

In outlying Eastern regions of Christendom, however, where the primitive conceptions of the religion lived on longer than in Rome, that great workshop of doctrinal changes, the idea of the baptismal regeneration of Jesus, and of his adoption in the Jordan as son of God, lived on for ages. In the West, as late as the beginning of the ninth century, Elipandus of Toledo, the primate of Spain, was condemned for holding it. The early Christian writers of Africa and Italy entertained it. It was held in Sicily, and the Fratricelli attributed it to their master and founder, St. Francis of Assisi. In the East it long remained a fundamental tenet of Syriac and Armenian Christianity. Among the Armenians it was not only believed that Jesus was anointed by the Spirit and became Christ and son of God at his baptism, but John the Baptist was believed to have then ordained him, by laying his hand on his head and imparting to him the triple dignity or grace of king, high priest, and prophet.

In the synoptic Gospels we do not meet with this idea that Jesus was reborn in baptism; but in all of them Jesus is regarded as having begun his higher spiritual life, his messianic and *quasi*-divine career, from the moment when the Spirit took possession of him. Thus Luke represents him as entering almost immediately his home synagogue of Nazareth, and appropriating to himself the words of Isaiah:—" *The spirit of the Lord is upon me, wherefore he hath anointed me to preach good tidings to the poor, hath sent me to proclaim to the prisoners forgiveness, and to the blind recovery of sight.*"

Of Jesus's life before his baptism by John the earliest gospel tradition, as reflected in Mark, knew nothing. In the perspective of the sub-apostolic age his baptism, his illumination by the Spirit, was the starting-point of his career; and accordingly the following words are, in Acts i. 21, set in the mouth of the chief apostle, Peter:—" *All the time that the Lord Jesus went in and went out among us, beginning from the baptism of John.*"

It is, then, natural that the earliest of the annual feasts of the Christian Church, not directly continued and taken over from the parent Judaism, should have commemorated the baptism. It was fixed by the followers of the Egyptian Gnostic Basilides, early in the second century, on January 6th, which was, it seems, the day on which the Egyptians solemnly blessed the Nile, and then filled their cisterns from it. Galleys were waiting in the harbour of Alexandria to convey the water thus blessed to the shrines of Isis all round the Mediterranean; and a Greek writer of the age of the Antonines, Aristides Rhetor, relates how the water thus consecrated was improved, like good wine, by keeping. It was better and purer at the end of one year than when it was first drawn up, and at the end of the second year than of the first, and so on even up to four years! Chrysostom, the great Greek Father, towards the end of the fourth century, in a sermon delivered at Antioch on January 6th, uses identical language of the water then drawn up, consecrated, and stored for use in baptisms. The water taken up and blessed at this feast was supposed to have the same grace for the healing of the sick and the remission of the sins of those who bathed in it as the waters of the Jordan. The hymns sung at this festival of the Manifestation or Epiphany embodied the idea of Jesus's spiritual birth at his baptism; and when, in the fourth century, the idea arose of feasting his physical birth, this new feast, for want of a better day, was tacked on to the earlier one of January 6th, so that both births, the physical and the spiritual, might be commemorated together. In Alexandria, Rome, Constantinople, and Antioch, the feast of the physical birth was, between 360 and 450, transferred to December 25th, the old Mithraic feast of the birthday of the sun—*natalis invicti Solis*. But the far-off Churches of the East rejected this innovation, which began in Rome, and taxed those who adopted it with sun-worship and idolatry. The Armenian Church to this day refuses to feast the birth from the Virgin on December 25th, and keeps the commemoration on January 6th, defending its usage on the ground that Jesus was baptised exactly on his thirtieth birthday, and that his human and spiritual births ought, for historical and symbolic reasons, to be feasted together.

Luke is the only authority who informs us that Jesus was thirty years old when he was baptised, and his statement lies under some suspicion. His text is much disturbed at this point (iii. 23), and it is not improbable that it originally ran thus:—"*And Jesus himself, when he began to be God* (or *divine*), *was about thirty years of age, being, as he was legally reckoned to be, son of Joseph.*"

Why thirty? Perhaps this number is due to the belief, vouched for by Jerome and his Hebrew teacher, of the Jewish rabbis of the first century, that when a man attains the age of thirty a new soul is born within him, transcending in moral dignity and value the soul derived from his mother at birth.

The legend of Zoroaster offers also a striking parallel to the story of Jesus. Of him it was related that in his thirtieth year he was enlightened by the descent upon him of the *Vohu mano*—*i.e.*, the Good Thought or Spirit. At the same time he overcame the evil spirit, Angra Mainyu, or Ahriman, who offered to him, as Satan offers to Jesus, rule over all the nations, if he would only renounce the good law and worship of Mazda, the good deity. The answer made by the old Persian Redeemer to the Evil One is similar to that returned by Jesus: "The words taught by Mazda, these are my weapons, my best weapons....... This I ask thee, Teach me the truth, O Lord." The Jews had lived much in contact with the Persians, and had been profoundly influenced by their demonology. It is, therefore, not impossible that, even if the story of the enlightenment and temptation of Jesus was not directly imitated from Mazdeism, it was anyhow under its influence that the enlightenment of Jesus was placed on his thirtieth birthday.

The Jewish Christians of Palestine at an early date taught that Jesus was chosen out to be anointed the Messiah because he was righteous above all men, and had kept the Jewish law as no man had ever done before him. Other men who attain an equal degree of moral perfection are to be considered and called Christs. Similarly Paul attests that Jesus, in his earthly life, "*was under the law*"; that he was "*a minister of the circumcision for the sake of God's truth, so as to give effect to the promises made of old to God's people*" (Rom. xv. 8). When he adds that he knew not sin (2 Cor. v. 21), he surely means that he entirely fulfilled the law, the transgression of which alone constituted sin to the mind of a Jew.

Perhaps, however, the Christology which made the baptism the moment of Jesus's promotion to the *rôle* and title of Anointed Messiah and Son of God was later than that which we can trace in the letters of Paul, and also in the Acts of the Apostles (see above, p. 175); for, according to these, Jesus was invested with the Sonship—that is to say, the *rôle* of son or servant of Jahveh—not at baptism, but in and through his resurrection. Thus in Romans i. 3 Paul asserts that he was "*born of the seed of David according to the flesh, and was constituted Son of God with power, according to the Spirit of holiness, through resurrection from the dead.*" However, this conception is not really incompatible with the view of the baptism taken by Mark; for according to this Jesus found, as Loisy says, in his baptism a sure revelation of his messianic *rôle*. The conviction of his divine sonship then took hold of him with a force which it had not before possessed, and which it was never afterwards to lose. This is probably the kernel of fact which underlies the traditional story in the simple form in which Mark tells it. But the Messiah of Jewish tradition was to play a far more glorious part than Jesus played. He crowned with a miserable death a life of physical weakness, having achieved no work worthy of the Messiah who was to come. If he was really Messiah, then his main task was still in the future; his glory still awaited him. Accordingly, a second advent was postulated, when he would come in power to judge the world, and make good the shortcomings and ill success of his first mission, when he came in the guise of weak and sinful humanity. The resurrection was the beginning of this new epoch of his activity. His followers were convinced, from his apparitions to them, that he was still alive and in heaven, seated on a throne at the right hand of his Father. He had triumphed here over all the incentives of human appetites and earthly ambition; he had even surmounted the supreme temptation and risk of death. The spirit communicated to him in the Jordan was eternal, and constituted him, its recipient, immortal life itself. He had died in order to live an ampler life, and had now entered into the glory which by nature belongs to the Messiah. Before the generation which knew him in the flesh should pass away, he was destined to return on the clouds of heaven, and bring about a restitution of all things, as sudden as it would be glorious. To his followers was left the task, as regarded themselves, of watching and praying for this second coming; as regarded others, of reforming and preparing them for the great event.

But what is interesting about this early phase of

opinion about Jesus is that in it he is not yet deified; until the baptism or the resurrection intervenes to advance and promote him, he is not regarded as other than a man born of men. A writer of the epoch 130–150, Justin Martyr, expressly testifies that this was the opinion of most Christians; and his testimony is the more striking because he was himself convinced—though on grounds of prophecy rather than of human evidence—that Jesus was miraculously begotten by the Spirit of a virgin, and was, from the moment of his supernatural conception, the incarnate Word of God. The passage I allude to is in an imaginary dialogue, or conversation, of about A.D. 135, held with a Jew called Tryphon. The latter has remarked that those followers of Jesus who reject the story of the virgin-birth—a pagan myth modelled, he says, on that of Danae—and who hold, rather, that Jesus was born an ordinary man, and was chosen out by Providence to be anointed *(kechristhai)*, and so became *Christ* (*i.e.*, the Lord's anointed or Messiah), appear to say what is the more probable. "For," he adds, "we all expect the Christ to be born a man of men, and that Elias will anoint him when he comes." Justin's answer to this criticism is as follows:—

> It is quite true that some people of our kind acknowledge him to be Christ, but at the same time declare him to have been a man of men. I, however, cannot agree with them, and will not do so, even if the majority (of Christians) insist on this opinion and impart it to me; for by Christ himself we have been commanded to base our conclusions, not on human teachings, but upon predictions set forth by the blessed prophets and imparted in his own teaching.

We gather from the above that the majority of

THE BAPTISM OF JESUS

Christians were more open to historical considerations and less ready than Justin to sacrifice them to *a priori* prophetic constructions. It is not, perhaps, rash to assume that this majority constituted the official Church of Rome, in which the Petrine traditions still flourished. For the point of view of "the majority," as Justin here represents it, is exactly that of Mark's Gospel, which was already regarded by Papias as in some special manner representing Peter's teaching. Alone among the Synoptics, it knows nothing of the legends which so soon grew up about the birth and childhood of Jesus; it is indeed, by implication, even hostile to them. There are also good reasons for believing that Justin, though he lived in Rome, was out of sympathy, perhaps not even in communion, with the official Church of that city. He never, so he says in the Acts of his Martyrdom, during his two terms of residence in Rome, frequented or attended any of the Christian conventicles there, with the single exception of the room over the bath-house of Martin Timotinus, in which he taught himself. He clearly avoided all the Roman churches but one. Why? The art of the catacombs testifies to the preponderating stress laid on the Baptism of Jesus in the Roman Church of the second century. Justin, on the other hand, transfers to the conception and virgin-birth the importance which the majority of Roman believers, being of a more primitive cast, still attached to the Baptism.

The earliest defence of Christianity written in Latin is probably a dialogue entitled *Octavius*, written about the year 163 by a Roman barrister, M. Minucius Felix.[1]

---

[1] Some critics, however, argue that it was written after Tertullian.

182 THE BAPTISM OF JESUS

In this dialogue the hostile interlocutor assails the Christians for paying divine honours to a crucified criminal. The apologist answers that his opponent is far from the truth when he supposes that a criminal deserved to be believed to be divine, or that an earthly man could be believed to be such by the Christians. And he hurls back the charge of anthropolatry at the pagan persecutors. They are the ones to be really pitied, because their entire hopes are set on a mortal man, who ceases to aid them when he dies. The Egyptians, for example, choose out a man and worship him, set themselves to propitiate him, consult him as an oracle about everything, slay victims in his honour. And yet he who, in the eyes of others, is thus made a god is surely, in his own, but a man, whether he will or not. He may deceive others; he cannot himself. The writer, after thus scathing the cult of Antinous, goes on to glance at Cæsar-worship. "Princes and kings," he says,

> might fairly be flattered as men mighty and elect, but the homage paid to them as gods is false. It is truer to bestow honour on a man because he is renowned, and sweeter to bestow love on him because he is best of his kind. But, instead of this, the pagans invoke the godhead of kings, pray to their images, appeal, when accused of aught, to their genius—that is, their demon; and so it is held less risky to perjure yourself by the genius of Jove than by that of the king.

Lactantius, another Latin apologist at the beginning of the fourth century, holds similar language, in a passage which merits citation because it so admirably sums up the earlier conceptions of Jesus entertained in the Church before his deification *à outrance*; for this was only accomplished later on, in the

THE BAPTISM OF JESUS

Councils called orthodox. The passage is in a work *On True Wisdom*, ch. 14 :—

> As to what were the ways of God and what his precepts, we are left neither in doubt nor in darkness. For God, when he saw that wickedness and the cults of false gods had grown so strong all over the earth that his name was almost effaced from men's minds, ...sent his son, the chief (*or* prince) of angels, as his deputy to mankind, to convert them from impious and vain cults to knowledge and worship of the true God; and likewise to lead their minds from folly to wisdom, from iniquity to works of justice. These are the ways of God, in which he instructed him to walk; these the precepts which he enjoined him to keep. But he in turn, in exemplary fashion, showed his faith in God, for he taught that God is one, and that he alone ought to be worshipped. Nor did he himself ever say that he was God, because he would not have kept faith if, after being sent to make away with polytheism and vindicate the one, he had brought in another beside the one. That would not have been to preach and proclaim the one God, but to push himself forward in the place of him that had sent him, and so to separate himself from him to manifest whom he had come. For the very reason that he proved himself so faithful, that he arrogated no honours whatever to himself, devoting himself rather to fulfilling the commands of him that sent him, he was rewarded with the dignity of being a priest for ever, with the honour of being supreme king, with the authority of judge, and with the name of God.

The same profound contrast with the Christology which boasts itself to be orthodox is found in many other early Christian writers; but I will only adduce a single other example. In Syriac and old Armenian are preserved twenty-three homilies, written by a Syrian Father, Aphraates, about the years 330–350. The seventeenth of these combats the Jews, who taxed the Christians with worshipping a crucified man— viz., Jesus—and calling him God; also with asserting that he was Son of God, whereas God has not sons. Aphraates's defence is hardly that of an orthodox Christian. "The venerable name of Godhood," he writes,

> has been given to just men themselves, and they have been held worthy to be called by it. And men in whom God has found pleasure he has himself called his sons and friends. Thus, when he chose Moses as his friend and beloved one and as leader of his people, and constituted him teacher and priest, he called him God. For he said to him: "*I have appointed thee God unto Pharaoh.*" And forthwith he gave him his priest as his prophet. "*Verily shall Aaron thy brother speak for thee to Pharaoh; unto him shalt thou be as God, but he shall be thy interpreter.*"......Again it is written, "*Ye are sons of the Lord your God.*" And about Solomon he said: "*He shall be to me as son, and I will be to him as father.*" We, therefore, in the same way do call Son of God the Christ through whom we have come to know God, just as he called Israel his firstborn son, and said of Solomon: "*He shall be a son unto me.*" We call him God, however, just as he called Moses with his own name.......Moreover, the name of Godhood is given by way of very great honour in the world, and God has imposed it upon whom he chooses. ......However transcendent and venerable be the name of Godhood, he has not denied it to the just.

Such was the sort of deification still accorded to Jesus in the fourth century in the Eastern Churches that lay outside the confederated Churches of the Roman

Empire. In them dogma was not yet brought up to date. These regions were too widely leavened with Jewish monotheism for the higher Christology, as it is called, to take root so early as the first half of the fourth century. Even in the Western world it was probably exceptional, until, with the defeat of Arianism, the last gleam of good sense and reason in Christian theology was extinguished.

Nothing is more certain than that the title *Son of God*, as applied to Jesus in the earliest evangelical texts, meant no more than *Servant of God* or *Messiah*. It was only when the religion was spread among pagans, accustomed to the idea of deified kings and emperors, that the deification of Jesus began to be possible. Aphraates even asserts that when the Church called Jesus God no more was intended than the promotion accorded to the Cæsars. Orthodox historians have sedulously kept out of sight this early and humanistic view of Jesus, which was the counterpart of the equally primitive view that at the baptism the descent of the Spirit constituted him Prophet and Messiah. Until this spiritual crisis was reached he was in no wise different from other men, except in his more complete righteousness. Between this early standpoint and the orthodoxy evolved by the doctors of Rome and Alexandria, in the fourth and fifth centuries, a great gulf yawns. The Mahommedan Koran reprobates as blasphemous the deification of Christ; in doing so it is far nearer to the primitive faith of the Church than any of the Christian creeds of to-day. "Jesus," we read in ch. 43 of that book, "is no other than a servant whom God favoured with the gift of prophecy, and appointed him for an example;...... and he shall be a sign of the approach of the last hour."

CHAPTER XII.

BIRTH LEGENDS

It is admitted, even by orthodox divines, as a reason why Mark's Gospel must embody the earliest form of evangelical tradition, that its author knew nothing of the birth and childhood of Jesus. It is also widely recognised by them that the story of the Virgin Birth was not divulged in the first apostolic age, nor revealed to the Church until Peter and Paul and the rest of the apostles had passed away; that the contemporaries of Jesus regularly spoke of Jesus as the son of Joseph, and that the apostles continued so to speak of him long after his death. Professor Sanday, indeed, would have us believe that Jesus's mother treasured up in her heart the miraculous experiences related in the first two chapters of Luke, and communicated them, as a sort of family secret, long years after the event, to her friend Joanna, wife of Chusa, Herod's steward, and that she in turn confided them to the evangelist. Such are the desperate shifts of latter-day apologetics! Other divines, well aware of the fact that the clause of the creed " born of the Virgin Mary " is fast becoming dead wood, warn their audiences that the Virgin Birth did not in itself constitute the Incarnation of the divine Word, but was only an interesting and important incident connected therewith. We are even told that God, if he had chosen to do so, might have incarnated himself in human form without having any recourse at all to such expedients. I am encouraged by such

BIRTH LEGENDS

admissions to deal frankly with a legend which is fast losing its hold on many religious minds. We have seen above that Paul speaks, in Romans i. 13, of Jesus as having been born "*of the seed of David according to the flesh.*" But in another passage, 2 Timothy ii. 8, he uses language of a kind to arouse our suspicions, for he writes thus: "*Be mindful of Jesus Christ raised from the dead, of the seed of David, according to my gospel.*"

Here the qualification *according to my gospel* seems to attach exclusively to the clause *of the seed of David*, and so contains a hint that there were others according to whose gospel Jesus was not *of the seed of David*. For Paul, when he thus speaks of *his* gospel, has in view the teaching of the true companions of Jesus— James, and John, and Peter. Did, then, these authorities reject this tenet? We know not; but one thing is certain, that in the tradition inherited by Mark[1] Jesus repudiated for himself a Davidic pedigree, for in Mark xii. 35 we read the following: "*Jesus teaching in the Temple said, How say the scribes that the Messiah is the son of David? David himself said, through the Holy Spirit, the Lord said to my Lord, sit thou on my right hand, till I place thine enemies under thy feet. David himself calls him* [*i.e.*, the Christ] *Lord; how, therefore, can he be his son?*"

The gist of the above argument is this: the Christ or Messiah cannot be a descendant of David, because David in an inspired psalm gives to the future Messiah a title—namely, *Lord*—which no man would assign to one of his own descendants. Such an argument is

---

[1] In Revelation xxii. 16, in the received text, Jesus says, "*I am the root and the offspring of David.*" It is significant that the old Armenian version reads *of Adam*. Revelation was written about the year 93.

rabbinic enough in kind, but none the less witnesses to an age in which the scribes alleged against the messianic claims of Jesus that he was no descendant of David. Jesus meets them with a mere denial of their major premiss. And yet, had he esteemed himself to be of Davidic origin, or had the authors or reporters of this conversation believed him to be such, the proper answer to the challenge was merely to assert the fact. No such assertion is made; on the contrary, the fact alleged is accepted, but denied to be any drawback. But there was also another way of meeting this objection of the scribes—namely, to invent Davidic genealogies for the master; and to this the Church soon had recourse. Of the imaginary Davidic pedigrees of Jesus thus called forth two survive to us, one of them prefixed in the first Gospel to the legend of the Virgin Birth; the other inserted by Luke immediately after the episode of the Spirit's descent upon Jesus in the Jordan—a position in which it serves to emphasise the point that the son of man has just been begotten anew, by spiritual unction, the son of God. The pedigree in the first Gospel in its original form ended (Matthew i. 16) thus: "*Jacob begat Joseph, and Joseph begat Jesus.*" End otherwise it could not, seeing that the aim and object of its compiler was to establish the Davidic descent of Jesus through his father Joseph. This original ending I myself discovered in an old Greek manuscript in the Vatican Library; it also stands in the earliest Syriac version of the Gospels, recently discovered in the Sinai convent. In all the Greek manuscripts of Matthew, however, the last clause of the pedigree has been botched in one of two ways, both intended to avoid its awkward attestation of Joseph's

BIRTH LEGENDS

paternity and adapt it to the later legend of the Virgin Birth.

The majority of MSS. read thus: "*Jacob begat Joseph, the husband of Mary, of whom was born* [or *begotten*] *Jesus called Christ.*"

In a smaller number of MSS. we find the following: "*Jacob begat Joseph, to whom being betrothed a Virgin Mary bore Jesus called Christ.*" The old Syriac text just mentioned has: "*Jacob begat Joseph: Joseph, to whom was betrothed Mary a Virgin, begat Jesus called Christ.*"

It is interesting to observe that the fourth evangelist, writing for the third or fourth generation of believers, is still incredulous of Jesus's Davidic origin, and, like Mark, he represents the Jews as disputing his claim to be Christ on the ground that he lacked it. Thus, in John vii. 40, 41, we read: "*Certain then of the people having heard these discourses said, He truly is the prophet: others said, He is the Christ. But some said, Nay, surely the Christ cometh not of Galilee? Doth not the Scripture say, that of the seed of David and from Bethlehem—the village where was David—cometh the Christ? So then there was a division among the people through him.*"

Such a passage as the above could not have been penned by one who knew for certain that Jesus was "*of the seed of David.*" It was, moreover, this evangelist's view that it mattered little what his human parentage was. As Christ and unique vehicle of the divine Word or Reason, he was not "*born of blood or of the will of the flesh, nor of the will of man, but of God.*" In this sense Christ declares in John viii. 14 that the Jews "*knew not whence he came nor whither he went,*" just because they "*judged according to the flesh*" only—*i.e.*, according to the accident of human descent.

But this passage of the Fourth Gospel preserves to us another objection brought by the Jews of the first age against the messianic claims of Jesus—this, namely, that he was not born in Bethlehem, the city of David. If the evangelist had heard any report of his having been born there, he would surely have revealed his knowledge of it, and, as he is so prone to do, have stigmatised the Jews as liars. But he gives no hint of it; and it becomes obvious that the story which Luke tells was invented to meet this particular objection of the Jews. Rabbinical interpretation of Old Testament prophecies required the Messiah to be born in Bethlehem, and not in Nazareth, as Mark assumes him to have been. It was, therefore, necessary to the fulfilment of prophecy that his mother be transferred to Bethlehem in time for her child to be born there; and Luke, or the form of tradition he followed, devised the following tale in satisfaction of the claims of prophecy, and as an answer to the objections of incredulous Jews: "*There went forth in those days a decree from Cæsar Augustus for a registration* [or *census*] *to be made of the whole world. This registration was first made when Kyrenios was governor of Syria, and all went to be registered, each to his own city. And, accordingly, Joseph also went up from Galilee, from the city of Nazareth, into Judea, to the city of David, which is called Bethlehem, because he belonged to the household and country of David, in order to be registered with Mary his wife, who was with child. And it came to pass while they were there the days of her pregnancy were fulfilled, and she brought forth her first-born son.*"

BIRTH LEGENDS

Nazareth lies north of Bethlehem about 130 kilometres, or 80 miles, as the crow flies, over very difficult country. Imagine a government which takes a couple of peasants all that way in order to fill up a census paper! And why take Mary, who, being of the house of Aaron, should have gone elsewhere? Nor, according to Luke, did Joseph and Mary alone have to go back to the city of his ancestor of a thousand years before; but everyone else all over the world did the same. Thus, we have a picture of hundreds of thousands of people all rushing in different directions at one and the same time from end to end of the Roman Empire, in order to fill up census papers which they could fill up equally well if they remained quietly at home. It is as if to-day every Scotch family of the name of Campbell were brought from London or the Antipodes in order to fill up income-tax papers in Argyleshire. Such is the monstrous absurdity which Luke calmly saddles on the administration of Augustus, the most practical of ancient rulers! He assumes that the Roman Government would register people, not by place of domicile, but according to who their ancestors were and where they had lived; as if everyone had his pedigree and family history ready at hand to inform him. Most of the Jews in that day knew nothing of who their remote ancestors were or where they lived, and, in order to fulfil this extravagant edict, would have been forced to sit down and forge pedigrees not unlike those which the authors of the First and Third Gospels have forged for Jesus.

If additional proof were needed of the legendary character of Luke's narrative, it is afforded by his mention of Quirinius or Kyrenios as the governor of

Syria under whom the enrolment was made in Judæa. This enrolment took place after Archelaus was deposed, on the occasion of Judæa being in due form incorporated in the Roman Empire. The aversion of Oriental races to being numbered is proverbial, and in the Old Testament Jahveh visited the Israelites with the plague because his favourite, King David, so numbered them. It is intelligible, therefore, that so obvious a reform could not be carried through in Judæa without resistance on the part of the Jews; and an insurrection of Judas of Galilee "*in the days of the enrolment*" (Acts v. 37) is attested by the historian Josephus. His testimony, however, is far from substantiating Luke's story; for, in the first place, the enrolment, or census, of Kyrenios was not of *all the world*, but only of the inhabitants of Judæa; and, secondly, it was not made until A.D. 6; whereas Herod—in whose days Luke i. 5 sets the birth of John the Baptist, and, by consequence, of Jesus also, since he was only six months John's junior —died in the spring of B.C. 4. Luke's dates, therefore, show an internal discrepancy of some ten years.

The first evangelist, Matthew, quite naïvely and unconsciously acquaints us with the genesis of the legend that Jesus was born at Bethlehem; for he makes King Herod, the least messianic of men, as Loisy well styles him, "*call together all the chief priests and scribes*," and ask them " *where the Christ should be born*," as if he shared in such beliefs and anticipations. " *And they said unto him, In Bethlehem of Judæa, for thus it is written by the prophet.*" And, without any further ado, Matthew assumes that Jesus was born in Bethlehem, and begins his narrative thus: "*Now when Jesus was born in Bethlehem of Judæa.*" He does not then, like Luke, invent episodes in order

BIRTH LEGENDS

to get Mary thither in time for the birth; and we feel that he reflects a later age, when the real facts were quite forgotten.

The legend of the Star of the Magi, in Matthew, ch. ii., has its parallels all over the world. In every age simple folk have believed the birth of famous men to be heralded by the appearance in heaven of a special star. "We saw his star in the East," say the wise men, as if it were a matter of course. This legend was generated, like others, out of a passage in the Old Testament, interpreted in current Jewish belief as a prophecy of the Messiah—viz., Numbers xxiv. 17, where the seer Balaam is made to say: "*I see him, but not now: I behold him, but not nigh: There shall come forth a star out of Jacob, And a sceptre shall arise out of Israel.*" We have already noticed a similar belief in the Testaments of the Patriarchs.[1]

In the targums of the Jewish rabbis the passage from Numbers is construed as a prediction of the future Messiah. The legend seems to have been redacted in a Greek text in Rome about the year 119 under Pope Xystus, and about that time it probably made its way into the Gospel text. The story of the Magi going with presents to worship Jesus may be an echo of the mission brought in A.D. 66 by the Parthian king, Tiridates, to Nero in Rome. With his train of three magi, laden with presents, Tiridates came before the Roman emperor. They "fell down and worshipped him," and hailed him as "Lord and God, even as Mithras." Now, Nero was the antichrist of early Christian legend; and so enduring was that legend that the Armenians have never had any other name

---

[1] See above, p. 169.

for the devilish counterfeit of Christ but *Nern—i.e.,* Neron. If the antichrist received such homage from three magi, the real Christ could not have received less. Hence the legend of Matthew.

The last seven verses of Matthew, ch. i., relate how Jesus was miraculously conceived of the Holy Ghost, his mother remaining a virgin, in flat contradiction with the pedigree which ended by declaring that *Joseph begat* him, so that he was *a son of David.* Matthew relates how "*when his mother Mary had been betrothed to Joseph, before they came together she was found with child of the Holy Ghost.*" Joseph was forthwith warned not even "*to put her away privily*" by an "*angel of the Lord which appeared unto him in a dream, saying, Joseph, thou son of David, fear not to take to thee Mary thy wife: for that which is conceived in her is of the Holy Ghost.*" Then follows the usual appeal to prophecy, the originating germ of the entire legend:—
"*Now all this is come to pass, that it might be fulfilled which was spoken by the Lord through the prophet, saying, Behold, the virgin shall be with child, and shall bring forth a son, and they shall call his name Immanuel.*"

In the sequel we read that "*Joseph arose from his sleep and did as the angel of the Lord commanded him, and took unto him his wife, and knew her not, till she had brought forth a son : and he called his name Jesus.*"

Here we find related of Jesus what was in antiquity a stock legend related of a number of celebrities. Let us notice a few of these parallels.

The philosopher Plato, very soon after he died, was reputed by his followers to have been born of a virgin, and his own nephew Speusippus told the story in nearly the same words as Matthew employs. Hear

Diogenes Laertius, the biographer of the ancient philosophers, who lived about A.D. 200, in his life of Plato :—

> Ariston (the putative father of Plato) tried to constrain Periktione (his wife), who was a beautiful woman, but failed. When he ceased to do so, he had a vision in which Apollo appeared to him, and in consequence thereof guarded her pure of the relations of wedlock until she brought forth Plato.

Diogenes invokes, beside the testimony of Speusippus, that of Klearchus, a pupil of Aristotle's, and Anaxilides, a Greek writer of uncertain date. Plutarch, in his *Convivial Disputations*, relates that Ariston not only saw the vision in his dream, but heard a voice which forbade him to approach his wife or touch her for ten months. And, after citing an old Greek poet to the effect that the currents of the winds impregnate hen birds, he continues as follows :—

> I see nothing absurd in the supposition that God, instead of approaching women in human wise, touches them to finer issues with other modes of contact, and so fills the mortal with divine offspring. The myth is not of my making, for the Egyptians say that Apis was thus conceived through touch and contact of Selene, the moon. The fact of the intercourse of a male god with mortal women is conceded by all, but it is not believed that mortal man can occasion pregnancy and birth in a goddess, because the stuff of which gods are made is air and spirit and certain forms of warmth and moisture.

This sort of myth, as we shall see, left its impress on Christian speculation about the birth of Jesus, and not a few Christian apologists of the third and fourth centuries, anxious to prove that Jesus was conceived of the Holy Spirit, compared his mother to the animals "which are wont to conceive by wind and air"—*quæ vento et aura concipere solent*, to use the words of Lactantius. The idea is an old one. Thus, in Virgil's *Georgics*, we read how the mares, "when in springtime the warmth returns in their bones, stand all on the top of the rocks, turning their mouths to the Zephyr, and gulp down the light airs, and ofttimes, without marriage union—marvellous to relate—they are made pregnant by the wind."

> Vere magis, quia vere calor redit ossibus, illæ
> Ore omnes versæ in Zephyrum stant rupibus altis,
> Exceptantque leves auras ; et sæpe sine ullis
> Conjugiis, vento gravidæ (mirabile dictu).

It was also related by an Egyptian writer, Asclepiades, that the mother of Julius Cæsar conceived him miraculously in a temple of Apollo, so that this first of the emperors was son of a god. The emperor Alexander likewise was conceived by a virgin. It is no matter for surprise that in the second century, when the legend of Christ's miraculous birth began to circulate in the Church, the Jews twitted the Christians with having picked up a pagan tale comparable to the story of Danae. The apologist Justin Martyr (see p. 180) tries in general to draw delicate distinctions between her case and that of the Virgin Mary, but sometimes, as in his first apology (ch. xxiv.), he chooses another line of defence, boldly admits the parallel, and asks, "Why are we Christians alone of men hated for Christ's name, when we do but relate of him stories similar to what the Greeks relate of Hermes and Perseus?" "What we teach," he says in the same apology (ch. xxiii.), "we learned from Christ and the prophets who preceded him, and it is a true lore and more ancient than that of all other writers that ever existed; but we claim acceptance, not because our stories are identical with those of others, but because they are true."

"When," he remarks in another passage (297 B), "I am told that Perseus was born of a virgin, I realise that here again is a case in which the serpent and deceiver has imitated our religion." Thus the parallel myths of the pagans were satanic imitations of Christian verities. And, addressing the Emperor Antoninus Pius in his first apology (ch. xxi.), he reminds him that the Christians, in asserting the word of God, Jesus Christ, their teacher, to have been born without parental intercourse, and to have been crucified and died, risen from the dead and gone up into heaven, imported no tenets either strange or new to those who were familiar with the tales of the sons of Zeus. "You well know," he continues, "how many sons of Zeus your most renowned authors enumerate—Hermes, the interpreter, Word and teacher of all; Asclepius, who ascended into heaven after being struck with lightning, although he was a healer; Dionysus, who was torn to pieces; Heracles, who, escaped from toil, consigned himself to the fire; the Dioscuri born of Leda; and Perseus, born of Danae; and Bellerophon, who, though of human parentage, ascended on the horse Pegasus."

Elsewhere (ch. xxii.) we read: "Even if we assert —and we do—that Jesus was born of a virgin, we contend that this too is a feature shared by him with Perseus. And when we tell you that Jesus healed the halt and paralytic and the maimed from birth, and that he raised the dead, you will see that here too we merely repeat things said to have been done by Asclepius." Such passages aid us to understand the rapid spread of the belief in the virgin birth and resurrection. Men's minds were already full of similar beliefs, and the ground prepared for their reception. The Christians claimed acceptance of their myths because the pagan religion was already full of similar ones.

The Jews of the *diaspora* were already, before the birth of Jesus, in the habit of throwing their messianic dreams into Homeric hexameters; these poems passed from hand to hand, and the Christian Fathers, when they inherited them, uncritically believed that genuine prophecies of the ancient Sibyls had fallen into their hands. A collection of such pseudo-oracles has come down to us under the name of the Sibylline poems. The passage of Isaiah vii. 14, "*A virgin shall conceive and bear a son*," may have inspired some such poem, and this have fallen into the hands of that most omnivorous of readers, the poet Virgil, who, pleased with the fancy, threw it into elegant Latin verse in his fourth Eclogue:—

> Ultima Cumaei venit iam carminis aetas:
> Magnus ab integro sæclorum nascitur ordo.
> Iam redit et Virgo, redeunt Saturnia regna;
> Iam nova progenies cælo demittitur alto.

"The last age of the Cumæan hymn is come: a great order of the ages is born afresh. Already the virgin returns—returns, too, the kingdom of Saturn. Already a new scion of the race is sent down from high heaven."

This passage of Virgil is interesting because it shows how widely such ideas were diffused. But it is not even necessary to go so far afield for parallels to the legend of Christ's birth. They were already to be found in the Jewish literature of the first Christian age. Philo, if he did not actually believe that Isaac was begotten of Sarah by the angel which came down to Abraham to predict his birth, was at least familiar with such a belief among his contemporaries, and uses it up for his allegory. In his tract *On Change of Names* he writes in similar strain that " Thamar was made pregnant of divine seed, and, as she saw not him who sowed—for, as it is said, she veiled her face, as did Moses when he turned away fearing with holy fear to look on God—so she, having scanned the symbols and testimonies and judged of them in her heart that they were not imparted by mortal man, cried out aloud, ' Of no man is this, by him (*i.e.*, God) am I with child.' "

In another of his works, *About Cherubim* (ch. xiii.), he allegorises away the wives of the Jewish patriarchs into the several virtues, but we feel that his allegory is suggested by the popular belief in miraculous or virgin births, when we meet with such phrases as the following :—

> Sarah is represented as becoming pregnant when God visits her in her solitude. And she brings forth not to him who so visited her, but to him who yearned to attain to wisdom, and who is named Abraham. Yet more clearly does Moses teach us in Leah's case, saying that God opened her womb, for to open the womb is a man's task. But she conceived and bore, not to God—for he alone is all-sufficing to himself— but to Jacob, who had willingly laboured for the good cause, that Virtue might receive the divine seed from the first cause and bring forth to that one of her suitors who should be preferred. Again, when Isaac, the all-wise, prayed to God, Rebecca, who is Patience, became pregnant by him to whom the prayer was offered. And without any prayer or supplication at all, Moses, having taken to himself Sepfora, who is

winged or soaring Virtue, finds her with child by no one mortal.

So, in Matthew i. 18, it is said that "*When his mother Mary had been betrothed to Joseph, before they came together she was found with child of the Holy Spirit.*" No one would affirm that Philo believed in the popular legends of miraculous births; but they suggested his allegory.

It is hardly necessary to insist on the mythological character of the first two chapters of Matthew, since even among the orthodox there is a tendency to sacrifice them to the wolves of criticism. Thus Professor Sanday allows that the birth-story in Matthew "appears to belong to that portion of the First Gospel which is latest and least certain" (*Critical Questions*, 1903, p. 148). Let us, therefore, return to our consideration of Luke's narrative of the birth, on which the latter-day apologist tries to make a final stand. This we have already criticised in respect of its location of the birth at Bethlehem. When we proceed to examine it from the point of view of language, we find it to be little more than a cento of phrases culled from the Septuagint or old Greek version of the Old Testament. This does not, of course, in itself forbid us to accept it as history; for it would be easy, with the help of a concordance to the Septuagint, to dress up a history of Alexander the Great or of Napoleon in phrases derived therefrom. Nevertheless, our suspicions are roused, for a genuine historian of real facts is unlikely to convey them to his readers in such a form. But when, in ch. i. 7, the narrative of the birth of John the Baptist begins with the statement that his parents, Zachariah and Elizabeth, had no child, because she was barren and both of them past the age at which married couples have children, we at once feel ourselves to be in the presence of a professional story-teller. For in popular legend and folklore it is almost incumbent on the hero to be born in such an abnormal manner. Thus we recognise in Luke's story what is vulgarly called " an old chestnut." He has derived both incident and *mise-en-scène* from the narrative of the birth of Samson in the thirteenth chapter of Judges, and from this he borrows phrase after phrase. If we compare the two texts, the justice of this criticism becomes evident:—

Judges xiii.	Luke i.
2. And there was a certain man of Sar-aa, of the portion of the kinship of Dan, and his name was Manoe, and his wife was barren and bare not.	5. There was a certain priest named Zacharia, of the course of Abijah, and he had a wife of the daughters of Aaron.... 7. And they had no child, because Elizabeth was barren, and they were both well advanced in years.
3. And the angel of the Lord appeared unto the woman, and said to her, Behold now, thou art barren, and hast not borne; but thou shalt bear a son. 4. Now therefore, beware, I pray thee, and drink no wine or strong drink, and eat not any unclean thing. 5. For lo, thou shalt conceive and bear a son, and no razor shall come upon his head; for the child shall be a Nazarite unto God from the womb: and he shall begin to save Israel from the hand of the Philistines.	11. And there appeared unto him an angel of the Lord....the angel said unto him....thy wife Elizabeth shall bear thee a son. 15. And he shall drink no wine or strong drink, and he shall be filled with the Holy Ghost, even from his mother's womb. 71. Salvation from our enemies, and from the hand of all that hate us.

It is not evident, however, that Luke intended his readers to regard Jesus as conceived in supernatural manner. He declares Joseph to have been of the house of David; whereas his wife Mary, being a kinswoman of Elizabeth, was presumably of the house of Aaron, and therefore incapable of transmitting a

Davidic strain to her child. Mary is already betrothed to Joseph when the angel Gabriel goes in to her at Nazareth and says :—"*Hail, thou favoured with grace, the Lord is with thee. But she was much troubled at the word, and pondered over what sort of greeting it might be. And the angel said, Fear not, Mary, for thou hast found favour with God. And behold thou shalt conceive and bring forth a son, and shalt call his name Jesus. He shall be mighty, and shall be called Son of the Highest, and the Lord shall give him the throne of David his father, and he shall rule over the house of Jacob for the ages, and of his kingdom there shall be no end.*"

Here we note that the Messiah promised is to be of the conventional Jewish type, a mighty king seated on David's throne, quite unlike the historical Jesus. But he will not be born in full possession of his temporal majesty; he will only be invested with it later on.

According to the oldest MS. of the old Latin version of Luke's Gospel, when the angel ends his address, Mary makes the following very suitable answer: "*Behold the handmaid of the Lord; be it unto me according to thy word.*" But the Greek MSS. set in her mouth the answer: "*How shall this be, seeing that I know not a man?*" The latter reading is absurd, for Gabriel had said not "*thou hast conceived,*" but "*thou shalt conceive.*" His message contemplates a near future, when she will no longer be merely the betrothed, but the bride of Joseph. This reading, then, is an interpolation, and a stupid one. And a second - century apocryph, called the Protevangel, which closely imitates Luke's narrative of the birth of Jesus, enables us to understand how the offending words came to be interpolated, for it tells the story thus :—

> And lo, an angel of the Lord stood before her, saying, Fear not, Mariam, for thou hast found favour in the eyes of the Lord of all, and thou shalt conceive by his word. But she, on hearing this, reasoned in herself, saying, Shall I then conceive by the Lord God who liveth, and yet bear as every woman bears children? And the angel of the Lord said, Not so, Mariam, for the power of the Lord shall overshadow thee. Wherefore, what is born of thee shall be called holy, a son of the highest. And thou shalt call his name Jesus. For he shall save his people from their sins. And Mariam said, Behold the handmaid of the Lord is in his presence. Be it unto me according to thy word.

In the text of Luke, then, as the author of this early apocryph read it, the Virgin made no such absurd answer as: "*How shall this be, seeing I know not a man?*" From what source, then, were these words interpolated in Luke? The answer is, from this very apocryph, which represents Mary as vowed by her parents from infancy "not to know a man all the days of her life," as the Syrian Father St. Ephrem put it. In this apocryph the phrase "I know not a man" occurs more than once, but always in contexts where it is appropriate and makes good sense. For example, when Joseph finds with child the Virgin whom, as her guardian, he had taken to his home, he chides her and says: "Thou hast forgotten the Lord thy God. Why hast thou abased thy soul?" And she, weeping, replies: "I am pure, and I know not a man." And Joseph said to her: "Whence, then, is that which is in thy womb?" Mary is next brought for trial before the high priest, who chides her in the same terms as

Joseph, and she repeats her answer: "As my God liveth, I am pure before him, and I know not a man." In both these contexts the words are as appropriate as in the existing text of Luke i. 34 they are inappropriate. The history of ancient manuscript literature supplies many examples of such interpolation. An earlier document A is imitated or commented on in another document B. Presently an amplification belonging to B finds its way into A. The Gospel of Mark was imitated or copied out with considerable modifications by Matthew and Luke. Some of these modifications have crept into the text of Mark, having been introduced by scribes desirous to assimilate to one another the various forms of the gospel story. In the same way Luke's text was contaminated from the Protevangel.

Some critics think the next verse also, Luke i. 35, to be an interpolation. It is this: "*And the angel answered and said to her: A Holy Spirit shall come upon thee, and a power of the Highest conceal* [or *overshadow*] *thee; wherefore also what is born* [or *begotten*] *holy shall be called son of God.*"

The above is generally interpreted as signifying an impregnation of the Virgin by the Spirit, and the words "*come upon thee*" and "*overshadow*" are understood by the oldest Christian Fathers in this sense. But they admit of another interpretation, for in contemporary Greek the word *episkiazô*, though literally it means *overshadow*, usually signifies no more than to *hide* or *conceal*. It was a common belief that women with child were peculiarly liable to the assaults of demons; and in Revelation we have a picture of a "*great red dragon*" who stood before the woman "*that was arrayed with the sun, and the moon under her feet, and upon her head a crown of twelve stars; and she was with child, and she cried out, travailing in birth and in pain to be delivered. And the dragon stood before the woman which was about to be delivered, that when she was delivered he might devour the child. And she was delivered of a son, a man child, who is to rule all the nations with a rod of iron."*

In the latter picture the heavenly Aeon or Power, the Church, is represented as the mother of the Messiah. The dragon lies in wait to devour him, and in the sequel he is saved by being caught up to God. Perhaps Luke also imagined that Satan lay in wait for the future Messiah, and dogged the steps of his mother, just as, after the baptism, he assailed him with triple temptation. If so, the *Power of the Highest* was to conceal his mother so that the devil should not molest him either before or after birth. Ignatius the Martyr, who died about A.D. 120, writes that "the virginity of Mary and the birth of Christ alike escaped the notice of the Prince of this world." He is the earliest writer in whom we can clearly trace the belief; and he supposed that Mary's virginity was a providential "blind" to hide from the simple-minded devil the fact that the Messiah was about to be born. Elsewhere Ignatius declares that the mother of Christ, the Word, was *Sigê*, or Silence—an heretical idea. By the Holy Spirit *coming upon* the mother, Luke may have meant no more than that the child, conceived as usual, received a peculiar sanctity before it was born, just as John the Baptist also (Luke i. 15) was "*to be filled with the Holy Ghost even from his mother's womb.*"

However this may be, the earliest Gospel, called of Mark, not only knows nothing, as we have above remarked, of the legend of the miraculous birth of Jesus, but by implication denies it. How could Mary and her sons have set out to place him under restraint, "because he was out of his mind," if she had really been the recipient of the Angel Gabriel's confidences? Here is an objection which no apologist even attempts to meet; we have shown above that the two later evangelists carefully expunged this incident from their texts. We will presently notice some other early and widely diffused documents which attest an epoch when, to say the least, the legend of the Virgin Birth was far from universally believed in the Church. But let us first pause to inquire what was believed by Jesus's own immediate following, the Christians of Palestine. These were, in the second century, known as Ebionites, or the Poor, and their enemies explained the name by reference to the supposed poverty of their doctrine; more probably it was suggested by the impoverishment which followed on their attempts to hold all things in common by way of preparation for the Second Advent. Now, these Ebionite Christians believed, so we learn from Irenæus and other second-century Fathers—of whom we cite another, Justin Martyr, elsewhere (p. 180)—that Jesus "was the son of Joseph and Mary according to the ordinary course of human generation." Their form of gospel, which was written in Aramaic, omitted, like Mark, the birth-stories of Jesus, and they continued for centuries to repudiate them as untrue and unworthy of the Messiah. It is additional evidence of how little idea the earliest Christians had of Jesus being the child of Mary alone that, the presidency of their first Church in Jerusalem being vested, according to Oriental habit, in the eldest surviving relative of the founder, James, the brother of the

Lord, was the first chosen to occupy this post of dignity. Yet his kinship with Jesus, supposing Mary was not their common mother, which is probable, could only be reckoned through the common father, Joseph. After the death of James, the dignity continued, for several generations, to be assigned to the oldest surviving representative of the family of Jesus, whose members were known as the *Desposunoi*, or kinsmen of the Lord. In Oriental lands it was, and still is, as I have stated above, the custom for the headship of a religious community to be assigned to the descendants of its founder. It was so in the Mohammedan religion, and the early messianic communion of Jerusalem formed no exception to the rule. One can trace a similar custom in the earliest Christian communities of Syria and Armenia.

The literature of the Christians during the second century is almost wholly lost. The pagans were not likely to preserve it, and the rapid change in Christian opinion in the third and fourth century soon made it antiquated and heretical. It was either not copied out or wilfully destroyed. Thus we cannot expect to discover much literary attestation of the early and naturalistic belief about Jesus's birth. Yet it has left clear traces. For example, in the so-called Acts of Judas Thomas, the apostle who was reputed to have gone to India and converted the Hindoo ruler Gundaphor, we have a document which goes back to the second century. It was written almost concurrently in Greek and Syriac, and was soon spread all over Christendom in Latin, Armenian, Coptic, and other versions. In this curious document Judas is represented as the twin brother of Jesus, and as on that account so like him in face and features that the very animals could not tell them apart. Such a document could neither be written nor accepted among Christians, for whom the birth from a virgin was a primary article of faith. In the so-called Acts of Pilate we have another early document, almost as widely diffused among the early Churches as the Gospels. It is a narrative of Jesus's trial before Pilate, and of his crucifixion, largely compiled from the existing Gospels. Its author seems not to have held the tenet of the miraculous birth; for, when the hostile Jews accuse Jesus to Pilate of being a son of fornication, twelve other Jews of substance and repute are brought on the stage, who testify that his parents, Mary and Joseph, were legally married, and that they themselves attended the wedding. The implication is that Jesus was their legitimate son.

The Jews of the second century, as they meet us in the pages of Justin Martyr (A.D. 130–150), though he is a hostile witness, yet contrast favourably with the Christians of that age. For they exhibit a higher and purer monotheism, in so far as they condemn as a pagan fable the story of God engendering a son by a mortal woman. It was, they declare, an echo of the myth of Danae and of her son Perseus, begotten by Zeus in a shower of gold. These second-century Jews were also able to interpret their old prophets in a more critical manner than the Christians. They pointed out, for example, that Isaiah's Hebrew text (Isaiah vii. 14), properly translated, means no more than that "a young girl (*or* maiden) shall conceive and bear a son"; and the Rabbi Aquila and Theodotion the Ebionite issued new Greek translations, in which the ambiguous Greek word *parthenos* or *virgin* was replaced by *neanis—a young woman*. They thus cut away the ground from under the feet of the Christians, who had, as we have seen above (p. 180), little except prophecy on which to base their legend. Nothing has so much excited the spleen of Christian and Catholic writers as this substitution of *neanis* for *parthenos*. But time has its revenges; and the recent revisers of the English Bible, timid time-servers as they were, yet felt themselves constrained to add at this verse the marginal note, " or *maiden*." For this, and not *virgin*, is the proper equivalent of the Hebrew word *alma*, which indicates not a woman's quality, but her age, so resembling the German equivalent *Jungfrau*. Let us note, in passing, that to the mind of healthy-minded Teutons a young woman is a virgin, and a virgin a young woman.

The Jews of that early age also showed some faculty in critical exegesis when they had to overthrow Christian beliefs; for they pointed out that Isaiah, in writing his seventh chapter, had in view, not a far-off Messiah, but Hezekiah, their king. It was only towards the close of the last century that the saner method of exegesis, thus anticipated by the Jews of the second century, began to be adopted by our divines; to-day no self-respecting Hebraist would venture to suggest that this or any other passage of Isaiah was any prediction of Jesus of Nazareth.

We must not suppose, however, that this passage in Isaiah sufficed, in and by itself, to generate the tradition of the miraculous birth. It was, of course, in that age regarded as evidence, and as the best sort of evidence; for, as John Chrysostom pregnantly remarks, " No argument was more cogent than the argument from prophecy, which outweighed even the historical facts themselves."[1] But other causes and conditions were at work in the early Christian circles, which rendered the growth of such a legend inevitable. In the first place, Gentile converts, when they heard Jesus Christ proclaimed the Son of God, were naturally prone to interpret the expression to mean that his physical generation was in some special way wrought by God; and they had, as I have said above, a number of pagan legends to shape their ideas of a miraculously arranged and providential genesis of the Saviour. To a messianically-minded Jew the title Son of God meant, no doubt, no more than the vicar or representative or servant of Jehovah. The Gentile converts shrank, perhaps, from the vulgar pagan idea of divine *liaisons* with mortal women; but the idea of a Holy Spirit operating divine results on earth supplied them with a middle term. The Holy Spirit, or *Logos*, which, according to Luke, entered Jesus at the Baptism in outward and material form, had already entered the Virgin, and in her womb been, as it were, coagulated with her flesh into the body of Christ.

But that which, above all else, predisposed Christian circles to accept the legend of the Virgin Birth was the impulse to continence and virginity, the determination to reject marriage and its ties and duties, which pervaded all the Churches. Minucius Felix (c. 160) sums up the matter in the following words, directed against those pagans who accused his co-religionists in Rome and elsewhere of habitual incest: "Most believers," he says, "enjoy inviolate a perpetual virginity of the body, but do not boast of it. So remote, in short, from us is the lust of incest that

---

[1] *Commentary on Acts*, ii. 16, Savile's edition, p. 637, 5.

some of us blush at the very idea even of a legitimate sexual union." The reasons for this feeling—which often amounted to a repudiation of marriage, as a contamination of the flesh—were many; and we can infer that they were already widely operative inside Judaism before Christianity was heard of, from the fact that most of the Essenes abjured marriage. In the time of Josephus, when their numbers were dwindling, their communion still numbered thousands of men, all living a monkish life. Philo also describes a similar society, in which women participated, called the Worshippers, or *Therapeutæ*, who had their headquarters at Alexandria, but ramified all round the Mediterranean, no less among Jews than among proselytes. These societies consisted of men and women living in separate cells, but meeting together on certain days for sacramental banquets, where prayer and praise led up to a sort of communion in bread and water, flesh and wine being excluded from the holy repast. The women, says Philo, were all virgins or widows. Within a few years of the crucifixion, Paul's Epistles reveal a similar impulse at work in the earliest Christian society of Corinth. It was urged that a believer should not touch his wife. Paul replies, with better sense, that if converts are married they had best remain so. Even unmarried men and widows, if they cannot keep chaste like himself, may without sin marry. Let everyone, he says, remain in the state in which the divine call found him. Paul next proceeds to speak of a special relationship, already in vogue among Christians, which may be described as a spiritual or platonic marriage, as follows :—

"*About virgins*," he says in 1 Corinthians vii. 25, "*I*

have no precept of the Lord." They had evidently asked him to regulate certain questions, and he modestly admits that about them he has had no private revelation. *"But,"* he continues, *"I give my opinion as one who by the compassion of the Lord is become one of the faithful. I deem, then, that this* [*i.e.*, virginity] *is best because of the present necessity* [probably the impending catastrophe of the Lord's advent] — *namely, that to remain thus* [*i.e.*, in virginity] *is best for man. Art thou tied to a wife? Seek not to loosen the tie. Art thou loosed from a wife? Seek not a wife. If, however, thou shouldst marry, thou hast not sinned; and, even if the virgin marry, she has not sinned. But such as these will incur tribulation for the flesh, and I would fain spare you it."*

Who is *"the virgin"* in the above who sins not even if she marry, and who in the sequel is distinguished from *" the unmarried woman "* (verse 34), though, like her, she *" is busy with the things of the Lord, so as to be holy both in body and spirit "*?

The sequel reveals to us that *" the virgin"* here is the woman who is living with a man as his spiritual or platonic wife; for in verse 36 Paul continues thus: *" If, however, anyone thinks he is behaving unseemly towards his virgin, if she is over the age of puberty, and it must be so, let him do what he wishes to. He sins not. Let them marry."*

The phrase *"his virgin"* indicates a relation between male and female believers both recognised and widespread. The Greek word *aschemonein*, rendered by *behave unseemly*, is a technical term for immodest behaviour towards one of the opposite sex. If a man is overpowered by his inclinations, says Paul, eminently practical teacher that he was, let

BIRTH LEGENDS

them marry, and substitute for the platonic union a tie of genuine wedlock. They will not sin in so doing. In the whole of this passage the only doubt is about the meaning of the word *huperakmos*, which I render *over the age of puberty*, but which, in the revised English version, is translated "*past the flower of her age.*" This may be the true meaning, for Philo specifies that the women in the contemporary Therapeutic societies were mostly *aged virgins*. On the other hand, Paul may be insisting, and wisely, that girls shall not marry until they are of mature age. In the canon law of the Eastern Churches are read many prescriptions against the child-marriages which are so unhappily common among Hindoos, and which were not unknown during the Middle Ages, even in the Western world. The English revisers, all through this passage, have added, after *virgin*, the word *daughter;* for the notion of fathers behaving unseemly to their virgin daughters, and then apparently marrying them, does not seem to have presented any difficulty to the excellent divines who prepared this new version for Anglo-Saxon readers.

Paul concludes by acknowledging that it is better to maintain the platonic tie in all its purity. "*He that remains stedfast in his heart, and has no necessity* [*i.e.*, overpowering desire], *but retains the mastery over his own inclinations, and is resolved on this in his own heart—namely, to keep and preserve his own virgin—will do well. Consequently both he that marries his own virgin doth well, and he that marries her not will do still better.*"

In one other passage Paul refers to this sort of relationship as in vogue even among those who formed the immediate *entourage* of Jesus. It is in a passage,

1 Corinthians ix. 1-6, where he is insisting on his equality with the other apostles: "*Am I not an apostle? Have I not seen Jesus our Lord? If in the eyes of others I am not an apostle, yet at least I am in yours.......Have we no right to eat and drink? Have we no right to lead about a wife that is a sister, even as do the rest of the apostles, and the brethren of the Lord, and Cephas?*"

Here the woman or wife (the Greek word signifies either), who is a *sister*, unquestionably corresponds to the virgin of ch. i. The great Benedictine scholar Muratori, writing to Montfaucon, about 1709, his tract *De Synisactis et Agapetis*, comes very near to this interpretation. They were not wives, he writes, but certain matrons of honest life, who supplied the apostles and other holy men with food, and made themselves their travelling companions, taking the name of *sister* by way of excluding all suspicion of married licence. St. Jerome's interpretation was similar. It may be remarked that Paul here uses the word *adelfos*, or *sister;* and that *adelfotês*, or *sistership*, was later on the technical term for this platonic marriage between Christian men and maids.

Here, then, we have a vivid glimpse into the earliest Christian society of Jerusalem, and realise the extent to which asceticism was at home therein from the first. For we must not forget that in that age the eyes of all believers were fixed on the future advent. Christ was to come again in glory on the clouds of heaven, before the generation had passed away that knew him in the flesh. Wherefore, then, propagate children and encumber oneself with the cares of offspring? Those that marry "*shall have tribulation in the flesh*," says Paul (1 Corinthians vii. 28). And he adds these words to encourage his converts in their efforts to keep chaste: "*But this I say, brethren, the time is shortened, that henceforth both those that have wives may be as though they had none.......For the fashion of this world is passing away. But I would have you to be free from cares.*" The same aversion from human marriage meets us in other books of the New Testament—*e.g.*, in Revelation, which reflects the feeling of the last decade of the first century. In ch. xiv. 4 of this book the seer beholds "*the Lamb standing on Mount Zion, and with him 144,000, having his name and the name of his father written on their foreheads. ......These are they which were not defiled with women; for they are virgins.*" The statement that they were virgins forbids us to suppose that they were men who had indulged in lawful wedlock; this was no less defiling than illicit unions.

And in the Acts of Paul and Thekla, a document which perhaps belongs to the first century and was anyhow written before 150, the Apostle's preaching is as follows: "Blessed are the souls and bodies of virgins, for they shall be pleasing to God, and they shall not lose the reward of their chastity."

In the messianic kingdom, which was to be preceded by a general resurrection of the just, but to be established on this earth, there was to be no marrying nor giving in marriage. It was only logical for those who believed in the imminent approach of this kingdom to abstain from marriage and leave family life to the incredulous. Terrible trials and tribulations, moreover, were to mark the approach of the end, and it was well, in view of these, for maidens not to become mothers. Marriage, indeed, was never admitted by the Church except as a *pis aller;* and nothing is further from the truth than the contention of modern divines that she from the first patronised and sanctified an institution which was in reality only imposed upon her by the Aryan societies which adopted, while modifying, her teaching.

It is wonderful how long this dream of the approaching end of this world haunted the minds of believers, predisposing them, even in the absence of other considerations, to a life of virginity. Hippolytus, in his commentary on Daniel, relates how, a hundred years later than Paul, a Pontic bishop had a revelation to the effect that the Lord would come again in a year's time on a certain Sunday. As the day approached the believers sold or gave away their properties, and the maidens abjured wedlock, and one and all trekked into the wilderness to the far-off mountain on which the Lord was to appear. The Sunday dawned, but no Lord appeared. Then thousands fainted from want of food, for they had expected the Lord to feed them in the wilderness. In a similar messianic exodus of Syrian Christians thousands risked being slain as vagrants and bandits by legionaries despatched against them by the Roman governor. Those who succeeded in regaining their cities only did so to find their homes and belongings lost to them, for the incredulous to whom they had given them away were little minded to restore them. In Pontus the brethren were scandalised; the men returned to the plough, and those who had rashly sold their possessions were reduced to begging. And, adds the good Hippolytus, as the final touch to his story, the virgins began to marry afresh.

The institution of spiritual wives continued to flourish in the Church for many generations; but, when the first enthusiasm flagged, it began to give rise to scandals, and was probably the ground of the accusation of incest levelled at the early Church by pagan writers, who misunderstood the Christian phrase *brothers and sisters*. In the *Shepherd of Hermas*, a Christian writing of the late first or early second century, there is much eulogy of it, and the virgins boldly invite the hero of the work to pass the night in their company. "Thou must sleep with us, they said, as a brother, not as a husband." This book was read out loud as holy scripture in Christian churches until the beginning of the fourth century! In the Churches of North Africa the scandals attendant on these spiritual marriages waxed so great towards the middle of the third century that Cyprian, the Bishop of Carthage, was constrained to forbid them; and innumerable deaconesses and virgins, victims of the institution, were expelled from the churches. Tertullian, fifty years before, had denounced the vice in scathing terms. However, the custom went on; and Gregory of Nyssa, an orthodox Father of the fourth century, glances, in many of his poems, at the *agapetoi* and *agapetai*—*beloved men* and *beloved women* who had contracted these unions. Here is one of his shorter poems on the subject:—

> O Virgin, thou hast Christ ever living as thy helper, and as
> Bridegroom of thy longings, and jealous of thy heavenly beauty.
> Accept not in his stead a being of flesh to be guardian
> Of thy miserable flesh, but avert the gossip of the malignant.
> Expose not to insults and disgrace the immaculate tunic of Christ,
> So inflicting on all virgins reproach and infamy.

In another poem he addresses the male companion thus:—

> Thou who art made of flesh livest with a beloved woman of flesh like thyself.

And what dost thou expect the foul-living to think of thee?
I grant that the chaste may themselves say nothing; but who can bear
The blame and ridicule excited in the many?

In yet another poem he writes thus to two persons so related:—

Before all, endeavour in very truth to be chaste;
And after that to rouse no suspicion in the disgraceful ones.
You are pure? Yes, purer than gold. And yet you wound me
By fixing on your beloved maid both your body and your eyes.
She is your beloved, you say. Verily this name is a holy one.
Alas, alas, if it cover an element of impure love!
There is naught, you say, of such impurity. Well, I believe you. And yet
You make yourself a path to lead men to live unholily with other women.
Clay and mud is man after all, even the chaste man
Who lives with a chaste woman. 'Tis to unmarried men and women I address myself.
Even if your conscience is free, nevertheless you should
Avoid people's tongues, for than such tongues nothing is more easily set in motion.
You say, Who will hold a flaming sword before my paradise?
Who will give me a guardian of my precious virginity?
Even so let no beloved man live within with you; but let the tongue
Of the envious pass thee by. The scandal-monger spares not even saints.

These poems reveal the situation most clearly. As late as the middle of the fourth century in Greece and Syria monks and clerics were still cohabiting, under the name of *Agapetoi*—*i.e.*, Beloved Brothers—with sisters, or *Suneisaktai*—*i.e.*, women who were brought in to live with them. Gregory admits that they often kept their purity, and that it was chiefly the cynics and scoffers who talked scandal about them. Yet, to avoid scandal, it was better the practice should cease. In Egypt and in the West Jerome, Augustine, Cassian, and others attest the same custom, as popular among the extremely pious as it was dangerous.

In the Syriac Churches of the fourth century such unions between the sons and daughters of the resurrection were by many still regarded as the culminating triumph of the Christian life; but Aphraates, about 350, expresses his disapproval of them in the same terms as Gregory of Nyssa. He also testifies that many who aspired thus to live the life of grace enjoyed by angels or by Adam and Eve in the garden before the fall of man retained the appearance without the reality of married life.[1] Being technically married, they were less to blame if they forfeited their chastity. In the literature of the early Celtic Church there are abundant traces of the presence of *Suneisaktai;* and Irish historians, unacquainted with the wider history of the Church, have wrongly supposed that they here had before them some primitive ethnological characteristic of the Celts. The custom lingered on into the Middle Ages, especially among those Cathars or Puritans who, regarding with horror all relations between the sexes, denounced marriage itself as the greater adultery. The custom and the ideas which went with it may have inspired the medieval notions of chivalry, among which is foremost that of the safeguarding, by a perfectly chaste knight, of a chaste maiden who remains all the time the focus of his admiration and love. The poet Dante devoted his genius to the glorification of his lofty and platonic love for Beatrice. The relation of the Messiah to the ideal Church was from the first conceived of in terms of such a passion, and the metaphor, we feel, has

---

[1] Mark xii. 25: "When they shall rise from the dead, they neither marry nor are given in marriage, but are as angels in heaven." In baptism, as Paul taught, the dead in sin rose from death into life together with Christ.

become rather mixed, when Paul writes that he has *espoused* the Corinthian Church, and desires *to present the same as a pure virgin to Christ* (2 Cor. xi. 2). Anyhow, Christ became the bridegroom, and the ever-virgin mother Church his bride; and many an early hymn to the Church was inspired by this idea. Such hymns were, in a later age, converted into hymns to the physical mother of Jesus; and most of the attributes and predicates of the heavenly æon, the *Ecclesia* or Church, were ultimately appropriated to her.

Outside the limits of Christendom, the Druses of the Lebanon are said to cultivate this purely spiritual union of man and woman; and this circumstance, if it be really so, must have been an additional reason to Laurence Oliphant and his wife for fixing their residence on the slopes of Mount Carmel. He had already learned from their American prophet Harris that philosophy of life which he expounds in his work entitled *Sympneumata* (London, 1885); but, as he states in the preface to that book, on the occasion of a visit to Palestine in 1879, he " became aware that the results of his life in California and of the knowledge there acquired might be more securely and rapidly increased by transferring the scene of his effort from the West to the East." Those who would fain understand the emotions of the *agapetoi* and *agapetai*, of the beloved brothers and sisters of the early Church, may learn them in the pages of this curious book. Take such a passage as the following (p. 130) :—

> It is not possible to say which thing seems the more marvellous to man in this change—that he knows God as different, or that he himself is different while he knows; that the rush to him of heat and power and

universal love is instinct with the rich tremors of a
subtle interaction, or that he finds beside him and
throughout him a presence whose twin particles take
up with his the interactive motion of these forces.
He asked—if he asked anything—if he had pain
enough to escape the creeping paralysis that invades
men's spirits in these days—for a little sense of God;
that he might not remain in the presence of grief and
death so all alone; and there comes, not only the god
of senses and of spirits as mighty arms thrown all
around his loneliness, but into it the stealing sweet-
ness of the lost Sympneuma's breath, its motion, its
delight.

It has been surmised by some that the revelation
of the reality of the Idea, its transformation from a
dialectical hypothesis into a real Presence, was effected
for Plato in such a moment of ecstasy as Oliphant
describes—ecstasy consequent, in Plato's case also, on
the forcible suppression of coarser instincts in the
presence of the person beloved. It is worth inquiring
whether the ecstasy of which we read so much in the
records of the early Christian Pneumatics or inspired
ones was not often due to a similar cause.

Oliphant, no less than the Christian ascetics, was
persuaded that this platonic love between man and
woman was an integral part of the revelation of Christ;
and he quotes, in support of this view, from Clement
of Alexandria, a second-century Father, the saying
attributed to Jesus, that the divine kingdom should
come "when two should be one, and that which is
without as that which is within, and the male with
the female, neither male nor female." "The missiles,"
he writes (p. 98),

> discharged through the faithful obedience of this man
> of burning purity to the high law of the peculiar

nature with which he stood endowed, almost annihilated at first in those who accepted in thought, and endeavoured to follow in life, the promise of his keen aspirings, all the sex-instinct that they possessed.

Oliphant also perceived in a dim manner the connection of medieval chivalry with early Christian asceticism in p. 99 :—

> This discovery of nascent knightliness, that the operative passion for a godly cause and the restrained passion for a pure woman were correlative motives for a high and manly living, was in fact the prophetic experience of the more vivid one which responds to-day to the ardent aspiration for knowledge of the dual in God, the dual in man, and the right devotion to the needs of the earth.

Elsewhere I indicate the probability that the mediæval rite—always religious, and conducted by a priest—of chivalrous initiation was a survival, as it were, in secular garb, of the rite of adult baptism, long corrupted and decayed in the purely religious sphere. It is significant that the new-made knight was expected to select a mistress, of whom, according to the *Codex Amoris* of Andrew, the chaplain of Pope Innocent IV., he was henceforth the *servente* or servant.

> The only senses allowed to be the vehicles of chivalrous love were the eyes and ears. The lover was forbidden to go beyond gazing on, or hearing, or thinking of his love.......When a knight was accepted as *ami*, he knelt before his lady, his two hands joined palm to palm between hers, and swore to serve her faithfully till death, and to protect her against all evil and outrage. She, on the other hand, accepted his services, promised him her tenderest affections, gave

him a ring, and raised him up with a kiss. Chivalrous
love was inconsistent with married love, because in
marriage the chivalrous subordination of the lover
to his mistress is impossible, the bounds of eyes and
fancy are passed, and the life is domestic, not ideal.[1]

The feudal character of this chivalrous rite must
not blind us to the parallelism with early baptism.
As it was for the fully-initiated knight that this final
trial of his worth and valour was reserved, so it was
in the earliest age for the baptised, who formed a sort
of aristocracy of asceticism. Later on it seems to
have been the privilege of deacons, monks, and clerics
to undertake the guardianship of the virgins, and
contract with them those angelic unions which
revived the life of Adam and Eve before the fall, and
were the foretaste and earthly counterpart of the
marriage of Christ, the heavenly bridegroom, with the
celestial æon, his virgin mother and bride, the Church.

Before nunneries were instituted in which they
could take refuge, many and cruel difficulties beset the
path of Christian women dedicated by vows to the
higher life of perpetual virginity. Who was to
protect them from the trials and temptations which
surrounded them in a society still mainly pagan?
"It is not to be wondered at," writes Muratori,

> that many virgins who had lost their parents and
> brothers, or who were driven to it by illness, poverty,
> or by other reasons, admitted homeless clerics and
> monks to live with them under one roof, that they
> shared in their wanderings—nay, that they sometimes
> shared with them their beds. Men and women felt
> themselves equally constrained by necessity—the latter

[1] From Richard Simpson's *Philosophy of Shakespeare's Sonnets*,
London, 1868, p. 21.

to seek the aid and ministry of another, the former to bestow it. And so it came about that clergymen or monks often took the place of parents and brothers for the custody, or rather for the ruin, of young girls. For who could have such strength of mind as to pledge himself never to catch fire, if he laid himself side by side with the flaming, burning fuel?

Gregory of Nyssa, in his poems, as I have said, Chrysostom in his orations, Jerome in his letters, and many other Fathers, had much to say about this aspect of the problem. There was hardly a single Christian Council, up to the seventh century, that did not discuss remedies for a practice of which certain Churches grew ashamed as early as the middle of the third century. Now, the relationship of the Virgin Mary to Joseph is exactly envisaged as that of an ecclesiastical virgin to her keeper both in the Protevangel and in the later form of the Acts of Pilate. In the former we read of how Mary was taken, in her infancy, to the high priest in Jerusalem by her parents, Joakim and Anna, and consecrated to the service of Jehovah. There she remains among other maidens, similarly consecrated, until she reaches the age of puberty. Then elderly and reputable Israelites are summoned by the high priest to the temple, where they draw lots for the virgins, who now stand in need of protectors. The lot assigns Mary to Joseph, who takes her to his home, not as his wife, but *eis térêsin*— *i.e.*, in order to guard and protect her in the life of virginity to which her parents long ago dedicated her. Similarly, in the later form of the Acts of Pilate, the charge that Jesus was born of fornication is met by the assertion that Joseph's relation to the Virgin was merely that of guardian of her virginity.

BIRTH LEGENDS

In some forms of this legend—for example, in a commentary attributed to Epiphanius (c. 350-400)—the memory of Mary as the real wife of Joseph and mother of his other children survives side by side with the tradition of the spiritual wife. For when, in the latter capacity, Mary reaches Joseph's home in Nazareth, she finds already installed therein another Mary, who is mother of the brothers and sisters of Jesus mentioned by Mark. This latter gives birth to a son named James (? Judas) almost at the same time that the spiritual wife bears Jesus by the Holy Ghost. In this form of the legend, therefore, preserved by Epiphanius as late as the end of the fourth century, Mary has been doubled into a real and a mystical partner of Joseph. The hagiological and homiletic literature of the first three or four centuries is largely inspired by such ideas, termed, at an early time, *encratite*, from *encratia*, a Greek word almost equivalent to our word *continence*. The encratites, says the learned French Abbé Pierre Batiffol, were not a sect, but a spirit diffused through all Christian Churches alike. In all of them we meet with the same *encratite*, or ascetic impulse. Tale after tale recounted the sufferings, and sometimes the martyrdom, of wives who forsook their husbands rather than live with them; of virgins, already betrothed, who refused to be wedded. The so-called Acts of Judas Thomas, of Peter and Paul, Andrew, and other apostles, which were forged in the second century and circulated all over Christendom in all languages, are full of morbid exhortations either not to marry at all or, if persons are married, to live as if they were not. Of this sexual *Schwärmerei*, which from the first pervaded all the Churches, the belief in the miraculous birth of

Jesus was not the cause, but the effect. And there was another contributory cause. There were even within the first century many teachers who denied that Jesus had ever been born at all of woman—who held that he had been all along what we to-day call a mahatma, who took literally Paul's statements (Romans viii. 3) that God "*sent his son in the likeness* [only] *of sinful flesh*"; that (Philippians ii. 7) Christ Jesus "*took* [only] *the form of a servant, was made in the likeness* [only] *of men, and was found in fashion* [only] *as a man*." These teachers—and in the second century the best thinkers and writers of the new religion were numbered among them—knew also how to appeal to the Old Testament. If it was objected to their view that Jesus ate and drank like other mortals, they answered that the angels who appeared to Abraham under the oak of Mamre did the same. We must not forget that in that age Jesus Christ was often regarded by Christian writers—*e.g.*, by Justin Martyr—as no more than a leading angel. The appeal to this Old Testament story was the more effective because Philo had taught that the three angels which appeared to Abraham were a vision of the triune God, of the One in Three and Three in One; and that one of them was the *Logos*, or Word of God, whom the Christians soon identified with Christ. Justin also held that the angel who appeared to Abraham with the two others in the form of a man was the Word. The same Word had appeared, in the past, to prophets and patriarchs. Such speculations made it much easier to affirm that Jesus, of whose birth nothing authentic was known, and who was appearing in dreams and trances to so many, had been a phantasm all along. If the Christ had revealed

BIRTH LEGENDS

himself in the guise of a man-like angel to the saints of the past, why not have so revealed himself to his disciples in this, the final age of the world? Such was the reasoning of these new teachers, who were called *Docetes*, as asserting that Jesus wore only the appearance, or *dokesis*, of human nature, was not a being of real flesh and blood, but was a divine being masquerading in human form. They rejected the idea of physical birth, as in the last degree degrading and unworthy of a divine saviour and teacher; the idea that he was begotten by a human father, of a woman, being, of course, still more repulsive to them. This form of opinion soon spread all over the East, and its advocates ever appealed to the Apostle Paul. If the early and fundamental tradition about Jesus had comprised any account of his birth and childhood, this party, which denied that he was born at all, could never have emerged. In the absence of any sound and authoritative tradition they were able to say what they liked. In the East, in Armenia, Syria, and Persia, we find this extreme denial of Jesus's humanity met by an equally uncompromising and Ebionite assertion thereof. At the present day we are so accustomed to the spectacle of orthodox divines defending the cause of the miraculous birth of Jesus against critics who affirm his full and absolute humanity that we can hardly imagine an age when it was otherwise. And yet it was otherwise for the space of over a hundred years, from about 80 until 200 A.D. It is hardly too much to affirm that, during this epoch, the main drift of Christian speculation, at any rate outside Judæa, was docetic, and that there was a great risk of the Church losing sight altogether and for ever of the fact that Jesus was a human being like ourselves. There was an ever-increasing tendency for the apparitional Christ of Paul's visions, the phantom of innumerable Christian ecstatics, to swamp and efface from Christian memory the peripatetic prophet of Nazareth. It is irrelevant to say that these docetic teachers—Marcion, Valentinus, and the countless Gnostics—were heretics, and outside the Church. In point of fact, they were not outside until the issue had been fought out; and that was not much before 160 A.D. Till then they were not technically heretics. Throughout this period it was the Ebionite party, as it was called later on—the party of those who affirmed the natural and non-miraculous birth of Jesus—that bore the brunt of the battle, and were the standard-bearers of historical Christianity. In the event neither side won. The contention that a divine being could not be born in the normal way found too much support in contemporary pagan legend and in the widespread encratism of the Churches for it to be wholly set aside. A compromise had to be effected; and the legend of the Virgin Birth was adopted by the Catholic Church as a *media via*, with a view to include as many as possible. The assertion that Jesus took his flesh from the Virgin was thenceforth regarded as a sufficient guarantee of his humanity, while the obscure part played in his conception by the Holy Spirit ensured his being divine. A tendency set in in Catholic speculation, as we shall explain below (p. 325), to put back the time or date of the divine affiliation from the baptism, where Luke set it, to the moment of conception; and this school of thought finally triumphed at the Council of Ephesus in 431, when it was laid down that Mary was the mother of God, or *Theotokos*. In a later age even this solution was voted inadequate, and the conundrum was propounded of how to shield Christ from original sin. It no longer seemed a sufficient protection to him that he was born without a human father. The Greek monks of the eighth century solved this new problem by supposing that Mary was conceived *immaculate*— *i.e.*, without the stain of original sin—by her mother Anna, who thus became, in a manner, the grandmother of God, her very name and personality being taken from the apocryphal Protevangel. These monks brought their speculations to Palermo, whence Norman divines of a later age carried them to Great Britain and Normandy. From Rouen they spread to Paris, and thence to Rome, where Pio IX., in 1854, solemnly proclaimed the immaculate conception of Mary as a new dogma necessary to salvation, and recorded it on lofty columns set up in the Piazza di Spagna and on the Pincio Hill.

I have dwelt so long on these strange and morbid growths of Christian opinion and practice because they help to explain the adoption and final triumph of the belief in the Virgin and of her cult. We must always bear in mind, however, that the cult of the Virgin was a plant of slow growth. Even as late as the end of the sixth century there were as yet no feasts of the Virgin in Rome. We have already seen that to the feast of Jesus's physical birth no special day was assigned till late in the fourth century. The feast of the Annunciation was fixed yet later, and wandered for centuries up and down the calendar before it was accorded a general recognition on a fixed day. In most cases these feasts were adaptations of older ones. Thus in Armenia the feast of the old goddess Anahité was appropriated to the Virgin, and doubtless much of her cult as well. In Asia Minor the Virgin took the place of Cybele and Artemis, in the West of Isis and other pagan goddesses. Latin hymns in honour of Isis seem to have been appropriated to Mary with little change; and I have seen statues of Isis set up in Christian churches as images of the Virgin.

Perhaps from some old Egyptian hymn came the line,

Quæ per aures concepisti

("Thou who didst conceive through the ears"), which meets us in mediæval hymns to the Virgin Mary.[1] For Herodotus related that a ray of light fell from heaven on the sacred cow which afterwards gave birth to Apis. Plutarch says it was a ray of moonlight. He also, in his book *About Isis and Osiris*, defends the old Egyptian worship of the cat on the ground that it symbolised the mystery of the generation of the Word, or *Logos*; for the cat, he writes, repeating an idea of old popular zoology, "conceives through its ears, and brings forth its young through its mouth; and the Word, or Logos, is also conceived through the ears and expressed through the mouth." As early as Tertullian, c. 200, we meet with similar ideas in Christian speculation about the genesis of Jesus. For he writes[2] that, when Gabriel visited Mary and announced to her that she should bring forth the Messiah, "a divine ray of light glided down into her and, descending, was made concrete as flesh in her womb," so that there was born of her a man mixed with God—*homo deo mistus*. Here we see turned into

---

[1] *E.q.*, in Bodley MS. Latin Liturgy x., fol. 91 vo.
[2] *Apologeticus*, 21.

incident an allegory often employed by Philo. For example, in his treatise on the Contemplative Life of the Therapeutæ, this writer describes the aged virgins who lived in the settlement near Alexandria (see above, p. 213), as follows:—

> They have preserved their chastity throughout, not, like some of the priestesses among the pagans, under compulsion rather than of their free will, but through zeal and longing for Wisdom, with whom anxious to mate they have despised bodily pleasures; yearning to bear, not mortal, so much as immortal, offspring; such as the God-loving soul is able to bring forth out of herself alone, so soon as the Father has sown into her beams of ideal light, wherewith she can contemplate the dogmas of Wisdom.

Elsewhere, in the tract *On Drunkenness* (Mangey ed., i. 361), he writes that "God mated with *Epistêmê* (science), though not as a man does, and sowed offspring. And she received the seed of God, and with throes that bring to perfection was pregnant with and brought forth the only and well-beloved sensible Son—to wit, this kosmos."

What is metaphor and allegory in Philo was turned into history by the Christians in connection with the mother of Christ. Yet current myths of parthenogenesis probably suggested it to Philo to write as he did. Ephrem, the Syrian Father, Ruffinus of Aquileia, and many others, describe how the Word of God entered, as divine seed, through the ears of the Virgin Mary. Old pictures and bas-reliefs equally depict the rays of light from heaven entering Mary's ears; and sometimes a manikin is being wafted along the ray, in token that Christ brought down a heavenly body with him—an idea soon denounced as heretical by the

Catholics, because it contradicted the belief that he took his flesh from Mary, and so was really man. Often a dove, symbol of the holy spirit, either emits, or floats along, the ray of light. In harmony with such a theory of Christ's conception as an emission of light from heaven, the monophysite Churches of Armenia and Syria, which only broke off from the Byzantine in the fifth century, taught, and still teach, that Jesus's body was made of ethereal fire; that he had no evacuations and no digestion, digestion being a sort of corruption, and his flesh being incorruptible. Asked what became of the food he ate, they ingeniously answer that it was consumed by the ethereal fire of which he consisted, just as a spill of paper is consumed when we hold it in a candle flame. His mother also, from the moment of conception, was, like her son, immune from the necessities of nature. Obviously these opinions come perilously near the old-fashioned docetism, which the monophysites profess to condemn as warmly as the Catholics.

A similar belief accounts for the name *Pearl*, which, first in Syria, it would seem, was given to Christ. Pearls were supposed to be generated by rays of sunlight striking down through the sea, on the floor of which they coagulated and took a material consistency in the oyster shell. They are thus a precipitate of sunlight. Jesus, engendered by rays of divine light or fire striking down through the Virgin's ears and consolidated within her, was by analogy and metaphor termed the Pearl, not, of course, without reference to the parable (Matthew xiii. 46) of the pearl of great price. The idea that spirits, especially evil ones, approach women through the ear, which these early legends of the Virgin Mary embody, was an old Rabbinic one,

BIRTH LEGENDS

found in the Talmud, in Philo, Josephus, and, above all, in Paul. The latter, in 1 Corinthians, ch. xi., forbids a woman "*to pray or prophesy with her head unveiled. She must carry on her head a talisman* (lit. power), *because of the angels.*" Tertullian, the earliest of the Christian Fathers to comment on this passage, explains that evil angels were ever lurking about ready to assail even married women, much more virgins, through their ears. From this point of view he penned his weighty treatise, *De Virginibus Velandis*— "On the Necessity of Veiling Virgins"; and the Church has been careful, in devising a dress for nuns, who are espoused to Christ, to cover up their ears and protect them from this class of risk. The ordinary hat worn in church by women hardly satisfies the Pauline prescription. The superstitions of the Arunta savages, in Central Australia, are the nearest existing analogue of the Pauline scruples, in supposed observance of which an Anglican clergyman in Cornwall recently expelled a lady from his church because, on a hot day, she had entered it holding her hat in her hand, instead of wearing it on her head. This fussy clergyman had, of course, no inkling of the quaint superstition which underlies this precept of Paul. It is a pity that a course of folklore cannot be introduced into the theological faculties of Oxford and Cambridge.

The *power* or *authority* which a woman is enjoined to bear on her head was probably a phylactery or talisman of a kind to avert evil angels. Connected with this was the precept to "*let the hair of the woman's head go loose,*" in the rite of ordeal described in Numbers v. 11 foll. A woman engaged in prophesying would be doubly exposed to risk, for in such moments a spirit was supposed to overshadow her, and the verb to overshadow was used, technically, of a spirit coming upon a woman and causing her to prophesy. Any pure or holy spirit visiting a priestess for this end would, according to Origen, a scholarly Greek Father of the third century, enter by her ears alone. The Delphic spirit, just because it entered the priestess of Apollo otherwise, was condemned by Origen as an impure and unclean demon. Those who demand the fullest instruction on such subjects will find it in the chapters devoted to Incubi and Succubi, in the philosophy of St. Thomas Aquinas.

Chapter XIII.

MAGIC USE OF NAMES

"What's in a name?" is a question we have all of us heard put—as a rule by persons unwilling to bow to some authority invoked by their fellows in argument. For we children of the nineteenth and twentieth century have learned to regard a man's name as something accidental and indifferent; as serving to distinguish one individual from another, but having no other use. It has as little to do with a man's self or personality as the number under which he is temporarily known in a large hotel. And yet the survival among us of such a phrase as " a name to conjure with" indicates that we have not long emerged from a phase of culture in which a man's name was regarded as mysteriously bound up with his personality, in such wise that, if he be himself gifted with powers beyond the ordinary, his name is the vehicle of similar power. We may even go further, and say that, in ancient religions, as in many folk-tales, a man's name was equivalent to his personality; and this belief so moulded language that we find authors writing of there being so many *names* in a city, where to-day we would say so many souls or persons. Thus, in Revelation xi. 13 we read that " *in that hour there was a great earthquake, and the tenth part of the city fell; and there were killed in the earthquake names of men seven thousand* "—that is, seven thousand souls. And in the same book, in the letter to the Church of

Sardis, it is said : "*Thou hast a few names in Sardis which did not defile their garments.*"

The sanctity or virtue of an individual belongs, in a measure, to his garments, his hair, nail-parings, even to his spittle, and, after death, as the cult of relics well illustrates, to his bones. It equally adheres to his name, which, if it cannot be touched and handled, can be invoked or uttered in speech. A thousand ritual observances have their root in this belief. Thus, one great bugbear of primitive peoples is the fear of being molested by the dead; and, accordingly, the name of a dead person must not be breathed out loud, lest his wraith be evoked together with his name. Among some races the name of a dead chieftain, which was often the name of an animal or plant, is tabooed, and a fresh name has to be invented for the natural object after which he was called. From this cause the vocabularies of such races are in perpetual flux.

Again, since a man's name is tantamount to his vital principle and personality, it must be concealed from his enemies no less than his picture and image. It is believed that to know another's name is to have power over him. This is why every ancient Egyptian had two names—one by which his fellows in this world knew him, and the other, his true or great name, by which he was known to the supernal powers and in the other world. An Abyssinian Christian similarly has two names given him at baptism—one his common name, the other a secret name never to be divulged. The guardian deity or patron saint of ancient Rome had a secret name not communicated to anyone, for he who learned it might harm the eternal city by tempting the deity in question to desert it, just as the Romans, by the rite of evocation, had won over to themselves the gods of many a conquered city. In parts of ancient Greece the holy names of the gods, that none might learn them and be able to profane them, were engraved on lead tablets and sunk in the sea. The same belief underlies our phrase " to take a name in vain "; and in more than one statute rash swearing is forbidden because it amounts to desecration of a holy name, and, with the name, of the personality named. In Oriental folklore—for example, in the *Arabian Nights*—he that would enlist a ginn or demon in his service must, above all things, master the name thereof; for, knowing it, he can use the spirit and its authority how he will. As in other ways, so in their assurance of the magic potency of names, the writers of the New Testament, and Jesus himself, announce themselves true sons of their age. Let us collect a few instances: "*He that overcometh,*" Christ is made to say in Revelation iii. 5, "*shall thus be arrayed in white garments; and I will in no wise blot his name out of the book of life.*"

Probably the name in question was a heavenly one, like the "great and true" name of an ancient Egyptian. Anyhow, the exclusion of the name implies that of the person named. In Revelation xiii. 1 the "*beast coming up out of the sea* has *upon his heads names of blasphemy*"—perhaps the names of Roman emperors, fraught with all the power with which posthumous deification invested them. In the same way Paul, who conceived of Jesus as having been mysteriously promoted, through his resurrection, to a new and higher grade of spiritual existence than he occupied in the flesh, writes, Ephesians i. 21, 22, that the "*father of glory raised him from the dead, and made him to sit at his right hand in the heavenly region, far above all rule and authority and power and dominion, and every name that is named, not only in this age, but also in that which is to come.*"

Here the words "*rule and authority*," etc., refer to the different grades of superhuman beings which tenant earth, air, and heaven; all these are "*names that are named*" in this world and the next—that is, names fraught with magic potency, and so invoked in order to control other inferior powers and forces of nature.

Names in themselves possess such potency in various degrees; and the divine father, according to the Pauline theosophy, has them in his gift, to confer them on whom he will. When he wished to reward Jesus after death for the trust and humility he displayed on earth, he raised him from the dead and "*exalted him highly, and gave unto him the name that is above every name; that in the name of Jesus every knee should bow, of beings in heaven and on earth and under the earth.*"

The name in question was that of Christ or Messiah. In receiving it Jesus was instantly exalted to the summit and sovereignty of the angelic and demonic creations. This passage reminds us of the old Egyptian legend of the God Ra, who owned a secret name by which he controlled men and gods, and which was only known to himself. Isis said to herself: "Cannot I, by virtue of the great name of Ra, make myself a goddess, and reign, like him, in heaven and earth?" And, by a stratagem, she forced Ra to transfer his magical name from his breast into hers, together with all its miraculous powers.[1]

---

[1] See Frazer's *Golden Bough*, ch. ii., § 3.

Matthew vii. 22 indicates that it was not long before many outside the pale of the Church used Jesus's name in their exorcisms: "*Many will say to me in that day, Lord, Lord, did we not prophesy by thy name, and by thy name cast out devils, and by thy name do many mighty works? And then will I profess unto them, I never knew you: depart from me, ye that work iniquity.*" In some of the magical papyri lately discovered in Egypt we find the name of Jesus so invoked. I adduce one such incantation from an ancient source, wherein also the demon is addressed in his own tongue:—

> Here is a goodly gift of Apsyrtus, a saving remedy, wonderfully effective for cattle. IAO, IAE, in the name of the father and of our Lord Jesus Christ and holy spirit, iriterli estather, nochthai brasax salolam nakarzeo masa areons daron charael aklanathal aketh thruth tou malath poumedoin chthon litiotan mazabates maner opsakion aklana thalila iao, iae.......And write the same with a brass pencil on a clean, smooth plate of tin.

That already during his Galilean ministry Jesus had won such fame as a faith-healer that his name was used by exorcists otherwise strangers to him we also learn from Mark ix. 37: "*John said unto him, Teacher, we saw one casting out devils in thy name; and we forbad him, because he followed us not.*" Thus his name, even before he quitted Capernaum, had already become, as we say, "a name to conjure with," though his disciples considered that they had a monopoly of its use. Jesus, however, said: "*Forbid him not: for there is no man that shall do a mighty work in my name and be able quickly to speak evil of me.*"

An incident narrated in Acts, ch. iii., illustrates very

neatly the nature of faith-healing in general. Peter finds a man "*that was lame from his mother's womb, whom they laid daily at the door of the temple which is called Beautiful to ask alms of them that entered.*" So to-day, at Lourdes, we see the sick and lame wheeled in their chairs before the shrine. Peter bids him walk "*in the name of Jesus Christ of Nazareth,* [and] *took him by the right hand and raised him up.*" And, later on, Peter explains to the people the nature of the cure. "*Why,*" he says, "*fasten ye your eyes on us as though, by our own power or godliness, we had made him to walk?*" Then he explains how the God of Abraham, Isaac, and Jacob "*had glorified his child (or servant) Jesus* [and] *raised him from the dead. Through faith in his name hath his name made this man strong.*" It was therefore the *name* which, as fraught with the personal power of Jesus Christ, operated the cure, though not without the pre-condition that the afflicted person had faith therein. On the morrow the priests hale Peter before them, "*And inquire, By what power, or in what name, have ye done this?*" Peter answers that it is "*through the name of Jesus Christ of Nazareth, whom God raised from the dead, doth this man stand here before you whole.*" The name, that is to say, like the relic of a later saint, has a virtue all of its own; and Peter goes on to claim for this name a sort of monopoly of saving and life-giving power: "*Neither is there any other name under heaven, that is given among men, wherein we must be saved.*"

Unquestionably, the name, *qua* name, of Brigham Young or Mary Eddy would have just the same virtue for their followers, supposing these latter-day sects had alive among them the old superstitious belief in the magical influence and importance of

MAGIC USE OF NAMES

names. I do not suggest that Jesus had anything in common with the charlatans I have named beyond an implicit confidence in himself which he succeeded in imparting to others. I only mean to say that, if our habits of mind were those of the first century, we should hear of cures being wrought in the names of Brigham Young and of Mary Eddy. They would enjoin their votaries to be baptised into their names, just as Paul was accused by his enemies of baptising his converts at Corinth into his own name (1 Corinthians i. 13)—a charge which he hotly disowns, on the ground that not he, but Christ, had been crucified for them. It was an age in which faith-healers and exorcists were ever on the look-out for new and powerful names wherewith to charge and weight their incantations; and among recently discovered Egyptian papyri we have many wherein the names of Abraham, Isaac, and Jacob, even of Jesus also, figure alongside of the *bizarre* titles of old Egyptian and Persian gods and demons. The Jews quarrelled among themselves and with the Christians about what names should be used in exorcisms; and on one occasion (Acts xviii. 16), when in Achaia the Jews rose against Paul, and dragged him before the judgment-seat, Gallio, the pro-consul, an eminently sensible magistrate, *drave them* away, saying: "*If, indeed, it were a matter of wrong or of wicked villainy, O ye Jews, it would be my duty to bear with you: but if they are questions about words and names and your own law, look to it yourselves.*" Similar scenes must often have taken place in British East India, between the votaries of Siva and Vishnu.

"In modern Egypt," remarks Mr. Frazer, quoting from E. W. Lane's *Manners and Customs of the Modern*

Egyptians, "the magician still works his old enchantments by the same ancient means; only the name of the God by which he conjures is different. The man who knows the most great name of God can, we are told, by the mere utterance of it, kill the living, raise the dead, transport himself instantly wherever he pleases, and perform any other miracle." Nor is it only men, demons, and gods whose names convey power. The virtues of a plant or animal equally reside in its name; and in old Rome the Flamen Dialis, or Priest of Jupiter, might not even utter the name of, any more than touch, certain impure animals and fruits, forbidden to him as food; for example, goat's flesh, ivy, and beans. Tertullian (*On Idolatry*, 15) believed that the use of demons' names, however empty and made-up they might be, yet, if employed for purposes of superstition, rapidly bring to one the demons and all unclean spirits by the binding power of consecration.

In the Gospels the demons have their names, and in Mark v. 9 Jesus asks of an unclean spirit: "*What is thy name?*" The demon answers: "*My name is Legion; for we are many.*" Jesus then sends them into a herd of swine. Perhaps this quaint legend recalls, as M. Salomon Reinach has pointed out, the circumstance that the Roman Legion, then forming part of the Palestinian garrison, had a sow as its badge.

It is no mere figure of speech, therefore, when, in Matthew xviii. 20, Jesus uses the words: "*Where two or three are gathered together in my name, there am I in the midst of them.*" Any other spirit would equally be in the midst of those who met in his name; for the name is an essential part of the being, and if, according

MAGIC USE OF NAMES

to the ancient Hebrew notions with which Jesus and his followers were imbued, a divine or powerful name could, like a divine spirit, dwell locally in a shrine, so much the more could it be immanent in men's hearts, and they and their lives within its sphere of influence. In countless passages of the Old Testament we meet with the idea of a divine name being enclosed in a holy place. Thus, in Jeremiah vii. 12, Jahveh "*caused his name to dwell at the first in his place at Shiloh.*" Later on he transferred it to the shrine at Jerusalem, over which it had been called. The psalmist (Psalms lxxiv. 8) laments that the enemy "*have set fire upon thy holy places, and have defiled the dwelling-place of thy Name.*" It was believed that, when the name of power was ritually pronounced over a building or stone, or any other material object, the unseen power, or *numen*, entered and dwelt within. Idols were consecrated in this way; and when the Christians—who, during the first three or four centuries, religiously eschewed pictures and images of Christ and the saints—twitted the pagans with their folly, in that they either fashioned with their hands objects in order afterwards to fear and venerate the same, or feared and venerated objects they had so fashioned, the pagans answered that it was not the idol they feared, but the being of whom the idol was the likeness and image, and by whose name it had been consecrated.[1]

In Christian rituals, from about the year 300 on, an altar, shrine, and any sort of building, and also "the natures" of oil, water, salt, candles, even of hassocks, have been consecrated by repeating over

---

[1] Lactantius, *On Origin of Error*, ch. ii.

them the formula "*in the name of Jesus Christ,*" or "*in the name of Father, Son, and Holy Ghost.*" Through such invocation any satanic taint there was is expelled, and a transcendental virtue, authority, or *mana*, as the Melanesian native calls it, inherent in the name passes over like an emanation into them. Similarly, the recitation at the beginning or end of a prayer of the words *in* (or *through*) *the name*, etc., sets in operation, in the transcendental sphere to which the prayer is supposed to ascend, the personality or spirit named. The modern church-goer is happily ignorant of the original meaning of the rites and forms of invocation which he daily hears repeated with so much unction. It is just as well, for he would be shocked if he knew their history, and realised that they are based on superstitious fancies, derived, through Judaism, from the ancient Assyrians, Egyptians, and Persians. Such, however, is the case; and in no other way can we interpret such phrases as "Hallowed be thy name," "The Lord's name be praised," "They that know thy name will put their trust in thee" (Ps. ix. 10), and "In the name of our Lord Jesus Christ."

Mr. Marett (in *Folk-lore*, vol. xv., No. 2) has shown that a prayer which relies on the use of a name of power is not far removed from a spell or magical incantation. The *mana* or authority (Greek *exousia*) with which Jesus controlled the unclean spirits, and which his enemies were prone to identify with the power exerted by Beelzebub, the prince of devils, over his subordinates, could be obtained and used in the absence or after the death of Jesus by invocation of his name. Here we are on the mental or religious plane of the modern Malay who exorcises the demons of disease, " grandfather smallpox " and his congeners, by invoking the spirit of some powerful wild beast (Marett, l.c., p. 157).

How deeply the magical uses and associations, prominent in other ancient cults, influenced also the mind of the earliest Church may be illustrated by two more examples.

In Matthew xvi. 19 Jesus confers on Simon Peter, who has recognised him as the Messiah, the power of binding and loosing, in the following words: *"I will give thee the keys of the kingdom of heaven; and whatsoever thou shalt bind on earth shall be bound in heaven, and whatsoever thou shalt loose on earth shall be loosed in heaven."* In Matthew xviii. 18 the same privilege is bestowed on all the apostles, and not on Peter alone.

What does the phrase *binding and loosing* signify in this context? This we learn from such a passage as Luke xiii. 10 foll., where Jesus heals a woman who for eighteen years had had *" a spirit of infirmity "* or weakness, and *"could in no wise lift herself up."* Probably she was crippled with rheumatism. From this spirit Jesus looses her: *" He called her and said to her, Woman, thou art loosed from thine infirmity. And he laid his hands upon her, and immediately she was made straight."* In the sequel Jesus speaks of her as *" a daughter of Abraham whom Satan had bound these eighteen years past,"* and he vindicates his right to *" loose* [her] *from this bond on the sabbath day."*

The writer of the above regarded disease as a spell laid on men by Satan. Dionysus, like Jesus, was credited with the power of loosing such spells, for Aristides the Rhetor writes in his panegyric of that God: "Nothing, it would seem, shall be so firmly bound, either by disease, or rage, or by any fortune, that Dionysus shall not be able to loose it."

The phrase, to bind and loose, was also used in reference to burdens of all kinds—of taxation, of sins, of the law. Thus Josephus, in his book on the Jewish Wars, i. 5, 2, relates how the Pharisees under Alexandra "got control of everything, exiled or restored to their land whom they would, loosed and bound." Diodorus Siculus, bk. i., p. 23, describes Isis as follows: "I am Isis, the queen of all the land, who was educated by Hermes; and whatsoever things I shall bind, no one is able to loose."

Ancient witches were believed to have a power of binding and loosing inanimate nature through their incantations. Thus Ovid says of Medea: "*Illa refrenat aquas, obliquaque flumina sistit; Illa loco silvas, vivaque saxa movet*"—"She chains back the waters and stays the slanting streams; She moves from their position woods and living rocks." And Virgil, in his eighth Bucolic, writes: "*Carmina vel caelo possunt deducere lunam*"—"Incantations (or charms) can even bring down the moon from heaven."

In popular magic binding and loosing are usually accompanied by the tying and untying of symbolical knots; and Dr. Frazer, in his *Golden Bough*, gives many examples of the magic knot or lock. It is "a Swiss superstition that if, in sewing a corpse into its shroud, you make a knot on the thread, it will hinder the soul of the deceased on its passage to eternity" (*Golden Bough*, vol. i., p. 401). In ancient Rome, according to Ovid, a witch pretended to shut the mouths of her enemies by sewing up the mouth of a fish with a bronze needle. All over the earth, no knots must be left tied about the dress of a pregnant woman, lest the birth of her child be impeded. Even the doors and boxes must be left unlocked, and husbands must not even sit with crossed legs, for in so doing they imitate the tying of a knot. If a sportsman in Laos wishes to keep his game preserve free from intruders, he knots together some stalks of grass and says, "As I knot this grass, so let no hunter be lucky here." And the spell binds the forest (Frazer, *Golden Bough*, vol. i., p. 399). In India the undoing of a knot may have an expiatory effect. Thus, if a novice has broken his vow of chastity, his teacher ties round his neck a blade of the *darbha* plant. Then he sprinkles over his fire grains of rice, barley, or sesame. Next he makes him wash in water mixed with *Sampâta*, and throws some fresh offering into the fire. Last of all he unties the necklace of *darbha*, and cries: "The indissoluble bond with which the goddess Nirrti has bound thy neck, I untie it and give thee life, vital force, and strength....... Homage to thee, O Nirrti of the sharp point. Loosen thy bonds of iron."

The above rite is from the old Sanskrit book of magic rites called *Atharva Véda*, my knowledge of which I owe to the late Professor Victor Henry's *La Magie dans l'Inde Antique*.

Vows and imprecations bound men and women with magical bonds, and involved many abstinences, restrictions, and taboos. Whether in the commission entrusted to Peter these are contemplated is uncertain, nor is it easy to fix precisely the meaning of the prescription that what is bound or loosed on earth is bound or loosed in heaven, and *vice versâ*. The words seem merely to indicate the universal and unlimited range of the power of interdiction and remission conferred on the Church by the founder; and we need not detect in it the idea that what is done ritually on earth is symbolically, and by a sort of magic sympathy, executed in heaven.

The giving of the keys of the kingdom of heaven has a magical sense analogous to that of binding and loosing. In Revelation i. 18 the Messiah is made to say: "*I was dead, and behold, I am alive for evermore, and I have the keys of death and of Hades.*"

So, according to an ancient treatise on agriculture called *Geoponica* (i. 14), farmers tried to ward off hail from their crops by tying keys to ropes all round their fields, and "to this day a Transylvanian sower thinks he can keep birds from the corn by carrying a lock in the seedbag" (*Golden Bough*, i., 400). As has been remarked above, it is the custom in many countries to open all the locks in a house where a woman is lying-in, for fear lest, if they be kept bolted, they should impede or prevent her delivery.

To sum up, then: the importance attached in the New Testament to the ritual use of the name, to binding and loosing, to the symbol of the key, savours of ancient magic. Of such matters we hear as little in the Old Testament as we do of possession by evil spirits. A kind of aristocratic intellectual influence excluded such ideas from the older Hebrew literature, as it later on kept them out of the Fourth Gospel. The later Jews acquired this whole circle of superstitious ideas—supposing they had not had them from the first—from their Persian, Syrian, Egyptian, and other pagan neighbours. As we encounter them in the New Testament they seem to have been especially acquired by contact with the Persians and Babylonians. Of ancient Babylon and Assyria Professor Sayce writes in his *Hibbert Lectures*, iv., p. 305, as follows: "Closely connected with the mystical

MAGIC USE OF NAMES 249

importance thus assigned to names was the awe and dread with which the curse or excommunication was regarded. Once uttered with the appropriate ceremonies, the binding of knots, and the invocation of divine names, it was a spell which even the gods were powerless to resist."

My other example is drawn from a passage already glanced at in an earlier chapter (p. 35). It is the episode of the withering of the fig-tree in consequence of a curse uttered by Christ, in Mark xi. 14: "*He answered and said to it, Let no man eat fruit from thee henceforward for ever.*" It matters little to our argument whether Jesus was really guilty of such an act of petulant folly as to curse a fig-tree because it had no figs on it when, as Mark adds, *it was not the season of figs;* or whether this monstrous story is the parable of Luke xiii. 6 foll., transformed by a blundering editor into an historical incident. The author of Mark as it stands, in any case, believed that his Lord cursed the tree, and saw in its being withered away from its roots an example of faith rewarded and prayer answered!

It has taxed the resources of orthodox commentators to palliate this tale. Thus Professor Swete denies that Jesus's words " can properly be called an imprecation or curse," as if he knew better than St. Peter, who, as they pass it the next day, says to his master, "*Rabbi, behold, the fig-tree which thou cursedst is withered away.*" " Planted in some sheltered hollow," adds this commentator, " it was already in leaf before the Passover, when other trees of its sort were only beginning to bud; and it was reasonable to expect a corresponding precocity in regard to the figs.......It is not mere fruitlessness which the Lord here condemns, but fruitlessness in the midst of a display which promises fruit."

Surely it were better frankly to admit that we have before us an example of the custom, common among primitive peoples, of cursing and threatening a tree that bears no fruit. In Lesbos the owner of an orange-tree that seems sterile will brandish an axe before it and say aloud, "Bear fruit, or I'll cut you down" (*Golden Bough*, i., p. 175). It was believed in antiquity that fruit-trees and crops could be withered and destroyed by magical incantations. So Tibullus: "*Cantus vicinis fruges traducit ab agris*"—"Incantation filches away their fruits from a neighbour's fields."

At Rome a special clause of the Twelve Tables was directed against anyone who ruined by charms his neighbour's fruit-trees. Even to-day, and in England, we encounter in remote villages the belief that a malicious person can overlook his neighbour's trees, and so wither and kill them. In Italy the evil eye is as potent against them as against human beings; and this is the circle of ideas within which the author of this story about Jesus moved.

CHAPTER XIV.

THE EUCHARIST

THE oldest account of the Christian Eucharist is in Paul's first Epistle to the Corinthians, xi. 23–25, as follows: "*For I received from the Lord that which also I delivered unto you, how that the Lord Jesus, in the night in which he was betrayed, took bread; and when he had given thanks, he brake it and said, This is my body, which is for your sake (broken): this do in remembrance of me. In like manner also the cup, after supper, saying, This cup is the new covenant in my blood: this do as oft as ye drink it in remembrance of me.*"

The words "*I received from the Lord*" imply that Paul derived this narrative of the last supper, not from companions of Jesus, but as one of the private revelations to which he was liable. It rests, therefore, on no basis of fact, but, like much of Paul's conception of Jesus, is partly, or wholly, an *a priori* construction of his own mind. I say *partly*, because the imagination of ecstatics generally works along the lines of what they have read or heard; and, if this was here the case, we have in the above account a nucleus of real tradition recast and expanded by Pauline fantasy. However this be, it remains true that this Epistle of Paul's became in time the norm of Christian eucharistic practice and thought.

A narrative wholly similar, except for the omission of the two clauses beginning "*this do*," recurs in

Matthew and Mark; while Luke is interpolated from this very passage of Paul. The Fourth Gospel ignores the entire episode. The redactors or compilers of Matthew and Mark took the words *this is my body* and *this is my blood* from Paul's Epistle. It does not much matter whether Jesus really used them, or Paul dreamed them. In either case their meaning is the same. What, then, do they mean?

Paul leaves us in no doubt about this. The sacred meal he describes was the Christian counterpart of the Jewish sacrifice to Jahveh, and of the sacrifices offered by Gentiles to their devilish gods. Just as through these old-world sacrificial rites was effected a communion between the worshippers on the one side and the god or gods on the other, so, by partaking of their own consecrated bread and wine, the Christians attained communion with Christ. It is in an earlier chapter of his Epistle that Paul assures us of this fact, and we must quote his words, because they show that he and his converts, in respect of what has become the central sacrament of the religion, were in exactly the same stage of religious and mental development as the ancient Jews, the pagans, and, we may add, as savage or primitive races all over the globe. Here, then, is what he says (1 Corinthians x. 14 foll.): "*Wherefore, my beloved, flee from idolatry. I speak as to wise men; prove ye what I say. The cup of blessing which we bless, is it not a communion of the blood of Christ? The bread which we break, is it not a communion of the body of Christ? Seeing that there is one bread* [or *loaf*], *we, who are many, are one body; for we all partake of the one bread* [or *loaf*]. *Look at Israel after the flesh: have not they which eat the sacrifices communion with the altar? What say I, then? that a thing sacrificed to idols is anything, or that an idol is anything? But* [I say] *that the things which the Gentiles sacrifice, they sacrifice to devils, and not to God: and I would not that ye should have communion with devils. Ye cannot drink the cup of the Lord and the cup of devils: ye cannot partake of the table of the Lord, and of the table of devils. Or do we provoke the Lord to jealousy? Are we stronger than he?"*

What does all this mean?

Let us remember that in Paul's age it nowise offended the popular mind and imagination to personify and elevate into divinities, not only a malignant virus like fever, but abstract qualities like peace, concord, fortune, fame, as Cicero relates in his book on *The Nature of Gods*, ii. 23 and iii. 25. Altars were raised to them; the sculptor rendered their features plain to the eye; with offerings of fruit and flowers men did them homage; with the blood and flesh of victims they appeased their wrath and nourished their shadowy substance. If abstract qualities could be thus venerated as active principles and spirits, the *rôle* and office of Christ, the messiahship, also admitted of being taken apart from the individual man Jesus, who was Messiah, and, as we say, hypostatised, or turned into a vague transcendental spiritual activity and impulse, untrammelled by the bonds and limits of the flesh, yet personal and self-conscious. Thus the Gnostic believers of the second century figured the Christhood as a pre-existent heavenly æon that had struck down from the highest through the many intermediate grades of being, and entered Jesus in the Jordan. Paul rather regarded the Christhood as a pre-existent ideal man, who had temporarily assumed a robe of flesh, and had through the resurrection recovered the divine attributes and glory which, in the time of fleshly infirmity, had been left behind in heaven. This risen Messiah was no longer Jesus Christ, but Christ Jesus, in token that the man and the Jew was left behind or had receded into the background. He was now an immortal, incorruptible, vitalising spirit, a pervading influence and impulse, blowing like a breeze through the chords of men's souls, and evoking from them a new harmony. From this mystical standpoint, the Church was the body of Christ, and he its head, or entelechy, to use an Aristotelian term. "*Now ye are the body of Christ and severally members thereof,*" Paul writes (1 Corinthians xii. 27) to his converts. And just before (verse 13) he has written: "*For by one spirit we were all baptised into one body, whether Jews or Greeks, whether bond or free; and were all made to drink of one spirit.*" The believers, accordingly, form a single organism, of which all the members suffer with one of themselves that is injured and rejoice with one that is honoured.

In full accord with this lofty ideal of the Church, Paul believed that each member of the same is a Christ in so far as he shares the single animating spirit. "*I live, yet no longer I, but Christ liveth within me,*" he characteristically exclaims in Galatians ii. 20. And so vivid was this belief that Christ is immanent in the believer that within a few decades it was not uncommon to represent saints and martyrs as metamorphosed in face and look into Christ. Thus the virgin Thekla, when she is haled before the judge by the youth whom she is pledged to wed, but has thrown over, looks round the court in search of solace and support, and her eyes fall upon Paul, and, as she gazes, his features give way to those of Christ. " As a sheep wandering among the hills in search of the shepherd, even so Thekla sought for Paul. And, as she looked round on all the men there, she saw the Lord Jesus sitting full opposite to her in the likeness of Paul.......And, while she kept her eyes fixed upon him, the Lord rose up, and went into heaven." Similarly, in the persecution at Lyons in A.D. 177, the faithful gazing on the female slave Blandina, who was being tortured, saw her "with their outward eyes" transformed into Christ, who had been crucified for them. In the apocryphal *Translation of Philip* Jesus appears to the faithful in the outward form of the saint, just as in the Fourth Gospel he appears to Mary Magdalene, watching at the tomb, in the guise of the gardener. Is it not possible that such ideas furnished the starting-point of the belief, noticed above (p. 207), that the Apostle Judas Thomas was physically the twin brother of Jesus?

Paul's conception of the Christian organism is a fine one, worthy of any philosopher, ancient or modern. The greater is the pity that he cannot sustain himself at its level, but deems it necessary to buttress up the noble spiritual unity he dreams of with a means suggested by and imitated from the pagan and Jewish religions of sacrifice—to wit, with the sacrament of the body and blood of Christ. From the heights of idealism we suddenly drop into the depths of primitive magic and fetichism.

The early idea of kinship contains elements to which to-day we scarcely give a thought. Thus an Arab whose bread and salt or other victuals you have shared regards you as his kinsman for such time, usually three days, as his food is supposed to remain in your blood. For so long he will protect you and your belongings, curse them that curse you, and bless them that bless you. As soon, however, as the taboo or sanctity, with which communion in eating invested you in his and his tribesmen's eyes, shall have worn off, he is as ready as ever to rob and murder you. Maybe the Arab is actuated in his hospitality by the fancy that, as without food man can neither think nor act, so communion in food involves common thinking and acting—in short, unity of life and spirit. By parity of reasoning, kinship, however created, is refreshed, sustained, and strengthened by common meals.

But the tie of kinship does not unite men alone; it equally binds together a kin or clan and the god worshipped by that kin or clan; and in this case also the tie, if not created, is anyhow strengthened and confirmed by sacramental meals in which the god either eats with or (under the figure of a holy animal) is eaten by the clan. In the one case the life and vigour of the god is communicated indirectly to the worshippers whose life and welfare are bound up with his; in the other case it passes directly into their heart and veins. The Jew or pagan never neglected an opportunity of reinforcing within himself the substance of his god or favourite demon. If he drank, he began with a libation to the god—that is, he poured out a little of his liquor, in order that the invisible god might drink it with him. If he slew an animal, he set apart the first bits cut off for the god, and in particular poured out the blood for the god to lap up. Similarly, the first fruits of the field were devoted to the gods, who consumed them, often in the guise of priests that personated them. If, like Jahveh, the god or his name inhabited a sacred stone, bethel, or altar, then the blood was poured over that, and the votaries smeared themselves with it in order to establish and complete communion with the god in what seemed the most effective way— that is to say, by material and physical contact.

The blood was conceived to be, if not the very life of the animal, at least intimately bound up therewith; since the mere emptying out of it from the veins and arteries entails death. As such it was in a special manner the food of gods and demons. In the *Odyssey* the shades of the departed have no strength to converse with Ulysses until he has given them draughts of black blood; and it passed unquestioned among the Fathers of the Church that, as the Jewish God Jahveh in Genesis viii. 21 snuffed up the savour of Noah's burnt-offerings and was appeased, so the demons that were the gods of the Gentiles battened on the blood and reek of their altars. Christians were taught sturdily to refuse to sacrifice to the old gods, in order to starve them out and reduce them to nerveless inanity.

This conception of the blood as essentially the life meets us in Genesis ix. 4, "*But flesh with the life thereof, which is the blood thereof, ye shall not eat.*" The underlying idea was this, that by consuming the blood of an animal you imbibe its spirit also; and the chance of harbouring in his entrails the spirit of a cow, goat, sheep, or fowl was one from which not the Jews alone shrank back in dismay. The neo-Pythagoreans of the late Hellenic period abstained altogether from flesh diet on this account, and Porphyry, in his work *On Abstinence*, ascribes the internal rumblings of the human gut to foul spirits introduced with a meat diet, and regards escapes of wind as their out-rushings. Such considerations as these explain why abstinence from meats strangled was one of the few rules of the Jewish law which the heads of the Jerusalem Church insisted that Gentile converts must observe. It is curious to note that this rule, so emphatically laid down by the earliest council ever held, has, except in the case of a few far-Eastern Churches, been for eighteen hundred years forgotten and rejected by orthodox Christians, in strong contrast with their meticulous observance of the Wednesday, Friday, and Lenten fasts. Why was the Apostolic rule so soon consigned to oblivion? Probably because the Jews observed it. If they went one way and kept one rule, the Church was careful to go another way and invent a different rule, making all the time hypocritical profession of her devotion to apostolic usage.

Another ancient custom, that of establishing a blood-brotherhood between persons not naturally akin, rests on the idea that the blood is the life and vital principle. One of the parties to the covenant cuts his arm or breast so that it bleeds, and the other sucks the wound. As their bloods are now mingled, so henceforth are their souls and lives. This rite still survives in South Italy among the members of the secret society known as the *mala vita*. In this case the chief brigand makes an incision under his left breast over the heart, and the neophytes apply their lips and suck a drop of his blood.

The custom is old and widespread. Oaths, says Herodotus, i. 64, are taken by the Medes and Lydians in the same way as by the Greeks, except that they make a slight flesh wound in their arms, from which each sucks a portion of the other's blood. Among the ancient Scythians, according to the same witness, the parties to an oath wounded themselves slightly with a knife, and, having mingled their blood with wine in a large bowl, repeated prayers and drank the sacred draught. Tacitus witnesses to a similar usage among the Armenians and Iberians of the Caucasus. Sir Samuel Baker, the traveller, in 1873, in the territories of Rionga, an African chief, "exchanged blood with him." Similar customs existed everywhere in the ancient world, and are still met with among savages. Human blood has a peculiar value in the ratifying of pacts, and the legend that Jews slay Christian children and eat their flesh in unholy communion is evidence not so much that such a custom ever prevailed among them as that their Christian accusers were familiar among themselves with the institution of such blood-brotherhoods. The early Christians were commonly accused by the pagans of such "Thyestean banquets." The religious rite of making another man into your brother, called *adelphopoiia*, and found in old Greek prayer-books, is a Christianised form of the rite which in its old barbarous shape still survives, as I have said, among South Italian brigands.

Let us apply these considerations to the interpretation of Paul's text. The born Jews, he says, "*which eat the sacrifices have communion with the altar.*" Sanctity belonged to the altar, because the God dwelt within it, as is recognised in Matthew xxiii. 19: "*Which is greater, the gift or the altar that sanctifieth it?*" For a victim or offering laid on the altar became taboo or holy, the magic virtue of the stone being communicated to it by contact and proximity. The same virtue is imparted to the believers who partake of the flesh of the victim after giving to the god his portion.

Paul recognised that the heathen, also, by laying their gifts or sacrifices on the altars of devils, imparted to them a magical or devilish virtue. The god may inhabit the image rather than the altar below it, but anyhow his influence extends to it and to the gifts laid on it. There is thus a sort of demoniac atmosphere all round, which contaminates the meats offered to idols; and this is why the early Christians so carefully avoided meats offered to idols, often condemning themselves, by their scruples, to a strict vegetarianism, for pretty well all the flesh exposed in an ancient market had been thus consecrated. Paul had two minds about this point: in the one he held that, as the idol was in itself nothing, there was no harm in eating meats offered to it; the more so because God had made all things good and pure, and fit for man's consumption. He even advises his converts to eat what is offered them and ask no questions; only if they are expressly told that the viand in question has been offered to an idol shall they abstain, in order not to appear to those present to do homage to the idol. In his other mind, as in the passage above cited, he takes a contrary line. The Gentiles have communion with the devils, to which they offer the blood and titbits of the victim, or pour off the first drops of the goblet. Paul would not like his converts thus to have communion with a devil and imbibe its influence; for Jehovah is a jealous God, and brooks no rivals. Here he regards the gods as real and living beings, emulous of a homage due to God alone.

For the Christian, then, the table of the Lord and

THE EUCHARIST 261

the cup of the Lord take the place of the victims and libations of the older religions. How was this? Clearly the bread and wine, over which Jesus had pronounced the words "*This is my body*," or "*This is my blood*," possessed for Paul and his converts a taboo value. The meal with its one loaf symbolised, of course, the ideal union of believers; but it was not merely symbolic. A magical value clearly attached to the elements in themselves, else why were they who "*shall eat the bread or drink the cup of the Lord unworthily guilty of the body and blood of the Lord*"?

This is the language of the ancient ordeal, where a taboo or holy food was given to the accused, whom it poisoned if he was guilty. "*He that eateth and drinketh eateth and drinketh judgment unto himself, if he discern not the body.*" These last words are obscure, and the word *discern* or *discriminate* must be a technical term of the occultists of that day. It seems a warning not to gobble down the consecrated bread, as if it were ordinary food, forgetting that it is the body of Christ. Because they did so, many of the Corinthian Church, adds Paul, are "*weak and sickly, and not a few sleep*"—*i.e.*, have died. The bread and wine, therefore, if taken with due care and solemnity, without gluttony or selfishness, formed a talisman and charm against sickness, and even death! Sixty years later Ignatius, the martyred bishop of Antioch, calls them a drug of immortality.

From the pointed manner, then, in which Paul contrasts "*the table of the Lord and the table of devils*," we can infer the working of his mind. It was this: As by sharing with a demon his sacrificial food we import into ourselves the demon's spirit, life, and qualities, so by eating food which Christ himself ate, and by so eating made and explicitly recognised to be his own body and blood, we establish a kinship with him. It was still the Lord's table, though he was dead, because he had once used the words *This is my body*. Those who sat at the table of the Lord, and rehearsed the scene of the last supper, still ate with him food that he ate; and, as it nourished in him a life that vanquished death, so it did in them. We cannot infer from Paul's addition of the words, "*This do in remembrance of me*," that it was part of the ritual for those who presided at the *agapês* or love-feasts of the Corinthian Church to repeat over the bread and wine the words *This is*, etc. But we find this ritual in a later age in certain heretical churches, in which the bishops or presidents or prophets were practically regarded as reincarnations of Christ. The Armenian dissenters to this day assert that the Pope, when he repeats these words over the bread and wine, converts them not into the body and blood of Christ—for he is no Christ—but into his own impure flesh and blood.

In any case, the bread and wine consumed at these feasts were, in Paul's eyes, charged with a certain influence of a holy sort, just as victuals of which a demon had received a first taste were charged with an unholy influence, which contaminated them. Having once gone to form and constitute the body and mind of Christ, the elements—that is, the bread and wine—if eaten and drunk worthily by his followers, constituted them the body of Christ and informed them with his vivifying spirit.

It has been suggested by some critics—*e.g.*, by Wellhausen—that the bread and wine were used by Jesus himself as surrogates for real flesh and blood. The sense of the word *surrogate*, first used by

Robertson Smith in this connection, needs to be explained. Let us take examples. A Chinaman, bound by filial piety to provide his dead parents with cash for use in the next world, and finding real coin of the realm to be scarce, makes paper images of money and buries these with the corpse. The paper is a surrogate for the metal. The manufacture of such mock-money for use of the dead is a large industry in China.

Again, the Hindoos, no longer allowed by the British Government to throw themselves under the wheels of the Juggernaut car, make images of men and women, and throw them under, so that the god may still reap the satisfaction of human sacrifices offered to him. In certain ancient cults dough or wax figures of men and animals were made and offered to the god in place of the archetypes, which were either beyond the means of the worshippers or out of fashion in a more civilised age.

From all this it follows that gods and ghosts are either easily deceived or so good-natured as to fall in with the make-believe piety of their votaries. Nor is the custom of substituting semblance for reality confined to gods and ghosts. It extends to magic. If I would wreak my spite on an enemy, I have but to make an image of him or her in wax, and melt it before a slow fire. As it melts, so my enemy will be consumed with disease. If I have no wax or moulding art, it will suffice to get a photograph or picture, and stick pins into it. Even an onion will do the turn. I can hang it up in my chimney, and as it dries up and blackens in the smoke, so my enemy will pine away. Such images and pictures are surrogates. Hence the maxim that, in magic and religion, "*ficta pro veris accipi*"—"feigned things are accepted for true."

Can we, then, suppose that the bread and wine were used in the early Christian Eucharist as were dough images in the cults referred to? Was the Eucharist, as established by Jesus or as dreamed by Paul to have been so established, an example of sympathetic or, as it is now termed, of homœopathic magic? Did the believers think that in eating and drinking the substitutes they reaped the same advantages as if they had eaten and drunk the real flesh and blood of their Lord?

I doubt it, and I do not think it much matters. It is, anyhow, clear that Paul believed that at the Lord's table—the Christian analogue of the tables of the demons—the bread and wine, having been once partaken of by Christ, and so become his body and blood, became so afresh, even after his death, if only a portion was offered or consecrated to him by blessing and prayer. As the offering of an *aparché* or first taste of a victim's flesh or of the fruits of the field to a demon brought all the rest of the carcase or produce into, as it were, a field of demonic influence and taboo, so with the bread and wine offered and consecrated by Jesus on the night in which he was betrayed. Solemn and ceremonial participation therein was an act of communion with him, by means of which his qualities passed into the participants, as those of the demon passed into his votaries whenever they partook of food and drink of which the demon partook. Whether, therefore, Christ himself instituted this sacrament, or whether Paul, under influence of his ecstatic revelations, merely fathered it on Christ, in either case ideas and conceptions which to-day we call magical underlay and motived it. For nearly four hundred years the divines of the reformed Churches have been trying, but in vain, to explain away these primitive and magical aspects of the early Christian sacrament. The Roman doctrine is really less remote than theirs from the mind of the primitive Church; and it only seems strange and absurd in this age because the ideas and atmosphere of the old sacrificial systems have long ago cleared away like a fog from our minds, and left the Eucharist hanging in the air naked and shorn of its old sympathetic background of pagan and Jewish superstition.

The other chief aspect of this sacrament was probably invented by Paul. It was to proclaim Christ's death until he should come again. Matthew declares the wine to be *the blood of the covenant, which is shed for many unto the remission of sin*, and of the bread Paul says that it is the body (broken) for believers. From this standpoint the sacrament is a rehearsal or repetition of the death regarded as an expiatory sacrifice. Here again we breathe an atmosphere of mythical and barbarous ideas. It took the Fathers of the Church many generations before they could make up their minds whether the death of Christ was a sop to Satan or to the offended Christian God.

It would be against all analogy that an institution so tainted with magic from the first as was the Eucharist, should not, as the ages rolled by, gather about it ever fresh accretions of superstition. Accordingly, long before the end of the second century the consecrated elements, and particularly the bread, which could more easily be carried about than the wine, became a mere fetish or talisman. If during the rite a portion fell on the ground, it was believed that Christ's body was wounded and bleeding afresh. Ladies carried a bit of the bread about in their pockets and swallowed it before dinner. It was sent about from one Church to another to strengthen and affirm their union with each other. Theories of how the consecration took place were soon evolved; and of these one of the earliest was this, that the Holy Spirit, or *Logos*, came down and abode either upon or within it, so that Christ enjoyed, as it were, a second sojourn upon earth within it. A fetish is a material object into which, by means of invocations or incantations, a spirit has been persuaded to enter, so as to dwell within it; this definition exactly fits the consecrated food of the Christian Eucharist. Later on certain thinkers in the Roman Church taught that the conversion into the body and blood of Jesus is only real, if the bread and wine be received with faith and worthily; but this attempt to moralise the institution was soon ruled out, and the consecration became a mere magical operation performed by the priest for the benefit of the living and the dead. The Aristotelian distinction of substance and accident was also called in to explain its nature. The substance of the bread, it was argued, becomes the substance of the flesh, even though the accidents of the bread—*e.g.*, colour, size, hardness, taste, weight, smell, etc.—remain; as if, forsooth, a bit of bread had any substance apart from the entire complex of its attributes. However, the substance of the body and blood having, on this view, replaced in the act of consecration that of the bread and wine, the recipient is declared to masticate, with teeth and tongue, the real flesh and

THE EUCHARIST

blood. It is only by the merciful providence of a God unwilling to shock and stupefy his worshippers, that the attributes or accidents are allowed to remain, and the holy bread or victim, as it is called, prevented from appearing on the altar as a bleeding mass of raw human flesh.

Let us, in conclusion, return to a question which has been touched upon in the foregoing pages—namely, whether the words *this is my body* and *this is my blood* can be supposed to have been used by Jesus himself. It is not an important issue; but the discussion of it serves to reveal upon how slender a basis of documentary evidence may rest the hugest dogmatic and ceremonial structures. Let us confront the three texts of Matthew, Mark and Luke:—

MATTHEW xxvi. 26.	MARK xiv. 22.	LUKE xxii.
And as they were eating Jesus *took bread, and, having blessed, broke and* gave it to the disciples *and said:* Take ye, *eat; this is my body.* And having taken a *cup* and given thanks, he gave it to them saying: *Drink* ye, all, of it, for this is my *blood* of *the covenant* which is poured out for many unto remission of sins. But I say unto you, I will not drink henceforth of this fruit of the vine until the day when I shall drink it new with you in the Kingdom of my father.	*omits* "eat" to them, and they *drank* of it all. And he said to them, This is *omits* "unto remission of sins." Verily I say *omits* "with you" Kingdom of God.	14. And when the hour was come, he lay down, and the apostles with him. 15. And he said to them: With desire have I desired to eat this passover with you before I suffer. 16. For I say unto you I will henceforth not eat it until it be fulfilled in the Kingdom of God. 17. And having received a cup he gave thanks and said: Take this and apportion it among yourselves; (18) for I say unto you I will not drink from now on of the fruit of the vine until the Kingdom of God be come. 19. And having taken bread he gave

268   THE EUCHARIST

> thanks, brake it and gave it to them, saying: This is my body [which is given for you. This do ye in commemoration of me. (20) And the cup likewise after the supping, saying: This cup is the new covenant in my blood, the (cup) which is poured out for you].

Let us consider, first, Luke's text. If the reader will look back to p. 251, where the text of 1 Corinthians xi. 23-25 is quoted, he will see that these verses of Paul's letter have been incorporated bodily in Luke's text, verses 19 and 20. So much also of these verses as is enclosed in square brackets is wanting in some of the earliest MSS. of Luke.

Remove these two verses from Luke's text, and what do we get? Surely no more than an anticipation of the speedy approach of the Kingdom; so soon will it come that, until then, Jesus will not again drink the wine and eat the bread of the passover meal. So remote from our minds to-day is the thought of a miraculous and sudden installation of a new era for humanity, as opposed to its slow and gradual evolution through piecemeal and painstaking correction of the evils and diseases of actual society, that the entire meaning of this last meal of Jesus with his disciples is hidden from the average reader. It needs too much effort to realise that Jesus believed that, by a sudden peripety, within his own lifetime and within that of his followers, the existing *régime* was to be upset and, to use Luke's phrase in Acts i. 6, "*the Kingdom restored to Israel.*" For the messianic aspirations voiced by this evangelist in the canticle ascribed to

THE EUCHARIST

Zacharias are to be fulfilled before that generation passed away. The "*Lord the God of Israel* [was] *to visit and effect the redemption of his people, salvation from their enemies and from the hand of all that hated them, to remember his holy covenant, the oath which he sware unto Abraham their father, to grant that they, being delivered out of the hand of their enemies, should serve him without fear, in holiness and righteousness before him all their days.*" John was conceived as the prophet who was "*to give knowledge of* [this] *salvation to his* [*i.e.*, Jahveh's] *people through remission of their sins.*" And this fifth act of the tragic drama of Jewish history was not to take place in another world, but in the promised land of Judæa itself. Jesus, having, as he thought, leavened the northern lands of Israel with his teaching, was come to Jerusalem, the focus of the religious life of his countrymen, to keep the yearly feast which commemorated their deliverance out of the land of Egypt. In the fervour of his enthusiasm he dreamed that it only remained to him to proclaim there also the immediate advent of the Kingdom; and Jehovah, who had been with him until now, would, even before his apostles had had time "*to go through the cities of Israel*" (Matthew x. 23), send "*the Son of Man*" to liquidate all existing things and inaugurate a new society. In the new era the twelve apostles will sit in Jerusalem on thrones judging the twelve tribes; and Jesus will preside among them at the passover table drinking new wine. Luke assumes that Jesus at this last supper foresaw his fate, and realised that this was his last passover before he should suffer. According to this perspective, his death was to intervene as a preliminary to the resurrection and second coming. In Mark, however, and Matthew, who servilely copies him out, we miss this perspective. In them there is no anticipation of impending death, but only of the day when he will drink "*the new wine*" with them "*in the kingdom of his father.*"

Now, is it possible that, as verses 19 and 20 of Luke's account have been interpolated from Paul's letter to the Corinthians, so also Mark interpolated therefrom his verses 22–24? I have italicised in Matthew's text (which is the same as Mark's) the words and phrases which agree with Paul's text. The agreement is so close and so extensive that either Mark must have copied Paul or Paul Mark. The latter hypothesis is ruled out by time considerations. It follows that Paul's text influenced Mark, or some early redactor of Mark. If we admit the second Gospel as it stands to be from the pen of Mark, we can quite well suppose that he had before him the letter of Paul to the Corinthians; for Paul, on the first of his missionary journeys, had Mark as his companion for part of the way. It is more likely, however, that the original text of Mark resembled in form and matter verses 14–18 of Luke's narrative. Then a redactor adjusted them to Paul's account in time for Matthew to copy them out. It would seem that Luke had an earlier form of Mark's text, not yet interpolated from Paul. The Pauline addition was not in his copy of Mark, or he would, like Matthew, have transcribed it. So it was left to a subsequent editor of his text to fill in the lacuna direct from Paul's Epistle. The fourth evangelist, in his narrative of the last supper, has no mention of the episode, and may not have found it in his copy of Mark. He was, however, familiar with the idea of Christ's flesh being the *living bread*, given

THE EUCHARIST

to man *for the life of the world*; and he sets in Jesus's lips the words: "*Except ye eat the flesh of the Son of Man and drink his blood, ye have not life in yourselves.*" Jesus, however, does not use these words at the last supper, but in Capernaum; and none but the unbelieving Jews are allowed to take the saying literally: "*The Jews therefore strove with one another, saying, How can this man give us his flesh to eat?*" Indeed, throughout the context the fourth evangelist is elaborating an idea, which equally meets us in Philo, of the Logos being *heavenly bread* and *the cup of God*. He probably knew of a Christian Eucharist whereat the believers deemed themselves to be really eating Christ's flesh and drinking his blood; and he tries to dissipate so gross and material an idea, and substitute for it that of a spiritual communion. He concludes: "*It is the spirit that quickeneth; the flesh profiteth nothing.*"

We may, then, sum up the probabilities about the origin of the Eucharist somewhat as follows: Other sects or heresies had, during the first century B.C., arisen in the bosom of Judaism, which had their sacred meals. Thus the Essenes, who by thousands rejected the temple sacrifices, rejected marriage, and lived apart among their date plantations near the Dead Sea, bathed in cold water, and met in white robes, every evening after their work in the fields was done, to partake of a holy repast, consisting mainly of bread and water. They had their own priests to bless or consecrate this repast, just as the Christians at first required prophets to do it, and later on consecrated priests for the purpose. The Essenes laid such stress upon the ritual purity of their food that they kept up special rest-houses in the various cities of Palestine, wherein their members might eat when engaged in travel; and members who, for having divulged the mysteries confided to them at initiation, had been excommunicated and expelled from the communion, had been known to die of hunger because they were denied the sacramental banquets of the sect, and could partake of no others without violating their oath and conscience. Here we have so close an analogue to the Church, with its equipment of priests and sacraments, that some writers—*e.g.*, De Quincey—have argued that the earliest Christianity was Essenism. The Essenes, however, were not, so far as we know, Messianists. Nevertheless, they may, in matters of organisation and discipline, have supplied the Christians with a model.

So also, in all probability, did the *Therapeutæ*, or *worshippers*, of Egypt, to whom we have already referred. They, too, had a sacred meal every fiftieth day, consisting of bread and water without flesh. The Scriptures were read and hymns sung in the course of this meal, which seems to have resembled the passover feast in all respects, except that there was no roast lamb. It was eaten in their synagogue or meeting-house, and their elders and deacons presided and ministered at it.

The first Christians, however, expected the end of the world and the second coming during their lifetime, and were but holding on until the great event should occur, preparing themselves for the restoration of God's rule on earth by mutual charity, forbearance, suffering of persecution, fasting, vigils, and prayers. Their great fear was to be surprised by the end ere they stood ready, with their lamps trimmed and their loins girded. Those who had means freely gave of

THE EUCHARIST

them for the support of the poorer; but there was no encouragement of idleness. The prophets and teachers were alone dispensed from the necessity of earning their livelihood; and in the *Teaching of the Apostles*, our earliest manual of their discipline and ritual, we find shrewd rules laid down even for the prophets. Any one of them who stayed for more than three days in a congregation was to be regarded as a false prophet. Once a week, presumably on Sundays, each Christian congregation met together for an *agapé*, or love-feast, whereat the prophet broke bread, using a single loaf, and distributing it in token of the spiritual union of the believers. This *fractio panis* (*klasis artou* in Greek), or breaking of the bread, was the most solemn episode in a solemn repast of love and charity, when the rich entertained the poor, and all alike were equal. With the bread was drunk a common cup of wine or water.

The Christians in Judæa may very well have imitated these solemn repasts from the Essenes and Therapeutæ. Outside Palestine the *Thiasoi*, or trade guilds (analogous to the castes of India, except that they were not so rigidly hereditary), supplied another model; for their members also met, at stated intervals, at a solemn repast, where all were brethren, and all gave homage to a patron saint or god.

The greatest moral and religious teachers are, after all, sons of their age, especially in intellectual matters; and we must not blame them if a certain tenacity in superstition accompanies their enthusiasm and moral fervour. So it was with Paul. With all his burning zeal for righteousness and brotherly love, overleaping narrow distinctions of Jew and barbarian, bondsman and free, he was singularly trammelled with the old magical ideas of vicarious sacrifice, of mystical communion with God or gods, reached through participation in the victim's flesh. Perhaps the idea that Christ's death was an atoning offering for human sin arose first in his mind, and suggested the revelation about the Eucharist. He would have all believers *present* or *offer their bodies as a living sacrifice holy and acceptable to God*, by way of rendering to him a *reasonable* or *spiritual worship* (Romans xii. 1). Christ had achieved so much, and more too, for he had actually been sacrificed as a sort of new passover victim (1 Cor. v. 7). It may be that this idea was suggested to him by the knowledge that the Syrian soldiery who crucified Jesus had invested his death with all the pomp and ceremonial of a human sacrifice. In any case, he, and no one else, seems to have started the idea that Christ's death was a genuine atoning sacrifice, in accordance with the old belief that " *all things are cleansed with blood, and apart from the shedding of blood there is no remission.*" The Epistle to the Hebrews, from which the above words are cited, though not Pauline, exactly expresses Paul's idea when, in ch. ix. 11, 12, it declares that Christ " *had entered into the holy place once for all and obtained eternal redemption, not through the blood of goats and calves, but through his own blood.*" The Jews, as the legend of the sacrifice of Isaac proves, had once held that Jahveh must have human blood; and the idea was, in Paul's day, still widespread among Syrians and Semites that human blood, especially the blood of a first-born son, is irresistible to the divine palate. Paul would have been nearly as much shocked to witness a human sacrifice as ourselves; and yet the idea which underlies such sacrifices was at the back of his head. The catholic Epistles are also pervaded with it, and as a good example we may cite 1 John i. 7: "*We have fellowship one with another, and the blood of Jesus cleanseth us from all sin.*"

What more natural than the transition from this idea to another that invariably accompanied it in the sacrificial scheme of Jews and pagans—this, namely, that the believers, who derive spiritual profit from the bloodshed, must also eat the victim slain for them, and so achieve spiritual union with the god in the most real and effective way? This extension of the idea came to Paul as one of his revelations direct from Christ. Of the real body and blood there was, of course, nothing left, and even Paul would have shrunk from the later Roman definitions. But Jesus might have indicated to his apostles in the last supper that the cup and bread he then blessed and broke to them symbolised his blood and body, soon to be broken on the cross. The ancient mind did not distinguish, as we do, between symbol and thing symbolised; nor does the savage of to-day, in whose *quasi*-magical rites the image or surrogate or substitute takes the place of the archetype in such a way that whatever happens to that happens also to this. The circumstance that at this last meal Jesus ate common food with his followers in itself constituted an almost physical tie between him and them, as it does among Arabs of to-day. By way of clinching the idea, Paul imagined Christ to have used the words "*This is my body, which is for you*," and "*This cup is the new covenant in* [or *through*] *my blood.*" By such means Paul assimilated the institution of the breaking of the bread as nearly as he could to the sacrificial meals of Jews and pagans. He lays special stress on the cup, which images the blood : it is the very covenant which binds Jesus and his followers into the one spiritual living body of the Church. He laid this extra stress on the cup, as Wellhausen remarks, because the blood was a better cement than the bread, and because, in popular belief, it was the life. In drinking the substitute the faithful, by all the rules of modern and ancient magic, drank the blood itself, and, in drinking it, imbibed the very life and spirit of Christ. "*Ye were all made,*" he writes in the context (1 Cor. xii. 13), "*to drink of one spirit.*"

If the Christians were to make headway against the pagans, they were bound to have a sacramental meal of their own, which they could pit against the *agapés*, or sacred meals, which accompanied every sacrifice. There must be a *table of the Lord*, to compete with *the tables of devils;* for the converted pagan did not lose, merely because he was converted, his fundamental religious needs and instincts. It was to satisfy these in the least objectionable manner that Paul had his revelation of what Jesus did and said in that last supper. His plan succeeded, and for centuries the Eucharist was the Christian sacrifice *par excellence*, and gathered round itself ever more and more the old sacerdotalism and the sacrificial customs, rites, and notions of Jew and Pagan alike.

The Pauline tradition thus originated has in Mark's Gospel been plastered, so to speak, on top of an older narrative of the last supper, according to which Jesus merely used the occasion to record for a last time his earnest faith in the immediate approach of the kingdom of God. Probably this addition to the tradition in Mark was the work of a reviser ; but it may have stood in the first draft of the Greek text, for Mark was at one time under Pauline influence, and must have met with it wherever he went outside Palestine. In any case, Matthew found, in his copy of Mark, the amplified text as we have it. Not so, it would seem, Luke, in whose text the Pauline addition is added in Paul's own words, and is clearly a mere interpolation from his Epistle to the Corinthians. If the words "*This is my body*," etc., and the idea they convey, were merely Pauline, and no part of the earliest evangelical tradition, we can also understand why the Fourth Gospel ignores them, and why, in the earliest eucharistic ritual we possess—viz., the *Teaching of the Apostles*—there is no trace of them.

Paul's language in speaking of the Eucharist was that commonly used by the pagans of their sacrifices. The Eucharist, or the *agapé* of which it was an episode, is *the table of the Lord*, in contrast with the *table of demons*. Among the papyri dug up on the site of the ancient city of Oxyrhynchus by Drs. Grenfell and Hunt is one (*Pap. Ox.*, i. 110) of the second century, which runs as follows: "Chaeremon invites thee to dine at the table (*or* divan) of the Lord Serapis in the Serapeum to-morrow, the 15th, at nine o'clock." Aristides, a Greek writer of the second century, further illustrates Paul's language when he remarks that men enjoy a real communion with Serapis in his sacrifices, in that they invite him to the altar, and appoint him to entertain and feast them. An old Greek inscription of Kos, describing the ritual of sacrifices to Herakles, speaks of the *table of the god*. Porphyry aids us to understand Paul's phrase, "*communion with devils*," when, in a passage I have already noted, he describes the demons as coming up and sitting close to our bodies when we eat flesh. "Most of all," he adds, "they delight in blood and in impure meats, and enjoy these by entering into those who use them." The meats in question had, of course, been previously consecrated or offered to the demons. Similarly, according to Paul, who here, of course, reflects the ordinary standpoint of his fellow Christians, the believer takes into himself in the communion the Lord Jesus Christ himself. The idea of a divine body being broken or torn to bits and eaten by the votaries meets us in the Orphic cult of Dionysus-Zagreus, who, according to the myth, was thus treated by the Titans. In this cult a victim representing the god was torn to pieces and eaten by the faithful. The myth here doubtless grew out of a primitive communion rite. In the Thracian cult of Dionysos or Bacchus the votaries ate the divine animal, and by doing so became Gods, Bacchi, themselves.

Chapter XV.

THE END

The story of the trial of Jesus before Pilate, of his condemnation and crucifixion, is, in main outlines, historical; but even here we can detect many touches added either in fulfilment of supposed prophecy or out of antagonism to the Jews. Luke in particular refashions the tradition so as to make of it a continuous polemic against the Jews. The guilt of the murder of Jesus had to be lifted off the Gentiles, in the person of Pilate, and loaded upon them. From Mark, through Matthew, Luke, the Fourth Gospel, into that called of Peter, we detect a veritable *crescendo* of animus against this unhappy race, of whom probably not one in a thousand ever heard of the crime until fifty years after it was committed; while the slender minority which actually witnessed it needed to be stirred up by the priests before they could approve of it. Set the pope and his cardinals in place of the Jewish priests, and in place of the Passover multitude met at Jerusalem a populace debauched by superstitious teaching, and we obtain in any one of the countless tragedies of the Roman Inquisition a parallel to that which fills the last chapters of the Gospels. Why any one of those victims of orthodox cruelty should be less worthy than Jesus to be venerated as a saviour and redeemer of our race I cannot understand.

As an example of how, under the persuasion of

passion, a real tradition can, little by little, be lost sight of, effaced and replaced by one that is false, let us examine the conduct of Pilate as represented in these different sources. In them we get all the stages of a myth in the very making.

According, then, to Mark, the Jewish chief priests, and the elders who composed the Sanhedrim, bound Jesus and brought him before Pilate, who "*asked him, Art thou the King of the Jews?*" Jesus merely assented, and lapsed into silence, utterly refusing to answer the many accusations levelled against him by the priests. Pilate "*perceived that for envy the chief priests had delivered him up,* [and] *asked, Why, what evil hath he done?*" The multitude, "*stirred up by the priests, cried out exceedingly, Crucify him. And Pilate, wishing to content the multitude.......delivered Jesus, when he had scourged him, to be crucified.*" Pilate's soldiers then led Jesus away, and put him to death, it would seem, as a human sacrifice, with all the frippery and pomp with which a mock king of the Saturnalia was slain.

It need hardly be observed that, if Pilate was really convinced of Jesus's innocence, he could have released him at once. But Jesus's admission before him that he was King of the Jews or Messiah, in a period when the Roman Government was perpetually menaced by such pretenders, left no alternative but to condemn him. How could Pilate know that the Messiah before him was not one of the ordinary physical-force kind, or that he would not, under pressure of his followers, shortly develop into such? In any case, if he was the unscrupulous and cruel Governor that Philo, his contemporary, represents him to have been, then the life of a Jewish enthusiast was of little account to him.

THE END

He would have thought much more of the death of his wife's pet sparrow than of a Jewish Messiah. The whitewashing of Pilate, then, has already begun in Mark. In Matthew it makes a stride forward, for we hear that "*when Pilate saw that he prevailed nothing, but rather that a tumult was arising, he took water, and washed his hands before the multitude, saying, I am innocent of the blood of this righteous man. And all the people answered and said, His blood be on us, and on our children.*"

The symbolism of washing the hands clean of guilt is wholly Jewish, and the words used by Pilate are taken from the Greek version of 2 Samuel iii. 28, where David exclaims, "*I am innocent of the blood of Abennêr.*" Thus Pilate is made to think, act, and speak, not as a Roman procurator would do, but as an ancient Jew might have done. The people equally answer in words taken from the Greek version of the Old Testament and from the same context. This evangelist, then, would have us believe that Pilate was wholly guiltless. In the cry of the populace we overhear the steadily growing irritation of the Christians of a later age against the Jews, who remained cold to their visions and predictions of the end of the world, and indifferent to the claims of their Messiah. If Pilate really "*washed his hands in innocency*" at one moment, and in the next "*scourged and delivered Jesus to be crucified*" (Matthew xxvii. 26), he but made himself chief actor in an absurd and wicked comedy. This, nevertheless, is what Matthew relates.

Luke handles the tradition of Mark independently of Matthew, and amplifies it, perhaps from a lost written source which he had in common with the apocryphal Gospel of Peter. Where Mark merely records Pilate's surprise at Jesus's silence in face of the priestly slanders, Luke asserts that "*he said to the chief priests and the multitudes, I find nothing of guilt in this man.*" Pilate then takes Jesus to Herod, the ruler of Galilee, who, having heard much of Jesus, "*hopes to see him work some sign*"—a queer ambition on the part of the murderer of John the Baptist. Jesus answers nothing, as before; and Pilate forthwith convokes the chief priests and magistrates and people, and assures them afresh that neither he nor Herod can find Jesus guilty of any crime that merits death. He "*will* [therefore] *chastise and release him.*" Luke, in accordance with his literary habit of repeating thrice any salient utterance, makes Pilate protest twice more his assurance of Jesus's innocence. Vain words! For, in spite of all his protestations, the procurator hands Jesus over to the Jews, that they may wreak their will upon him. In the immediate sequel, Luke is careful to omit the episode of Pilate's soldiery crowning Jesus with thorns, of their smiting him and spitting on him, though it stood in Mark, his source. For he wishes his readers to believe that the Jews themselves, and not a Gentile soldiery, carried out the execution. Nor can he admit that *both* the malefactors crucified with Jesus died reviling him, though Mark and Matthew expressly affirm that they did so. Accordingly, one of them repents and prays Jesus to remember him whenever he shall attain unto his kingdom. Jesus answers: "*Verily, I tell you, this day shalt thou be with me in paradise.*" For such a rewriting of his source few will blame Luke; none the less, it is not history, though it is good dramatic art.

The fourth evangelist walks in the steps of Luke.

Far from keeping silence before Pilate, Jesus explains to him the character of his sovereignty. "*My kingdom is not of this world,*" he tells him, in flat contradiction of the real expectations of Jesus and his apostles. In a second conversation, at which the Jews assist, Pilate asks: "*Whence art thou?*" And, when Jesus answers nothing, adds: "*Knowest thou not that I have power to crucify thee, and have power to release thee?*" Jesus answers: "*Thou hadst not any power over me, were it not given thee from above. Wherefore he who has betrayed me to thee hath greater sin.*" Pilate forthwith sought "*to release him: but the Jews cried out, saying, If thou release this man, thou art not Cæsar's friend: everyone that maketh himself a king opposeth Cæsar.*" To this sort of argument Pilate yields after a struggle, and delivers Jesus to them to be crucified, as in Luke. The drift of the entire narrative is to exonerate Pilate by demonstrating that he was overawed at the prospect of an informer accusing him to the emperor whom he served.

Of the so-called Gospel of Peter, written about A.D. 150, we have but the last portion, which begins towards the end of the trial of Jesus. But what remains of it is enough to show that in it the process of exonerating Pilate was carried even further than in the canonical Gospels, for it begins thus: "*But of the Jews not one washed his hands, neither Herod nor any one of his judges. And as they would not wash themselves, Pilate stood up. And then Herod the king bade the Lord to be brought along, and said to them: Whatsoever I have ordered you to do, that do unto him.*"

The author of this Gospel, therefore, saddles the guilt of handing over Jesus to his enemies, not upon

Pilate, but on the half-Jewish Herod. The exculpation of Pilate is complete. Herod and the Jews are alone responsible.

The feelings of awe and horror which thrilled the mind of the early Christians as they brooded over the death of their Saviour are stamped on their tradition of the last moments. "*When it was the sixth hour,*" write the evangelists, "*there was darkness upon the whole earth, until the ninth hour*"—that is to say, from noon until three in the afternoon. And Luke adds the words: "*because the sun was eclipsed.*" The Greek word he uses is the technical term for an eclipse due to the interposition of the moon, and it is difficult to suppose that so cultivated a writer in that age was ignorant of this explanation of an eclipse, or that he used the term merely in the sense that the sun failed to shine, as it may do when obscured by a cloud. Yet, if we are to interpret the phrase in the usual sense, we must accuse Luke either of great ignorance or of great carelessness, for Jesus was crucified at the Jewish passover, and this was held at full moon. The synoptic evangelists do not minimise the miracle, but declare that it extended all over the earth, so that it was not confined to Judæa alone. The fourth evangelist omits it, for he regarded Christ's crucifixion as a final glorification, over which nature had no reason to be sad. How long after the death could such a story arise? On first consideration, one is inclined to postulate a long period; and yet in less than fourteen years a similar myth had grown up in connection with the death of Julius Cæsar. For that is just the number of years which had elapsed when Virgil, in his Georgics (i. 463), records it among other wonders:—

> Solem quis dicere falsum
> Audeat? Ille etiam cæcos instare tumultus
> Sæpe monet, fraudem que et operta tumescere bella.
> Ille etiam exstincto miseratus Cæsare Romam,
> Cum caput obscura nitidum ferrugine texit,
> Impiaque æternam timuerunt sæcula noctem.

"Who will venture to call the sun a false prophet? It is he that often warns us that blind tumults are at hand, and that treachery and hidden wars are brewing. He, also, when Cæsar was slain, felt pity for Rome, since he veiled his shining head with murky rust, and the impious age feared an everlasting night." So the author of the *Consolatio ad Liviam* (in Baehrens, *Poetæ Minores*, i., p. 104–121) assures us (verses 405–408) that on the death of Drusus "the stars fled from heaven; that Lucifer, the morning star, quitted his ordinary path, and failed to rise all over the globe."

> Sidera quinetiam cælo fugisse feruntur,
> Lucifer et Solitas destituisse vias :
> Lucifer in toto nulli comparuit orbe.

Around the death of Augustus a similar legend gathered. It was inevitable that such a story should soon be related of the death of the Messiah by the Christians.

Another miracle occurred, according to Mark, at the moment when Jesus gave up the ghost: "*And the veil of the temple was rent in twain from top to bottom.*" This much suffices for Mark, but Matthew accumulates wonders, as we remarked above (p. 79), and adds that "*the earth trembled, the stones were riven asunder,*" and many saints rose bodily "*out of their tombs after his resurrection, entered the holy city, and appeared unto many.*" The latter part of the legend is found still further adorned in an old source, the Dialogue of Timothy and Aquila,[1] as follows:—

[1] In the *Anecdota Oxoniensia*, 1898, p. 101.

The mountains were shaken, and the rocks riven asunder, and the tombs were opened, and many bodies of those that slept rose up and entered the holy city, and appeared to many. And they asked them that were so risen, Art thou not so and so? Quoth he, Art thou not, then, he that died so many years ago? And the other said, I am. And others in turn asked others of the risen other questions, and heard the same. So he said again to them, But how were ye raised from the dead?

And in the sequel the risen relate how Jesus went down to Hades, and broke open the gates of Hell in spite of their bolts, and how he bound Hades or death, but ransomed the dead and raised them up to life with himself. A clause to the effect that Jesus "*descended into hell*" found its way into the earliest creed, and whole epics were composed on the theme of Christ's invasion and plundering of Hell. Similar legends were current long before among the Greeks of Orpheus and Pythagoras. In the Catacombs Christ is often depicted as Orpheus, and we may safely attribute to the influence of the old Orphic hymns and mysteries this class of Christian myth.

The idea of the dead being called up from their tombs was a familiar one in antiquity. The witch of old was able, as we read in the story of Jason and Medea, to "move the woods and bid the hills tremble, and the ground to groan, and the dead to issue from their sepulchres."

> Et silvas moveo, jubeoque tremiscere montes,
> Et mugire, solum manesque exire sepulchris.
> —Ovid, *Metamorph.*, vii., 205-6.

Of all this complex of myth there is, then, but one element which is not so banal as not to need much explanation. Why should the veil of the temple be rent asunder ? The following is probably the explanation of this curious addition. It was Paul's idea that the death of Christ in a mystical manner brought mankind into the presence of the God Jahveh; and, as the latter was believed to be a real presence within the holy of holies, which was separated by a curtain or veil from the rest of the sanctuary of the Jewish temple, the unknown author of the Epistle to the Hebrews, ch. vi., 19, 20, speaks of Jesus as "*having become a high-priest for ever after the order of Melchisedek*," and as having, after the manner of the high-priest, who was privileged to enter the holy of holies once a year, "*entered as a forerunner for us into the place which is within the veil.*" Here, then, we have the symbolism which underlies the mythical narrative of the Gospel. Figuratively, the veil was rent at the moment of his death, and Jesus, as the representative of a new humanity, and superseding the Jewish high-priest, passed within. Evangelic tradition has changed the allegory into an historical event and incident of the crucifixion. In ch. x., 19, 20, of the same Epistle, the flesh of Jesus is described as a *veil* through which, as by *a new and living way*, the *brethren* have courage *to enter into the holy place*. This metaphor, equally with the other, may have served to generate the legend in question.

Let us pass on to the story of the resurrection. In this also we are able to catch the various phases and stages of a myth constantly in process of growth and amplification. The earliest and only strictly historical stage is to be found in a passage of Paul's first Epistle to the Corinthians, xv. 5-8, cited above (p. 17). As a stone flung into a pond generates ever-widening circles of disturbance, so the first appearance of Jesus to Peter, or Cephas, was succeeded first by one *to the twelve*, and then by one to as many as five hundred brethren at once. Having become so widely diffused, the belief had gained such prestige and authority as to impose itself even on recalcitrant minds; and there followed an appearance to James, Jesus's brother, who, in Mark's Gospel, is represented as incredulous of his teaching and hostile to his messianic claims. Jesus next appears to all the apostles, and the series is complete when the persecutor Paul, smitten with remorse and impressed by the patience with which his victims suffer, himself beholds the risen Messiah. In such experiences *c'est le premier pas qui coûte*. In the earliest form of gospel tradition Peter is the leader and spokesman of Jesus's followers; if he was once convinced that Jesus had been raised from the dead and had appeared to him, he was sure to suggestionise the rest of the twelve companions into seeing visions like his own; they in turn would be capable of suggestionising the much larger number specified by Paul, of whom many were yet alive when the letter to the Corinthians was written. In the history of religious enthusiasm we find nothing so contagious as visions. Let a number of persons be confined in a room, and by means of fervent prayer and singing of hymns brought to a sufficiently high pitch of nervous tension; then let one in higher ecstasy than the rest cry out that he sees a dead saint, a Christ, or a Madonna, and the entire assembly will, in a few moments, share the illusion. It is impossible to collate or compare such visions with one another, so as to determine whether or no they agree. Each enthusiast will, of course, behold the lost saint or teacher in the guise in which he best knew and loved him. In Paul's Epistles we have vivid glimpses of early Christian gatherings, where all would be talking with tongues at once, swept off their feet by common ecstasy. In the Shepherd of Hermas we have similar pictures. Actual persecution, or the fear of it, helped to keep these early believers in a fever of religious excitement. Is it surprising that the apparitions multiplied so rapidly as before long to overtake James the incredulous and Paul the persecutor? How significant is the statement in Acts xiii. 31 that Jesus "*was seen for many days, but only by them that came up with him from Galilee to Jerusalem, who are now his witnesses unto the people.*" In other words, he was seen by those whom his personality had most deeply impressed. On the experience of Cephas, then, the entire history of the resurrection hinges. Was his a supernormal vision of the dead, or just one of those apparitions, hardly less vivid and intense than waking reality, to which even normally constituted subjects, much more men of ardent and impetuous natures, such as was his, are so liable when death has suddenly robbed them of a friend and loved teacher or leader on whom they have leaned and fixed their hopes?

Those who approach the question with open and critical mind will, I think, adopt the latter view, especially when they bear in mind that, in the age and generation to which Peter and Paul belonged, there was a general inability to distinguish between subjective and objective experiences, between dreams and waking reality. It was an age in which few except the aristocrats of intelligence regarded their dreams as do educated people of to-day—*i.e.*, as private phantasms referable to trivial disturbances of the digestion and nervous system. The ancient Jews, like all primitive races, esteemed their dreams to be revelations of another world. And not the Jews alone. Rich men among the Greeks and Romans kept interpreters of their dreams, just as rich men to-day keep their private chaplains or confessors. The story of King Pharaoh and his interpreter of dreams in the tale of Joseph will occur to everyone; and, according to the meaning put upon their dreams by these interpreters, who were not consciously charlatans, the great ones of the earth directed their conduct and formed their plans for the future. The *Sacred Discourses* or *Hieroi Logoi* of the Greek Rhetor Aristides, a friend of the Emperor Marcus Aurelius, bring home to us the importance anciently attached to dreams and visions. Here we have a *journal intime*, as it were, in which the writer recorded day by day his dreams and apparitions all through a long and painful illness. He even became the despair of his physicians, because he insisted on taking the odd remedies enjoined in their many epiphanies by gods and goddesses and heroes, such as Æsculapius, Apollo, and Athênê. He relates his interviews and conversations with these sacred personages, just as the ecstatic girl of Lourdes related hers with the Virgin Mary. We have not only the letters of Paul, but the authentic acts of St. Perpetua, and of a score of other early martyrs, to convince us that the Christians in no wise differed from their pagan contemporaries in the reality and importance they attributed to omens, dreams, visions, voices from heaven, and what not. The dreams and visions of children were held especially sacred, as we know from the works of Cyprian, who died A.D. 258. The custom of incubation—that is, of sleeping in temples (*e.g.*, of Æsculapius), in order that the god may visit the sleeper in his dreams—was continued in Christianity, and in some Eastern Churches (*e.g.*, in the Georgian) still survives, or, at least, survived till yesterday. A lower or middle-class Italian seldom dreams a dream without at once consulting one of the many dream-books, and buying a lottery ticket of the number which corresponds to the objects he dreamed about. Many factors contributed powerfully in Peter's case to establish such a psychological attitude towards the dead Jesus as must generate apparitions, and the assurance that he was not dead, but alive in heaven. He was the earliest of the disciples to leave all and follow Jesus. He had discerned in him the hope of Israel—the man sent from God to restore the glorious kingdom of David. That hope had been rudely dashed. He had seen his master betrayed and arrested; and, when he was himself taxed with being a Galilean and a follower of Jesus, his courage had failed him, and he had with emphasis denied all knowledge of him. Then he had fled back to Galilee, probably without waiting even to see how the trial before the Roman procurator would end, and certainly before the death agony on the cross supervened. In the solitudes of the lake of Gennesaret, where he had resumed his vocation as a fisherman, keen remorse must have assailed him for his desertion of his leader. The influence of his leader's personality must quickly have reasserted itself over him in a region full of personal souvenirs, and in which he had originally fallen under its spell. In such conditions Peter could not admit that his hopes and expectations had been in vain, and they revived. In the present day we see even men of science duped by the legerdemain of such charlatans as Eusapia Palladino, Home, and Madame Blavatsky. Some day or other the entire vulgar mechanism of trickery is exposed; yet the once convinced, the true believers, will seldom own to themselves or others that they were duped. Rather than do so, they will frame the most roundabout hypotheses, to save themselves from an admission so humiliating. I do not suggest that Jesus was a charlatan, or Peter a goose; nevertheless, the same law held good in his case, for man is ever the same. Accordingly, when Jesus appeared in visions to Peter, as to a man of such a temperament he could not fail to do, the old messianic hope, the old confidence in the kingdom of God about to be set up afresh, revived in his breast. Thus the true resurrection was that which ensued in the hearts of Peter and his companions. They saw Jesus still alive, surrounded with glory in heaven, and knew instantly that the joyous consummation was only delayed a little until the Messiah, like Daniel's Son of Man, should come back in glory on the clouds of heaven. The admission made by Luke in Acts, that Jesus appeared to none but the faithful, establishes the subjective character of the apparitions. The terms, moreover, used in describing the risen Jesus belong to the stock phraseology of apparitions. Thus in Acts i. 3 the Greek word *optanô* is used, a technical term for *seeing* a ghost; and the noun *optasia*, formed from this verb, is used in Acts xxvi. 19 to describe Paul's vision on the way to Damascus. This vision was, in Paul's mind, co-ordinate with, and of the same real quality and importance as, the visions vouchsafed to Peter, to the apostles, to the five hundred, and to James, the Lord's brother.

Starting from Paul's statement, the only one at all near in point of time to the events themselves, let us try to understand the legend of the resurrection and of the empty tomb, as it insinuated itself, with ever fresh growths of legendary detail, into evangelical tradition. In Mark we have the tale in its earliest and simplest form. He merely relates that Jesus was buried on Friday afternoon, in a tomb hewn out of rock, against the door of which a stone was rolled; that certain women, who had followed him from Galilee, visited the tomb early on the Sunday morning, bringing spices in order to anoint the body; that they found the stone rolled away and the tomb empty. Such is the theme, which in the other evangelists receives ever fresh accretions of miraculous detail.

From Paul himself we merely learn that Christ, having *died for our sins according to the Scriptures, was buried, and raised* [or *resuscitated*] *on the third day*, equally *according to the Scriptures*.

The scripture which dictated a resurrection on the third day was probably Hosea vi. 1, 2 : " *Come, and let us return unto the Lord : for he hath torn, and he will heal us ; he hath smitten, and he will bind us up. After two days will he revive us : on the third day he will raise us up, and we shall live before him.*"

The true explanation of this passage is, of course, to be sought in the immediate circumstances and conditions under which Hosea penned them, for they limited his outlook and determined his ideas. The messianic exegetes of the early Church rummaged the Old Testament for passages which even remotely seemed to echo events in a future Messiah's career.

These they took out of their context, misunderstood and even garbled, in order to fit them out as prophecies of Christ. Not seldom the passages thus mangled and misinterpreted generated new details in the evangelical tradition, as we have noticed above, p. 81.

Now, Paul does not say that Jesus was raised in the flesh, and his maxim that corruption cannot inherit incorruption precludes such an idea. He probably believed that Jesus was equipped at the resurrection with an ethereal or, to use the jargon of modern spiritualists, with an astral body; with the uncorrupted body which Adam wore before the fall; with a tunic of incorruption, left behind him in heaven when, descending to earth, he put on sinful flesh, and *was found in semblance and form as a man.*

Exactly how, when, and where arose the Marcan tradition that Jesus's dead body was resuscitated we do not know. But there were many influences at work in the lands that were the cradle of Christianity to suggest it. Josephus (*Antiq.*, xviii. 1, 3) attests that the Pharisees believed that the souls of the just have power to revive and live again, and (*B. J.*, iii. 8, 5) that in the revolution of ages they are sent afresh into pure bodies. We are therefore not surprised that Herod Agrippa, as we read in Mark vi. 14, supposed, when he first heard the fame of Jesus, that he was *John the Baptist raised from the dead*, while his entourage declared him to be Elijah similarly resuscitated. It was believed all over the East a little later on that the slain Nero was still alive and soon to return. Whenever the promised Messiah should appear, the dead, it was believed, would also arise out of their tombs. It was an age, moreover, in which the dead still had to be carefully tended, housed, and regularly furnished with food and drink. Adjoining Syria and Palestine, and through seaborne commerce in daily contact with Rome and Antioch, lay Egypt, where from time immemorial the bodies of the dead had been mummified, to keep them from corruption, in view of a bodily resurrection; and Egypt was full of Greeks and Jews, who had in such matters learned to feel and believe as the ancient Egyptians felt and believed. The Christian belief in a resurrection of the flesh is an ancient Egyptian belief, inherited through various channels. In this connection we may refer to the picture of the resurrection of the righteous found in the book of Enoch. It is summarised by Dr. Charles, in his *Critical History of the Doctrine of a Future Life in Israel, in Judaism, and in Christianity* (p. 188), as follows:—

> The righteous......rise with their bodies; they eat of the tree of life, and thereby enjoy patriarchal lives, in the messianic kingdom on a purified earth, with Jerusalem as its centre. All the Gentiles become righteous, and worship God. In this messianic kingdom, in which there is, however, no Messiah, but the immediate presence of God with men, the felicity of the blessed is of a very sensuous character. The powers of nature are increased indefinitely. Thus the righteous will beget 1,000 children; of all the seed that is sown, each measure will bear 10,000 grains; and each vine will have 10,000 branches, and each branch 10,000 twigs, and each twig 10,000 clusters, and each cluster 10,000 grapes, and each grape twenty-five measures of wine.

"The allowance is liberal," comments Dr. Charles, who adds as follows:—

> We must not, however, neglect the ethical side of

this felicity. Thus "light and joy and peace and wisdom" will be bestowed upon them; and "they will all live, and never again sin either through heedlessness or through pride"; and "their lives will grow old in peace, and the years of their joy will be many in happiness, and the peace of their age all the days of their life."

Such, or nearly such, was the vision of the impending kingdom of God which floated before the fancy of Jesus at the last supper, when he promised his disciples that he would not again drink with them of the fruit of the vine until he should drink it with them newly made in the kingdom of God.

The legend, however, that it was on the third day or after three days that Jesus was raised from the dead, was not generated by prophecy alone; for it was a popular belief that the spirit or soul of a man remains by his corpse for a period of three days—a belief glanced at in the legend of the raising of Lazarus. "*Lord, by this time he stinketh: for he hath been dead four days,*" says Martha, his sister, to Jesus, as soon as the latter orders the stone to be lifted off the tomb. We see that the task of restoring life to the dead was accounted hopeless after the lapse of three days, because by that time corruption had begun its work. Thus Psalm xvi. 10 was generally accepted as a prophecy of the resurrection: "*Thou wilt not leave my soul in Hades, nor allow thy holy one to see corruption*"; but for this to be applicable to Jesus it was essential that he should rise again not later than the third day.

Who buried Jesus? Paul, in his Epistle, 1 Cor. xv. 4, merely says that he was buried. In a speech, however, which either Luke (Acts xiii. 27–31) or Paul's travelling companion sets in his mouth at Antioch of

Pisidia, it is declared that "*they that dwell in Jerusalem and their rulers, who, though they found no cause of death, yet asked of Pilate that he should be slain, when they had fulfilled all things that were written of him, took him down from the tree and laid him in a tomb.*"
It was, then, the unbelieving Jews who buried Jesus, according to this form of the story; and it may well be Paul's own, since in the context we meet with the thoroughly Pauline thought that the text of Psalm ii. 7, "*Thou art my son, this day have I begotten thee,*" is a prophecy, not of the descent of the Spirit and affiliation of Jesus at baptism (see above, p. 172), but of the resurrection, when the Father by the power of the Spirit raised him from the dead, and constituted him Messiah and Son of God. But in his Gospel Luke has followed Mark in a wholly different story, according to which Joseph of Arimathea *boldly went in unto Pilate and asked for the body of Jesus*. Pilate was surprised that death should have supervened so soon; but, having through a centurion assured himself of the fact, gave the body up to Joseph. The latter wrapped it in a linen cloth bought for the purpose, *laid it in a tomb hewn out of the rock, and rolled a stone against the door.*

The Abbé Loisy suggests that Jesus was more probably thrown into the common pit reserved for crucified malefactors, and that the episode of his burial by Joseph was invented by his followers at a later day to save him from the reproach of a dishonourable interment. The words ascribed in Acts xiii. 29 to Paul certainly favour the Abbé's view, and Joseph, if he was *a councillor of honourable estate*—that is, a member of the Sanhedrin—may possibly be identifiable with *them that dwell in Jerusalem and their rulers.* Luke, however (xxiii. 50), is careful to assure us that as *a good man and righteous he had not consented to the plan and deed* of his fellow councillors; and Mark, in adding that he was *expecting the kingdom of God*, hints plainly that he was favourable to Jesus. The Pauline speech, however, cited from Acts expressly identifies those who clamoured for the death of the innocent Messiah with those who took him down from the cross and buried him. Here, then, we have an echo of an earlier tradition, which, since it absolutely contradicts the miraculous story of the empty tomb accepted by the Church, is surely older than it and more genuine.

The tale which follows in Mark was designed to confute the incredulous Jews who denied that Jesus rose from the dead. Mark knows of no one who saw him actually emerge from the tomb; but the same women, *Mary Magdalene, Mary the mother* (in some old texts *daughter*) *of James*, who had, together with Salome, watched Joseph and seen where he laid Jesus, are paraded in the immediate sequel both as witnesses of the empty tomb and as recipients of the message of *a young man, clad in a white robe, sitting to the right hand of it.* He addresses them thus: "*Be not surprised; ye seek Jesus the Nazarene, the Crucified. He is not here. Behold the place where they laid him. But go ye and say to the other disciples and to Peter that he goeth before you into Galilee. There shall ye see him, as he told you.*"

The story-teller, however, has to invent some reason why the women should have been present at the tomb just in time to find it empty. What could bring them there? They went, we are told, with spices in order to anoint the corpse. Matthew, on the contrary, attributes their visit to the mere desire to see the tomb or the body. If the fourth Gospel (xix. 39) is to be credited, Nicodemus and Joseph together had already bound up the body on Friday evening in linen swathes, using 100 litres of myrrh and aloes to anoint the same. It is difficult to understand why the women needed to anoint afresh on Sunday morning a corpse already anointed on Friday in so regal a manner. A hundred litres was nearly equal to a modern hundredweight, a litre being equal to twelve ounces!

Mark's story is full of improbability and self-contradiction. If Joseph rolled against the door of the tomb a stone so large that the three women together despaired of moving it, and that, according to an ancient reading in Luke, it took twenty men together to roll along, he must have done so with a view to the definite and lasting interment of Jesus. When the women reach the tomb on Sunday morning they exclaim, "*Who will roll away for us the stone from the door of the tomb?*" And yet they had seen Joseph (unaided, so it would seem) deposit the stone there on Friday afternoon. Why, then, did they not bring men with them to open the tomb? Why not have informed Joseph, as they watched him bury Jesus, that they intended to come back later on and anoint the corpse? And why wait so long to anoint him? It is not usual, especially in the East, where decay is so rapid, to wait so long. Even if they had to wait until the Sabbath was over—that is, until sunset on Saturday—to buy their spices, why delay another twelve hours before going to the tomb? Evidently the story of the anointing is a clumsy device on the part of the evangelist to get them there at dawn on Sunday, and not before. And why on Sunday? The tradition which fixed for the rising of the Christ from the dead the moment of sunrise on the day of the sun must surely have been generated by the same symbolism which dictated to Luke or his source the hymn of Zacharias, which speaks of

......*the tender mercy of our God,*
Whereby the dayspring from on high shall visit us,
To shine upon them that sit in darkness and in the shadow of death.

The resurrection of Jesus was, as we have seen, the birth of Christ, according to the old belief underlying the passage (Acts xiii. 33) already cited. If Christ so risen was the daystar, when else could he appropriately be born except at the moment of dawn on the Sunday? Guided by the same symbolism, the Church of Rome at a later day deliberately fixed the feast of his physical birth on December 25th, the Mithraic Feast of the birth of the unconquered sun, *dies natalis invicti solis,* as the old pagan calendars term it. The large body of oriental Christians known as Manicheans actually saw in the sun the outward and visible symbol of Christ, and gave corresponding homage to the heavenly body. Augustine of Hippo tells a story of a dispute between an orthodox lady and a Manichean. While it was raging a ray of sunlight penetrated the shutter of their window, and glinted across the floor of the room in which they sat. The orthodox lady instantly jumped up, and, dancing over it, cried, "Behold, I stamp upon your God."

But let us return to Mark's tale. In it the youth in white is the conventional angel. Matthew, however, knew of a slightly variant text which made of him Christ himself. Of this more anon. In spite of this figure's exhortation to the women not to be astonished, "*they went out and fled from the tomb*," beside themselves with fear and trembling, and, so the story ends, "*said nothing to anyone, because they were afraid.*" The message then seems not to have been delivered after all to Peter and the apostles. Nor is it evident how it could be, since they had fled away to Galilee two days before—for that they so fled is a legitimate inference from the words set in the mouth of Jesus in Mark xiv. 27. The last supper was ended, and, having sung a "*hymn, they went forth into the Mount of Olives. And Jesus said to them, Ye shall all be scandalised, for it is written: I will smite the shepherd, and the sheep shall be scattered. But after I have been raised, I will go before you into Galilee.*"

The word *proaxô*, rendered *I will go before*, means not that Jesus started before the disciples, but only that he got there first. The words were perhaps ascribed to Jesus *après coup*, after the event; whether they were or not, nothing short of the actual flight explains their presence in the tradition.

Such was the story as Mark found it to tell. It was designed, firstly, to refute the Jews who denied that Jesus had risen at all from the dead; secondly, to establish that he had risen in the flesh—an idea which, as we have pointed out, was foreign to Paul, but not to the beliefs and outlook of that age. And, thirdly, in the absence of the apostles, this tale provides witnesses to the empty tomb in the persons of the women, who, having followed Jesus all the way from Galilee, might be deemed to be trustworthy.

Let us compare with Mark the story of Matthew, and see how quickly a legend of this kind was amplified and embellished, in answer to objections supposed to be raised by Jewish opponents.

Matthew, then, drops out Mark's statement that Joseph of Arimathea was a member of the Sanhedrin, because he wishes us to suppose that that Jewish council had been unanimous in demanding the death of Jesus; and he ignores Pilate's sending of a centurion to see if Jesus were really dead, for he contemplates an ampler mission of Roman soldiers to the tomb. He is careful to tell us that Joseph chose a *clean* linen cloth to wrap the body in, and that the tomb in which he laid it was *his own new tomb*. So Luke here adds the touch that *never yet had man lain* in the tomb chosen by Joseph. Such elements in the narrative have no chance to be historical, but are due to the same symbolising fancy which leads Mark and Luke to note that in his messianic entry into Jerusalem Jesus, the new Adam of Paul, rode on the back of an ass *whereon no man ever yet sat*. The genuine tradition of Jesus having been cast by his enemies into the common pit reserved for malefactors still survived among the Jews, and the most effective way of meeting it was to assert an honourable interment in a new tomb.

In Mark, then, the tradition has merely got as far as the story of a tomb which three devout women found empty, and of an angel sitting by it, commissioned to reveal to them that Jesus was risen. The growth of the legend could not stop here, and friends and foes alike united to extend it. Jewish critics, real or imaginary, objected that an empty tomb proved little enough, for might not the disciples of Jesus have come by night and stolen the body? Matthew supposes that the Jews foresaw this contingency, and so went in a body to Pilate, recalled to him Jesus's prediction that after three days he would rise again, and petitioned him that "*the sepulchre be made sure until the third day, lest haply his disciples come and steal him away, and say unto the people, He is risen from the dead.*" Pilate accordingly gives them a guard, and they seal the stone. In order to anoint the body the tomb would have to be opened, but this could not be if it was sealed and soldiers set to prevent it. Matthew accordingly pretends that the women came merely from curiosity *to see the sepulchre*, and ignores the flimsy pretext provided by Mark in explanation of their movements—namely, that they desired to anoint Jesus; but in Matthew they arrive at an impossible hour—namely, "*late on the sabbath day, as it began to dawn towards the first day of the week.*" The writer imagines that the sabbath ended at dawn on Sunday morning, so evincing extraordinary ignorance of Jewish reckoning.

However, they arrive in time to witness a conventional earthquake, of the kind defined by Professor Sanday to be "a natural event opportunely timed"; and they see an angel of the Lord descend from heaven, roll away the stone, and sit upon it! In his description of the angel's appearance Matthew betters Mark: "*His appearance was as lightning, and his raiment white as snow.*" The watchers quake, and are dead with fear; but to the women the angel addresses the same exhortation not to fear, etc., as in Mark. Instead, however, of "*saying nothing to any man*" because of their panic, as in Mark, the women in Matthew "*ran to bring the disciples word.*" According to one form of Mark's tradition, the *young man* in white raiment of Mark was Jesus himself, and Matthew tacks this form of the story on to the other, without perceiving it to be a mere doublet. For, so he relates, as the women "*departed quickly from the tomb with fear and great joy, Jesus met them, saying, All hail. They came and took hold of his feet and worshipped him. Then saith Jesus unto them, Fear not: go tell my brethren to depart into Galilee, and there shall they see me.*" Note that the words here assigned to Jesus are in Mark assigned to the young man in white. But— the Jewish unbeliever may be supposed to have objected, when he was told about the guard of Roman soldiers and the sealed tomb—why, if they witnessed the earthquake and other wonderful circumstances of the resurrection, is their testimony not invoked by the Christians? Why do the latter rely exclusively on a handful of scared and ecstatic women? The soldiers were there to see that the disciples did not come and steal the body; nevertheless, this calumny about the stealing "*was spread abroad among the Jews until this day*"—that is, until the time when this last chapter of Matthew was penned. If so, why was the evidence of the soldiers themselves never appealed to by the faithful in refutation of the calumny? If the Christians had their independent testimony to the resurrection, why not use it? Here is another objection which the incredulous Jews may have raised. In order to combat it Matthew invents a fresh episode, and adds it to his story. Some of the soldiers, he tells us, did return to the city, and told the chief priests of all that had happened; and they, having conferred with the elders, paid a large sum in hush-money to the soldiers, saying, "*Say ye, His disciples came by night, and stole him away while we slept. So they took the money, and did as they were taught.*"

This Gospel closes with an apparition of Jesus to the eleven disciples on a mountain in Galilee, where he had arranged to meet them. It is interesting to notice how, in relating this episode, Matthew preserves to us a memory of the doubts entertained about the resurrection among the apostles themselves : "*When they saw him, they worshipped, but some doubted.*" We would like to know if they were ever cured of their doubts. It may, anyhow, be inferred from this passage that the belief in the resurrection did not triumph in a day, or even in a week, and that at the first there were companions of Jesus who were sceptical. Even among Paul's congregation at Corinth, twenty-five years after the crucifixion, there were some who questioned if there be any resurrection of the dead. "*How say some among you that there is no resurrection of the dead?*" he writes in 1 Corinthians xv. 12. But it is not clear whether their doubt extended to the resurrection of Christ, although Paul contends that logically it must do so. In other early documents we hear of similar doubts—*e.g.*, in the Acts of Paul and Thekla, where Demas and Hermogenes, companions of Paul, assert that men find their true resurrection in their children. Hegesippus, an early Christian writer of Palestine, recorded that James, the ascetic and brother of Jesus, made a vow neither to eat nor drink until he had a vision of him risen from the dead. Rigorous fasting is a recognised means of inducing visions, and, as such, is practised among the American Indians and other primitive religionists all over the world.

The tradition which is reported in the last verses of Matthew's Gospel has foreshortened history and cramped into one last scene on an unknown hilltop in Galilee apparitions which, as we know from Paul, were numerous and widely diffused. The same evangelist masses together, in a single sermon on a mountain, precepts delivered by Jesus all through his ministry. In the last scene Jesus, seen in a vision on the same or on some other hilltop, delivers, like the second Moses that Matthew conceives him to be, a last address to his followers. It is, naturally enough, inspired by conceptions of Christ and of his mission which the Church only formed long afterwards—partly under Pauline influence, partly under the assumption, which it did not take a long time for his followers to make, that he was the Son of Man described in Daniel vii. 13. The post-resurrection discourse of Jesus, in Matthew xxviii. 18 foll., is as follows: *"All authority hath been given unto me in heaven and on earth. Go ye, therefore, and make disciples of all the nations in my name* [so Eusebius], *teaching them to observe all things whatsoever I commanded you: and lo, I am with you always, even unto the consummation of the world."* So, in the Septuagint version of Daniel, we read of the Son of Man *" beheld in the night vision "* that there *" was given him authority and kingly honour, and all the nations of the earth, race by race, and all glory worshipping him: and his authority is an agelong authority which shall not be taken away."*

This is not the same Jesus who, in Matthew x. 5–7, forbade his disciples to *" travel in the path of the Gentiles or enter a city of the Samaritans,"* but charged them rather *" to visit the lost sheep of the house of Israel, and to go and preach, saying that the kingdom of heaven is at hand."* Nor are the disciples in this last scene those who, a generation later, are still bitterly opposing Paul's plan of admitting into the kingdom of promise the uncircumcised Gentiles. It is the Church herself that here addresses us in the person of the risen Christ. The aims and aspirations of Christians towards the close of the first century are here attributed to the risen Jesus; and the contrast with the real Jesus is yet greater, if we substitute for the words *in my name*, or *and they shall believe in me*, read here by Eusebius and the Syrian Aphraates, the later interpolation: "*baptising them in the name of the Father, Son, and Holy Spirit.*" It was, indeed, Jesus of Nazareth that died and was buried; but he that rose again was the universalist and divine figure of orthodox Christology, ordaining sacraments and *credenda* altogether alien to the real man of Nazareth.

I will not weary my readers with an equally detailed examination of the forms which the legend of the resurrection assumes in Luke and in the fourth Gospel. I have already pointed out (p. 101) that the former, in open contradiction of Matthew and Mark, makes the city of Jerusalem the scene of the visions of the apostles. He takes from Mark nothing but the tale of the empty tomb and the women, and that he handles in the very free manner in which he always treats his source where it is in conflict with later developments of tradition. The author of the fourth Gospel follows Luke, and, guided by symbolism, or anxious to magnify Jesus, amplifies the legend with sundry new details and episodes. Nor did the mythoplastic imagination of believers rest content with the accounts furnished by the four canonical Gospels. Still ranker growths of legend lie before us in the so-called Gospel of Peter and in the Acts of Pilate.

The former of these two documents was probably composed between 100 and 130, and is, therefore, nearly contemporaneous with the supplementary chapter xxi., added by some editor to the fourth

Gospel. The author of it, who pretends that he is St. Peter, in the same way as the author of the fourth Gospel pretends to be an apostle and eye-witness, used Matthew and Mark; but it is probable that the copy of Mark which was in his hands did not end, where ours does, with the words "*for they were afraid,*" but went on to describe the flight of the apostles back to Galilee and a vision they there had of the risen Jesus.

The most noticeable extension of the resurrection myth made by Peter—as we will term the author of this apocryph—is a picture of the actual resurrection of Jesus from the tomb. The earlier tradition was felt to be faulty and imperfect, in so far as it did not narrate the actual exodus of Jesus from his tomb. Following, therefore, the clue afforded by Matthew, Peter makes the Roman guards witnesses of this event, and even associates the elders of the Jews with them, as follows:—

> Now, on the night when the Lord's day was drawing on, as the soldiers kept guard by two and two in a watch, there was a great voice in heaven, and they saw the heavens opened, and two men descend thence with much light and approach the tomb. And the stone which had been laid at the door rolled away of itself and made way in part, and the tomb was opened, and both the young men entered it. The soldiers, therefore, when they saw it, awakened the centurions and the elders (for they were also there keeping watch); and as they told the things that they had seen, again they see three men coming forth from the tomb, two of them supporting the other, and a cross following them; and the head of the two reached to heaven, but that of him who was led by them over-

passed the heavens. And they heard a voice from the heavens, saying, Didst thou preach to them that sleep? And a response was heard from the cross, Yea.

The risen body is of marvellous dimensions, and the tale resembles a legend current among certain Christians of Palestine and related by Epiphanius, that a figure of the risen Jesus was seen in that land so gigantic that when they measured it against a neighbouring mountain it overtopped the same. The talking cross often reappears in early hagiological stories, and it was currently believed in many Eastern churches that Jesus took his cross up into heaven with him, having first deposited therein his soul, as if for safe custody. This last must appear to modern Christians an unnecessary precaution; but they forget that Justin Martyr, in the first half of the second century, believed that when Jesus died the demons of the air were on the watch to waylay his spirit or soul in its heavenward ascent, and would probably have succeeded, had he not prudently entrusted it to the hands of God, "*crying* [as Luke says] *with a loud voice, Father, unto thy hands I commit my spirit.*"

But although Peter, in the passage above cited, excels the New Testament accounts in love of the miraculous, he transmits other more sober details which have more chance to be historical, since they so utterly contradict the later story (preferred by Luke and John), that the first appearances of the risen Jesus to disciples were in Jerusalem. He attests, for example, that Peter, with his fellows, hid themselves when Jesus died, because the Jews were seeking for them as malefactors who were minded to burn the temple. On the last day of the unleavened bread, the feast being at an end, the twelve withdrew to their homes, which were in Galilee, weeping and full of sorrow for that which had happened. Simon Peter, in particular, and Andrew, his brother, took their nets and went to the sea; and there was with them Levi or Matthew, the son of Alphæus.

Here the fragment breaks off, just at the point, evidently, where Jesus was about to appear in a vision to them. Such a vision is described in the appendix to the fourth Gospel, ch. xxi., which begins as follows: "*After these things Jesus manifested himself again to the disciples at the Sea of Galilee. Simon Peter and Thomas called Didymus and Nathaniel of Cana in Galilee, and the sons of Zebedee, and two others of his disciples, were there together, and Simon Peter said to them, I go a fishing. They say unto him, We also come with thee. They went out and entered into the boat.*"

There follows in John an apparition of Jesus while they are fishing. In the preceding chapter (xx.) of this Gospel apparitions in Jerusalem to Mary Magdalene and to the disciples have been narrated. It would seem as if the older tradition of the apostles' flight into Galilee was too persistent to be wholly neglected, and as if some early editor of the fourth Gospel, by way of completing it, added ch. xxi. It is impossible to say whence this editor took his story; the compiler of the Peter Gospel, however, probably took his information from a lost conclusion of Mark, for the fragment closely follows that evangelist in its last paragraphs, as is seen if we juxtapose the two texts:—

MARK xvi. 4–8.	PETER GOSPEL, xi.
And looking up, they see that the stone is rolled back: for it was exceeding great. And entering into the tomb, they saw a	So they went and found the tomb open, and they came near and stooped down to look in there; and they see there a young

young man sitting on the right hand, arrayed in a white robe; and they were amazed. And he said to them, Be not amazed. Ye seek Jesus, the Nazarene, who has been crucified. He is risen. He is not here. Behold the place where they laid him. But go, tell his disciples and Peter, He goeth before you into Galilee: there shall ye see him, as he said unto you. And they went out, and fled from the tomb; for trembling and stupor had come upon them; and they said nothing to anyone; for they were afraid.

man sitting in the midst of the tomb, fair and clothed with a robe exceeding bright, who said to them, Wherefore have ye come? Whom seek ye? Him who was crucified? He is risen and gone. But if ye believe not, stoop down and look in and see the place where he lay, for he is not here; for he is risen and gone thither whence he was sent. Then the women fled, being afraid.

xii.

Now it was the last day of unleavened bread, and many went out of the city, returning to their houses, the feast being at an end. And we, the twelve disciples of the Lord, wept and were in sorrow; and everyone retired to his home, sorrowing for what had happened. But I, Simon Peter, and Andrew my brother took our nets and went to the sea; and there was with us Levi, the son of Alphæus, whom the Lord....

We see how closely pseudo-Peter follows Mark as far as the words *"for they were afraid,"* with which his text as we have it ends; and this makes it very probable that the sequel, ch. xii., is matter derived from the same source. The end of Mark may very well have been mutilated by someone who disliked its subject-matter, and preferred to believe that all the apparitions of Jesus took place in the holy city to apostles and faithful ones who, being full of faith and undismayed by the tragic end of their Messiah, had never fled back to Galilee at all. The evangelist Luke satisfies the conditions, and it is not impossible that, if the Gospel of Mark was really mutilated, as most scholars opine that it was, he was the offender; and that all our copies have come down from the single one which he thus mutilated. This supposition accords with the animus against Mark which Professor Harnack detects in his writings.

The account of the resurrection in the *Acta Pilati* deserves more attention than it has received, for it adheres closely to the story as we have it in Matthew and Mark, altogether discarding the story of the apparitions in Jerusalem related in the third and fourth Gospels. No more than one apparition is attested in Galilee, on the top of a mountain of which the name is variously given in the MSS. as Mamilch, Mambêch, Malêk, Mofêk, or Monfê.

CHAPTER XVI.

BAPTISM

THE church-goer of to-day, whose horizon is limited by the Book of Common Prayer, finds it hard to understand that the Church was not always such as he sees it—namely, an organised body of which all members hold certain cut-and-dried opinions embodied in written creeds; in which bishops and clergy conduct services and administer sacraments according to prescribed forms; of which every member is initiated at birth by a rite of baptism, and sealed or confirmed, at twelve to sixteen years of age, by imposition of the episcopal hand.

In the first age charity and fervour took the place of creeds and organisation. The words, "*Yea, I come quickly. Amen; come, Lord Jesus,*" form the closing message of the book of Revelation, written about A.D. 93, and are the last in the New Testament. They express the ethos of the earliest believers. For a community intoxicated with such a belief there were needed, not bishops and priests, but apostles and prophets; and these they had. In the first age we barely hear of bishops or overseers, and that only in contexts which imply that they were not distinguished from the presbyters or elders in the faith. Bishops, or overseers—for such is the meaning of the word—were officers appointed to watch over and administer the funds contributed by the richer converts for the support of widows and orphans, and to represent the particular congregation in its relations with the outside world. Their prestige waxed as that of the primitive prophets and teachers waned; and they soon aspired to be guardians of doctrine no less than to keep the bag or alms-chest, as Judas Iscariot is reputed to have done for the circle of Jesus, so becoming the first Christian bishop, though not the last of them to betray his master.

If we examine the oldest ritual texts of the Christians, we find that their rite of initiation was made up of three chief steps. On the eighth day after birth a child was taken to the porch, or *narthex*, of the church, and the priest or elder—in some churches making the sign of the cross on its brow, in others not—gave it a Christian name—that is, a name not taken from the pagan mythology; he also offered up a brief prayer that it might be rightly and religiously trained by its parents, and be vouchsafed health and strength to grow up until it should reach the right and fitting age to receive baptism and gain admission into the Church. This rite, which among Gentile converts replaced Jewish circumcision, and which corresponds to the old custom of fating children—*i.e.*, to their dedication to the household gods and fairies—is entitled the rite of sealing, or of giving to a child a name. Thus consecrated, a child might die with impunity: the malignant spirits which haunt the air could not snatch its soul.

This rite was followed, on the fortieth day, by that of *churching* the child. The stain of birth and parturition was now supposed to have vanished from mother and child alike. Consequently, she also was now allowed to enter the church, which her presence no longer soiled; she carried her baby up to the steps of the altar, and the priest, laying his hands on their heads, offered up one or two more prayers similar in purport to the one already used in the rite of name-giving. This rite corresponded to the presentation of Jesus in the temple, described in the second chapter of Luke; and the prayers recited commemorated that incident.

Years are now to elapse before the rite of baptism proper is undergone. The child is, in a loose sense, a catechumen. It will rest with him to choose the fitting moment for his full initiation. Probably puberty will be reached and left behind long before that moment arrives. Tertullian, in his treatise on baptism, exhorts the faithful to get over the business of marriage and propagation of children before they incur the awful responsibilities of baptism. This was about A.D. 200. He complains that a custom was growing up of admitting girls and boys to baptism, merely because they clamoured for it. Those, however, who favoured their admission never contemplated the baptism of speechless and unconscious babies, for they quoted the text (Matthew vii. 7) : "*Ask, and it shall be given you; seek, and ye shall find; knock, and it shall be opened to you: for everyone that asketh receiveth; and he that seeketh findeth; and to him that knocketh it shall be opened.*" Tertullian replies that people must be of an age not merely to ask, but to understand what they ask for. He dwells on the *pondus sacramenti*—the weighty character of this sacrament—and asks: "*Quid innocens aetas festinat ad remissionem peccatorum?*"—"Why should innocent children be in a hurry to have their sins remitted?" A century and a half later, when Augustine, a boy of fourteen, clamoured in illness to be baptised, his very conservative mother, Veronica, bade him wait till he was older and had acquired a deeper sense of responsibility. Her counsel prevailed, and he waited until he was perhaps married, and anyhow past thirty, for that, as the age at which Jesus was baptised, was regarded as the most suitable by the old-fashioned pietists of the fourth century. Many, however, put baptism off until the deathbed, like Augustine's friend Verecundus, who esteemed marriage incompatible with the state of grace. But there was held to be a risk in deferring it so late; for some who did so were, after all, unable to receive it, because their tongues were paralysed and unable to make the responses, or their minds wandering and unable to grasp the meaning of the words. Gregory of Nazianzen and other preachers of that age constantly warn their flocks of such dangers, and the former goes so far as to recommend baptism for children who have reached their third birthday; for, he says, at that age they can speak clearly, so as to make the responses and understand what is said. Here we note a change of attitude since the age of Tertullian; and a very few generations after Gregory infants were regularly baptised in the Greek Church on the fortieth day. This change was, no doubt, due to the solicitations of mothers, anxious that their children should, as soon as possible, undergo a rite which protected them from the demons which specially beset infancy, and from the possible prejudice of malign constellations; for the power of the stars over an individual ceased abruptly at the moment of baptism.

The rite of baptism proper fell into two halves— the washing with water for remission of sins, corresponding to the baptism of John the Baptist, and the rite of receiving the holy spirit by imposition of hands, to which was added later on anointing with holy oil. Jesus himself was supposed in Jordan to have received the sevenfold grace of the spirit, and to have handed it on, in the form of the Consoling Spirit or Paraclete, to his disciples. They, by imposition of hands, passed the gift on to the faithful at large. Many of the medieval dissenters, known as the *Cathari* or *Puritans*, retained this second half alone of the baptismal rite, and called it *consolamentum*, or the rite of consoling. Except in the case of their leaders or bishops, they put it off until the deathbed, so adhering to an early custom. In the high society of the Middle Ages the old rite of adult baptism seems to have lived on, only laicised, in the initiatory rite of chivalry. For the young squire who aspired to knighthood was first stripped and immersed in a bath of purification. Emerging therefrom, he was clad in a white tunic, a red robe, and a white coif. A rigorous fast of twenty-four hours followed, and he passed the night in church, praying alone or in company with a priest and his sponsors. The next morning he went to confession, and then received the sacrament.

The surviving documents of the third and fourth century enable us to picture to ourselves the rite as it was in those ages. The candidate waited for the season of the Epiphany or Easter feast, the one of which commemorated the baptism, the other the death, of Jesus. He needed two sponsors to bear witness that he was a person of sober and virtuous life, led on to enter the Church, not by hope of gain or temporal advantages, but by spiritual inward call; not under compulsion, but of his own free will. Armed with such credentials, he approached the bishop, and inscribed his name seven weeks or so before the feast-day. He was then handed over to an exorcist, who, laying hands on his head, blew in his face, and so rid him of evil spirits. Then for weeks he attended the lectures of a catechist, who instructed him in the monotheistic views of the world and creation, and in Christian doctrine and practice. Thus prepared, the candidate became a *competens*, or asker for baptism. Hence our word " competent," in the sense of a duly qualified person. More than one collection of such lectures survives. Throughout the period of preparation the catechumen had to give himself up to fasting and prayer. On the eve of Easter Sunday, or on the day of Epiphany, the candidate was stripped stark naked, and led down by the deacon, or if a woman by the deaconess, into the font, generally a shallow basin through which ran living water. In the Greek and Roman Churches he turned first to the west, and thrice solemnly renounced Satan and his angels and works. Then, turning to the east, he thrice vowed to side henceforth with Christ. The priest then poured three handfulls of water over his head, and perhaps immersed him thrice as well. Such triple affusion or immersion was customary in ancient lustrations, as many ancient authors testify. Thus Aristotle, in his book *On the Heavens*, i., p. 268, wrote thus: " Having received, as it were, from heaven the number three, we use it in the holy rites of religion." And an old scholiast, Acro, explains the phrase " *thrice purely*," used by Horace, by saying that " those who would expiate their sins must dip themselves thrice." And an old Greek writer, Eratosthenes (c. 240 B.C.), remarks that " the gods vouchsafe moral improvement to those who have thrice wiped themselves clean." It is evident, then, that the Christians adopted it from the pagans; but they interpreted

it symbolically, discerning in it, in the Eastern
Churches, a commemoration of the three days passed
by Jesus in the tomb ; in the West, an act of homage
to the triple name of Father, Son, and Holy Ghost,
in which, except in a few outlying Churches, like the
early Armenian and Celtic, baptism soon came to be
administered. The candidate repeated some form of
creed, dictated to him by the priest, who recited
appropriate prayers, in which it was particularly
mentioned that the candidate had come of his own
free will, and under no compulsion, to baptism. His
inward call and impulse was an essential condition.

Confirmation, or reception of the spirit, generally
followed as a completion of the baptism with water. The
bishop and deacon smeared, with consecrated oil, the
candidate's organs of sense, as well as certain other
parts of his person ; the bishop's hand was laid on
his head, and, in response to proper invocations, the
holy or pure spirit was supposed to enter into him.
Meanwhile, he was robed in white, in token that he
was liberated from Satan, and a crown set on his
head. This he wore for eight days, when he returned
to the church, where the priest, with fresh prayers,
lifted it off.

The earliest rubrics enjoin the use of live or
running water in baptism, for the orientals think
it important that in lustrations the water should
incessantly run past and off the body, so as to carry
away the physical contamination of sin. Still and
stagnant water did not suffice. In the third century
still water stored in a receptacle was permitted, but
not until it had been consecrated, the evil spirit being
expelled and the pure induced by adjurations and
invocations of the name of Christ or of the Trinity.

320 BAPTISM

For the pure spirit, like the impure, was conceived of as an attenuated form of matter, like vapour or smoke, and was held to be dissolved in the water like salt, or, as we should say, held in suspension. The oil used in confirmation or sealing was, in the same way, a solution of holy spirit. The object of anointing the organs of sense was probably to block them against the evil spirit; hence the use of the word *to seal.* For, in the East, a jar of wine is kept good by floating a little oil on the top of it, in the neck or narrow spout; and this use of oil may have suggested the rites of anointing, common to pagan and Christian alike. Salt was exorcised in the same way as water and oil, and occasionally mixed with the eucharistic bread. In ancient sacrifice it was similarly used. All these uses were borrowed direct from earlier religions.

We have dwelt on the tendency shown in the early centuries to put off baptism. It was greatly due to the belief that mortal sin, committed after baptism, could no longer be expiated. Such a sinner put himself outside the Church, which could never again receive him into its bosom. For him there was no second repentance, no hope of salvation: he was eternally lost. This Draconian view of baptism prevailed already in the first century, and is inculcated in the Epistle to the Hebrews, vi. 4–8 and x. 26–27, in the former of which passages we read this:—
" *For as touching those who have once been illuminated* (*i.e.*, baptised) *and have tasted the heavenly gift, and been made partakers of the Holy Ghost, and have tasted the goodness of God's word and the powers of the age to come, but have then fallen away, it is impossible to renew them again unto repentance. Like a field which, in*

spite of the copious rains of heaven, brings forth not herbs useful for them that tilled it, but only thorns and thistles, so these sinners receive no blessing from God, but are rejected and nigh unto a curse; whose end is to be burned." And in the second passage: *"For if we sin wilfully after we have received the knowledge of the truth, there is left no sacrifice for sins, but only a certain awful expectation of judgment, and a fierceness of fire which shall devour the adversaries."*

Such puritanism was too much for human frailty. The baptised, in spite of it, must often have relapsed into idolatry, homicide, fornication, and other sins; and nearly as often have repented. Something had to be done in order to reclaim them and restore them to the Church. Rome, as always, made the change—in this case most necessary, if the Church was to continue to exist. Pope Calixtus, therefore, invented, about 218 A.D., a rite of *Exhomologesis*—*i.e.*, of outright confession—which is yet to be found in some old service-books; *e.g.*, in those of the Armenian Church. It was a repetition of the rite of baptism, of which all the formalities were repeated except the use of water. But this "medicine of repentance," as the rubrics which still exist prescribe, could be used only once. If the Christian relapsed a second time, then he was really lost. Old-fashioned believers, like Tertullian and Hippolytus, railed against this innovation, which yet later generations found insufficient. Re-admission but once was not enough for sinners, and it was found necessary to permit it a second and third and fourth time; and finally it became the existing sacrament of penitence, which is inspired by the very convenient and roomy doctrine that, no matter how often and how wilfully a man sins, he can always, by confession and penance, expiate his guilt and be reconciled to the Church.

Such was baptism in the primitive Church. So far as water—and, later on, holy oil—entered into the rite, it was analogous to the magical purificatory rites of other religions; but, in other respects, it was the expression of a lofty ideal, and in profound contrast with the later travesty of itself known as child-baptism. In the early Church the baptised formed, as it were, an aristocracy of picked individuals, who had voluntarily renounced the world and, like the sages in the Platonic Republic, dedicated themselves to the higher life. The professional clergy could not, under such conditions, stand out in relief against the laity as they did later on. The beginnings of clerical orders are obscure; but it would seem as if, at the first, priestly ordination, which was by laying on of hands, was no other than that rite of sealing with the spirit which constitutes the second half of the baptismal rite. The idea of one man transmitting to others a special spiritual value through his finger-tips laid on their heads is common to many primitive religions; and the belief which underlies Christian confirmation and ordination meets us in other religions. In the old Hebrew religion of sacrifice an animal was devoted by the priest laying his hands on its head before its life-blood was shed on the altar. More than one idea was at work in such imposition of hands. The sins of the people might be translated or transferred to the victim, which would then, like the scapegoat, be turned adrift in the desert, or sold to the nation's enemies. Or, instead of sin, it might be a spirit of wisdom or holiness which was so communicated. Thus, in Deuteronomy xxxiv. 9, Moses laid his hands upon Joshua and imparted to him the spirit of wisdom. Such imposition might also serve just to identify the parties with one another. In Acts viii. 17 the apostles Peter and John lay their hands on converts, who instantly receive the holy spirit. In Acts xix. 6 the same rite induces, together with the spirit, speaking with tongues and prophesying. In Mithraic bas-reliefs Mithras lays his left hand on the head of a human figure representing the sun. In savage religions a most dangerous supernatural influence, or *mana*, is turned upon and into one who incautiously touches a chieftain charged therewith.

The holy spirit could also be communicated by blowing, and so in John xx. 22 Jesus *breathed on* the disciples and said: "*Receive ye the holy spirit: whose soever sins ye forgive, are forgiven unto them; whose soever sins ye retain, they are retained.*" In the Hermetic papyrus, edited by the late Professor Dieterich (Leipzig, 1903—*Eine Mithrasliturgie*), the votary addresses the sun-god thus: "O Sun, Lord of heaven and earth, god of gods, thy breath is powerful, powerful also thy might." And also thus: "May I be in mind born again, may I be hallowed and the holy spirit breathe in me."

Similar in origin is the priest's use of the extended hand in blessing a congregation. Examples of such a use of the hand meet us again and again in our anthropological studies and in folk-lore. The use of extended hand and pointed finger to-day in Italy to ward off the evil eye—a compendious name for all devilish influences—has come down from a remote antiquity. In many museums we have preserved models of hands with the fingers extended in the same way as an orthodox priest to-day extends them.

These were amulets to keep off demons. Ovid, in his *Fasti*, describes how the ancient head of a household scared away the demons of the unburied dead from his house by pointing his joined fingers and thumb at them, while someone else rattled the brass cauldrons. The gesture of the Christian priest has the same pedigree. He nominally blesses the congregation. In reality, he is pointing off the demons, as a Neapolitan with his finger or coral hand points off the evil eye.

In ancient Lycia there was a local cult of Zeus Sebazios, whom the Jewish colonists of that part of Asia Minor identified with the god of Sabaoth on account of the similarity of title. This cult spread westwards in the Roman epoch, and with it the ritual use, perhaps for healing purposes, of votive arms and hand. The arm is given from the elbow downwards, and the hand and fingers exactly reproduce the gesture made by a Greek orthodox priest in the act of blessing. It is supposed that it was through Jewish channels that this gesture came into the Christian Church. In the Middle Ages metal reliquaries, to contain the remains of saints, were made exactly on this device; and these may have been used to point off or avert demonic agencies and influence. The cornelian stone in a bishop's ring had the same meaning, for the cornelian stone is a great prophylactic against demons. I have traced back this belief among Christians as early as about A.D. 430. The ring in itself has a magical use of the same kind, and one of the three great relics kissed by Christian pilgrims to Jerusalem in the fourth century was the ring with which King Solomon controlled the demons and forced them to help him build his temple. The other

two relics were the true cross and the column of
scourging. The latter is now shown in the church
of St. Pudenziana at Rome. It is made of green
travertine; but when St. Chrysostom saw it in
Jerusalem about A.D. 400 it was made of wood.

One other circumstance is noteworthy in connection with the degeneration of the primitive baptism
into the lifeless and superstitious *opus operatum*
which, except among the Baptist sects, it is to-day.
It degenerated exactly as the modern orthodox
Christology grew up. We have seen how, in the
synoptic Gospels, the descent of the spirit upon Jesus
is regarded as the moment of his becoming the
Messiah and Son of God. Presently the legend of
the miraculous birth was diffused, and paved the way
for a new apprehension of divine sonship, according
to which he was Son of God and Messiah from the
moment in which the holy spirit impregnated his
mother. This new point of view, of course, emptied
the story of his baptism of all sense and meaning; for
if he was God incarnate from the first moment when
he was conceived, what was added to him by the
illumination in Jordan? He did not need it, and it
merely overloaded him.

Thus Archelaus, Bishop of Kharkhar, a champion
of Eastern orthodoxy, about A.D. 300, in an imaginary
dialogue with Mani, who deified Jesus to the extent of
denying his humanity altogether, says: "Tell me on
whom it was that the holy Spirit descended as a dove?
Who is it, too, that is baptised by John? If he was
already perfect, if he was already Son of God, if he
was already the power of God, it was impossible for
the Spirit to enter him; as impossible as it would be

for kingship to enter kingship." "Among men born of women," he continues, "Jesus was as inferior to John, who baptised him, as he was superior to him in the kingdom of heaven."

In other words, Jesus was a mere man born of men until the descent of the spirit constituted him the Elect Son of God and first-born in the kingdom of heaven. The dialogue assumes that he was really the son of Joseph, and Mani attributes this view uncontradicted to his orthodox opponent. "To me," says Mani, "it seems more reverent to suppose that the Son of God did not need anything to facilitate his advent upon earth; that he could have done without the dove and the baptism, without a mother and brethren, perhaps even without a father, who, according to you, was Joseph."

The new Christology, however, accustomed men to regard the working of the spirit, not as an inward development of the mind and heart, but as a process mechanical and external to the self, like any of the natural processes by which the organism is built up in the womb. This is what is meant by the Latin phrase *opus operatum*—i.e., a *work performed*, without the conscious co-operation of the individual's self. But if the spirit worked thus in the case of Jesus Christ, why not in the case of his followers? Why wait until a child could speak, act, and think for itself, in order to baptise it? Why not perform the rite immediately after birth? Thus the baptism of Jesus and the baptism of believers lost their primitive meaning *pari passu*, and together. The former came to be regarded as a mere pantomime which signified no spiritual advance, growth, or promotion of Jesus. The latter became a bit of idle magic, a washing with water bewitched and a greasing with oil enchanted. No room was left for the idea of a convert self-regenerated and renewed through active repentance of sin and profession of faith. It is marvellous to hear modern divines railing against the Jews for their superstitious retention of the rite of circumcision, and, at the same time, insisting for new-born babes upon a rite every whit as superstitious, and even physically useless, which circumcision probably is not.

One other point merits notice. Jesus himself insisted, not on baptism, but on faith in the kingdom about to be revealed. His immediate followers, however, continued the baptism of John, and, according to traditional Jewish custom, insisted upon it as a first step in the moral reformation which prepared men for the kingdom. Soon it was found that impostors and heretics could baptise in the name of Jesus, or in that of Father, Son, and Holy Ghost, just as much as the Catholics; in the same way as already during Jesus's lifetime others than his followers had been found to exploit his name. But, if the sacraments thus carried the Church, instead of the Church the sacraments, how were heretics and impostors to be kept out of it? The Roman Church in the second century, as against the Eastern communions, made the question doubly acute by deciding that the baptism of heretics was valid so long as it was administered even with the shorter formula "in the name of Jesus Christ." The difficulty was got over finally by augmenting the power and authority of the bishops, the visible heads of the congregations, and by commissioning them to exclude heretics from church union even though they were correctly baptised. Thus the importance originally attached to continuity of baptism came to be attached to continuity of bishops; and each orthodox Church tried to trace back the succession or *diadoché* of its bishops to an apostle. By way of checking still further the infiltration of heretics, the rite of laying hands on the baptised, or confirming them with the gift of the spirit, was reserved to the bishops alone; and the episcopate itself was at a later time still further hedged round by the rule that presbyters should not consecrate a bishop, but only fellow-bishops.

Chapter XVII.

MARCION

Darwin, in his autobiography, penned no more memorable passage than the following:

> I had gradually come by this time—*i.e.*, 1836 to 1839—to see that the Old Testament was no more to be trusted than the sacred books of the Hindoos. The question then continually rose before my mind, and would not be banished, Is it credible that, if God were now to make a revelation to the Hindoos, he would permit it to be connected with the belief in Vishnu, Siva, etc., as Christianity is connected with the Old Testament? This appeared to me utterly incredible.

Darwin's life was given up to more important researches; yet, if he had had leisure for incursions into the domain of Church history, how pleased he would have been to find that, in the opinions he here broaches, he had been anticipated in the second century by one Marcion, a converted pagan and the greatest anti-Semite of antiquity!

It is unlikely that the latter approached the new religion by the path of Jewish proselytism. He seems, rather, like most of those to whom Paul turned in his later missionary work, to have passed direct from paganism to Pauline Christianity. Marcion went through no intermediate stage of initiation in Jewish monotheism, of disciplined respect for the Jewish scriptures; no such training obscured for him the abrupt contrast between the Sermon on the Mount and the dispensation of Jahveh.

This contrast seemed to him so absolute that he denied any affinity of the spirit whom the Jews adored, and who inspired their scriptures, with the god who appeared on earth in the guise of Jesus. The former was a just god, indeed, visiting the sins of the fathers on their children; a jealous god, devoid of compassion for those who infringed his harsh law and barbaric prescriptions. He was also the author of Nature; for Nature's laws, like Jahveh's, are of iron—pitiless against the weak, and often contradictory of themselves. Alike in the history of Jahveh, as it is pictured in the Old Testament, and in nature, " red in tooth and claw with ravine," we have all shades of conduct, ranging from bare justice and resentment to arbitrary malice, from tenacious obstinacy to crass stupidity, but all alike falling short of real goodness.[1]

The ancient Stoics, anxious to rehabilitate and purify the popular religion, had applied the method of allegory to the poems of Homer, which were the old Greek Bible. Whatever was offensive, immoral, or scandalous in the Court of Olympus was interpreted to mean something else than the texts, if literally interpreted, conveyed to the reader's mind. In this way the immoralities of the ancient gods were explained away, and the pious enabled to preserve their respect for texts traditionally holy. The Hellenised Jews of Alexandria followed, in respect of their own scriptures, the example set them by philosophers whose wisdom they had assimilated; and in the Greek version of the Bible executed in the third

[1] I quote from Harnack's *History of Dogma*, bk. i., ch. 5.

and second centuries before Christ not a few of the worst anthropomorphic traits of Jahveh were already glosed over and effaced. As early as 150 B.C. an Alexandrine Jew, named Aristobulus, issued for Gentile reading a commentary on the Pentateuch, in which he at once sought to prove that the Greek philosophers, Pythagoras, Socrates, and Plato, even Homer and Hesiod, had plagiarised the best of their wisdom from Moses, and also explained away such passages as attributed to the Jewish God hands and arms, face and feet, and represented him as coming down and walking about in the Garden of Eden. Philo, a contemporary of Jesus, followed Aristobulus in discarding the literal interpretation of Jahveh's record, especially where it conflicted with the higher notions of divine agency which Greek philosophers had thought out. He even went so far as to condemn as mythical sundry of the more disgraceful episodes in the history of Jahveh and of his prime favourites, the Jewish Patriarchs. In the second and following centuries such allegorisation was the recognised Christian method of Biblical exegesis; and Clement of Alexandria, Origen, Eusebius, Ambrose of Milan, and other Fathers of the Church, appropriated in their commentaries, without acknowledgment, page after page of the Philonean lucubrations.

Yet, after all, the method was a subterfuge, and in reading Philo we are aware of the disquietude of a mind which has already transcended, in religious and moral development, the standpoint of religious books inherited from a relatively barbarous past. Marcion was too honest—shall we not say too sensible?—to tolerate such a subterfuge. How, he asked, can the God who in Exodus demands eye for eye and tooth for tooth be he who, incarnate in Jesus, bids us turn the other cheek to the smiter, love our enemies, and pray for them that persecute us? How can the God who in Deuteronomy addresses his chosen race in the words, "*Thou shalt lend unto many nations, and thou shalt not borrow*," be he who declared, through Jesus, that "*Blessed are the poor, for theirs is the Kingdom of God*"; he from whom we have the precept: "*To one who asks of thee give; and from one who would borrow of thee, turn not away*"?

Marcion, in a book which, to the eternal scandal of the orthodox, he composed and called *Antitheses*, drew out the numerous contrasts and contradictions between the gospel of Jesus and the conduct of Jahveh, whom he denominated the just God in opposition to the good God who inspired Jesus, and whose sole attributes are love and mercy. He did not, of course, question the literal truth of the early chapters of Genesis, in which the creation of man and of the world is described; for, like the rest of the early Christians, he was not competent to distinguish history from fable. To Jahveh, however, as creator, he gave the name of Demiurge, and held that he made not only man's body, but, it would seem, his soul as well. The one and the other were hopelessly evil, and alien to the good God; but the latter's grace and mercy were all the more signally revealed when he set himself to rescue from the burdens of the Jewish law and the abominations of idolatry a human race in whose creation he had taken no part. In his benevolent work of salvation the good God ignored, said Marcion, the self-righteous Pharisaic Jew who, having kept the law, imagined himself to be justified; and addressed himself to the sinful Gentiles, who the more readily accepted his message because they were humble. He came not to call the righteous, but sinners to repentance.

In writing and preaching Marcion was thus at pains to take Jesus out of his Hebrew frame, to detach him from all Jewish associations, and to represent him as having been from the first the universalist teacher which, according to Paul, he became when God raised him from the dead. To those who objected that the twelve apostles kept the law, and represented their Master also as having insisted upon its observance, Marcion replied that the apostles were backsliders, and had falsified the record. He seems to have been acquainted with works of the apostles, possibly genuine, which were more uncompromising in their Judaism than any of the documents which have survived to us. In answer to those who objected that Jesus was born of Jewish parentage, and had been divinely recognised as the Jewish Messiah when John baptised him, Marcion denied all three of these facts. Jesus, he taught, was never born, never baptised, nor ever became the Jewish Messiah foretold by the Hebrew prophets. The latter, in accordance with those prophecies, was, he said, yet to appear and play a purely Jewish *rôle*. It was necessary for Marcion to have a written Gospel for his converts; so he took that of Luke, the companion of Paul, but not without mutilating it and cutting out the stories of the birth and baptism. It was comparatively safe and easy for him to eliminate the legends of Christ's birth and childhood; for, as we have said above, these were no part of the earliest body of evangelical tradition. In trying to suppress, also, the narrative of John's baptism of Jesus, Marcion anticipated the orthodoxy of later generations, which found in that narrative nothing but an awkward tradition needing to be explained away. From the Epistles of Paul, which he was the first to collect together in one book, Marcion excised many passages which violated his ideal of Jesus. At the expense of his theory, however, he admitted the fact of the crucifixion, forgetting that a divinely appointed being, who had dropped straight out of heaven, could hardly undergo crucifixion in the flesh. His Gnostic contemporaries, who denied Jesus to have been born, more consistently held that he was never crucified either; but on this point the teaching of Paul was for Marcion authoritative, and he did not see his way to resist it.

I have dwelt so long on the arguments of Marcion because they are curiously apposite in the present day. The Manicheans, after the extinction of Marcion's Church, continued to diffuse his *Antitheses;* and as late as the end of the thirteenth century thousands of Cathars, as they were called, perished at the stake all over Europe for affirming that the Old Testament was inspired by an evil Demiurge. The Church burned them, but was, nevertheless, so put to shame by their arguments as to withdraw the book as much as possible from the hands of the laity. The so-called reformers of the sixteenth century, having divorced themselves from the unity of the Catholic Church, and being in quest of some authority upon which to base their teaching and discipline, tried to substitute the Bible for the Pope; and thousands of misguided people still imagine that the ends of piety are served by thrusting barbarous translations of the Pentateuch into the hands of savages. Educated Anglicans, however, are visibly uncomfortable about it, and begin to realise that it is hardly appropriate for their white-robed choirs of small boys to be chanting daily such vindictive imprecations as Psalm 137, to take a single example, contains :—

> O daughter of Babylon, that art to be destroyed;
> Happy shall be he, that rewardeth thee,
> As thou hast served us.
> Happy shall he be, that taketh and dasheth thy little ones
> Against the rock.[1]

And what is to be said of such advice as the book of the Proverbs of Solomon supplies (ch. xxiv. 17) ?—

> If thy enemy falleth, exult not over him. And when he is overthrown, be not puffed up, Lest the Lord see it, and it displease him, And he turn away his wrath from him.

What are divines to do? The old methods of allegory are discredited and out of date; and modern Hebrew scholarship, Assyriological research, and the comparative study of religion render it impossible any longer to deny that the compilers of the Pentateuch borrowed their tales from older pagan sources; that before the age of Saul and David the narratives of the Old Testament are almost wholly legendary; and, lastly, that the Hebrew religion of taboo and sacrifice was in any essential manner distinguishable from or superior to similar cults among pagans both ancient and modern.

The Darwinian idea of evolution, so long decried and denied, is at the eleventh hour caught at by these distressed theologians as supplying a way out of their difficulties; and we hear proclaimed from many a

---

[1] Verses 8 and 9, according to the Revised Version.

pulpit a new and strange doctrine—that the Bible is the record of a progressive revelation.

Let us examine this conception. It implies that a being, denominated God, omnipotent and morally perfect, desiring to reveal his nature to mankind, was obliged to do so piecemeal and by slow degrees. Had he flashed upon mankind all at once his full-orbed perfection, it would merely have dazzled their eyes, confounded their faculty of comprehension, and contributed nothing to their moral advance. So he began with humanity, as parents to-day begin with their children, by instructing them in myths and legends, and by initiating them in barbarous rites and cults, such as animal sacrifice, which hinted at and foreshadowed, but did not yet accurately embody, the truer sacramental worship of the Catholic Church. Nor is the talk of progressive revelation confined to one set of religionists; and just as the Catholic pretends that the sacrifice of the Mass is the ultimate stage of religious evolution, so the Calvinist considers it to consist in a belief in Predestination. As taught by the High Church clergy of the Anglican communion, this new conception is a quiet way of discarding much in the Bible that is notoriously at variance with modern ideals of propriety, and of substituting for the authority of the scriptures that of a miracle-working caste. Often in the pulpit, however, old and pious commonplaces about God's Book continue to be repeated which in private conversation are relegated to the intellectual lumber-room. The few among the clergy who have seriously attempted to think it out have begun to discern the logical outcome of their new conception, which is this, that, if the cosmogonic and theological notions of Genesis and Exodus are to be regarded as an early step or stage in a divine but progressive revelation, then no less must be admitted in respect of the old Assyrian and Egyptian religions, the indebtedness to which of the Pentateuch is apparent to modern scholars. Nor can the claim to be similarly imperfect revelations be denied to the religious systems of Persia, India, Greece, and Rome. Thus the title of revealed religion must in the end be accorded to every cult, however savage, that human awe has ever generated; and, instead of there being one chosen people, the Jews, to whom the divine being vouchsafed a knowledge of himself, there have been many. It is idle to pretend that the Pentateuch has a moral standard and value which the works of Confucius or of the Buddhists have not. If we admit lections in church and chapel from the Pentateuch, then why not from other equally worthy sources? I will not deny that much of the Bible is as superior in literary and moral respects to the Zend Avesta as a play of Shakespeare to an ill-written cookery book; I realise that Christianity triumphed over Mithraism, its rival of the second and third centuries, because the latter was weighted with too many myths immoral and inane. But if the Bible triumphed long ago over other sacred literatures just because of its intrinsic superiority, is not that fact a good reason to-day for cancelling in daily worship all passages redolent of the earliest and most barbarous stage of progressive revelation? The evil result of singing and reading out such literature in church and chapel must have impressed every student of the history of religion in Europe. For the persecutor has ever found in the precepts of Jahveh an armoury of cruel texts, justifying by reason of their supposed divine authority the worst excesses of religious fanaticism. The bibliolatry of the reformed Churches was even less humane in its results than the sacerdotalism of Rome.

It is not clear, then, that the theory of a progressive revelation as applied by the clergy is anything more than a lame excuse for adhering to old, but false, weights and measures. It also rests on a fallacy. The full truth, it argues, could not from the first be revealed to man, and God was obliged, if we may use a phrase from mechanics, carefully to dose his revelation. But how many crude conceptions, culled either from the Old Testament or from the New, especially from Paul, and enshrined long ago in catechisms, liturgies, and articles of religion, continue to be thrust upon children, congregations, and curates under the high-sounding title of religious education and divinity? Do we, then, live in the first and barbarous stages of human development, that this should be? Where is the English bishop who has the courage to urge a better way? The one idea of the English higher clergy is rather to keep the Church together; and as this aim entails much quiet suppression of the truth, they sit on their bench in the House of Lords timorous and tongue-tied. The crescent moon is no less bright than the full orb of fourteen nights; but do the fables of the Garden of Eden, of the talking serpent, of the vindictive God punishing his own creatures because they desire knowledge, of Noah and his Ark, give us any light at all? Are they more respectable than the myth of Prometheus chained to the rock by Zeus because he revealed the use of fire to mankind? And yet it is on such fables that the doctrine of human redemption, as formulated by Paul and promulgated in catechisms, reposes. And how is it possible for any educated person of to-day to acquiesce in the hypothesis of a chosen people, acceptable above all others to the creator of heaven and earth? And will not anyone who studies candidly the historical books of the Old Testament exclaim with Marcion " Like creator, like people "? What claim had the Jews to be taken at their own estimate? Did the ancient Assyrians and Egyptians, the Greeks and the Romans, contribute less than they to our science and civilisation? And, after all, is not the very idea of one people being chosen above others, as it is presented in the Old Testament, utterly mythological—on a level with the story of the patronage of Aeneas and the house of Augustus by Venus, or of the Argives by Hera, the spouse of Zeus?

The adversaries of Marcion complained that by separating Jesus from history, by taking his portrait out of its Jewish frame, he effaced all his lineaments and left but an empty shadow. For nine-tenths of early Christian literature consist of a laborious demonstration that Jesus was the promised Messiah foretold by the Jewish prophets; and Marcion, by denying both premise and conclusion, at a single stroke made all this literature idle and superfluous. But does the modern divine do less when he accepts, as he must accept, the results of modern Hebrew scholarship? For this interprets the text of Isaiah and the rest of the prophets by the circumstances and outlook of the ages in which they wrote, and dismisses almost contemptuously the old view that they wrote with their eyes fixed on events which were only to transpire seven or eight hundred years later. If we discard the Jewish idea of a Messiah, as belonging to a lower and exploded stage of progressive revelation, or—what is the same thing—of religious evolution, what meaning is left to the terms Christ and Christians? Is their retention more than make-believe? Our forefathers could honestly call themselves Christians, because they shared with the Jews the old conception of Messiahship; but that conception to-day has been consigned to the lumber-room.

Let us pass on to another aspect of the teaching of Marcion. He was not content to deny that Jahveh was the good God who reveals himself in Jesus. He equally denied the visible, sensible world to be the work of this good God. Here again he touched on a problem which more and more exercises the mind of our own generation, rendering impossible the old facile optimism of Catholic Christianity. The question forces itself on us: Can we, apart from man and the higher animals, especially the mammals, in some of which we discern the rudiments of a conscience, detect anywhere in nature the workings of a mind actuated by love and mercy? Our race has been able to establish a foothold on this earth late in its geological development. But our tenure is frail and precarious; and our origins were as much the result of accident as the emergence of any other form of life. Our mother earth in her frequent convulsions has no respect for our cities and centres of civilisation; and we can easily imagine a cosmic catastrophe, such as a sudden increase or decrease in the solar temperature or the impact of a foreign body, solid or gaseous, on the solar system, which would in a moment carry death and desolation all over our globe. How, moreover, can we reconcile with the conception of a Providence, of a Creator who watches over us as a parent over his children, the great volume of human suffering and disease? We daily see children born maimed, crippled, or tainted with hereditary disease and madness. It is poor comfort to read that God is a jealous god, who visits the sins of the fathers upon the children to the third and fourth generation. It is all too true that they are so visited, but the intelligent and all-powerful being who should be responsible for the infliction of so much suffering upon innocent beings, would be wickeder than the wickedest of our human criminals—would, indeed, be the evil Demiurge that Marcion declared the God of the Jews to be.

Nor is it on the moral side only that the old monotheism is impossible. What sense can we attach to the words in which the Roman Church placed on record, in the so-called Apostles' Creed, its rejection of Marcion's dualism? I mean the words: "I believe in God the Father Almighty, maker of heaven and of earth." The little ones, of course, figure to themselves a stupendously exaggerated man taking matter in quasi-human hands, and fashioning it into this and that. Paul compared the Creator to a potter working clay into vessels, and used the simile in order to demonstrate what is to our minds a wholly unmoral— we would rather say immoral—conception of Deity. God, he declares (Romans ix. 18), "*hath mercy on whom he will, and whom he will he hardeneth.*" The obvious answer is that those who are fashioned to wickedness by their Creator cannot be blamed, for they cannot help being wicked; and this thought arose in Paul's mind, for he continues thus: "*Thou wilt say then unto me, Why doth he still find fault? For who can oppose his will?*" Paul answers the imaginary objector as follows: "*Nay, but, O man, who art thou that bandiest words with God? Shall the thing formed say to him who formed it, Why didst thou make me thus? Or hath not the potter a right over the clay, from the same lump to make one part a vessel unto honour, and another unto dishonour?"*

This idea of an arch-potter or omnipotent agent making the universe will not bear examination. Inside the universe of our experience we can with our hands, and perhaps using tools as well, divert already-existing properties of matter, or contrive new combinations, new actions and reactions, at which unassisted nature would never arrive, but which we require for our needs. But the matter we thus work up into new forms was never formless, and the contemplation of our activity does not really assist us to explain how the universe arose. We merely pay ourselves with words when we talk about the necessity of a First Cause. Inside our experience—that is to say, inside the world—one object or agent or material state causes another; but every such relation of causality is between part and part of the universe, and not between it and a being that is not the universe. I avoid saying a being that is outside the universe, for here again we use a category or way of looking at the matter under discussion which is inadequate. Objects inside our universe or inside our experience (which is the same thing) are outside, as they are also beside, one another. But outside the universe there can be nothing. In other words, space and spatial relations are real, and hold good, inside the universe or inside experience alone. If we think it out, we shall find that no categories under which we can envisage material reality are applicable to the universe as a whole, and we fall into contradictions so soon as we try to apply them. Thus the world as a whole is neither in space nor not in space, neither limited nor unlimited, neither caused nor uncaused, perhaps neither in time nor not in time. It is as difficult to invent formulæ that adequately represent it as to invent similar ones for the mind. The least insufficient way of describing it is to say that it is the known or knowable; and John Stuart Mill was not far wrong in defining matter to be the permanent possibility of sensation. Its *esse* is *percipi*; its reality lies in its being perceived.

To the untutored person this sounds the rankest nonsense, and he will ask: "What, then, becomes of reality when men are asleep or all of them dead?" He has never asked himself the question: "What becomes of colours or sounds or tastes or smells in the absence of a self which sees, hears, tastes, and smells?" The permanence and continuity which we attribute to matter are qualities rather of the knower than of the known, of the percipient than of the perceived. Nor is the difficulty raised about sleep so insoluble as it at first sight seems to be. Our individual selves are continuous across intervals of sleep, for we wake up the same persons we were before, and to the same world. In other words, the self or spirit has not slept, but merely not manifested itself for a time through sensible agencies or percepts to those who kept awake. Death, viewed from a psychological standpoint, is the same fact as sleep. "But," the champion of common sense will object, "where and how was my world before I was born?" I should reply: "Exactly where and as it is when you are asleep. As a self and percipient of a real world, you neither sleep nor die. On the contrary, your judgments have all a universal range; and when you say, 'This earth is round,' or 'The three angles of a triangle are equal to two right angles,' you do not think it necessary to add, 'so long as I am awake,' or 'since I was born.'"

The untutored man, who undertakes, like Dr. Johnson, to refute Bishop Berkeley with the arms of mere common sense, is firmly persuaded that the universe persists as a system in space and time and a complex of contrasts of colour, sound, and so forth, no matter whether he perceives it or not. He is, in a sense, right. But he is also clearly wrong, so far as he makes abstraction of mind and of the work mind has done in construing to him his sensations, in selecting them, and arranging them into an order or cosmos. Mind, the objectifying or world-making faculty of thought, is ever at work in each of us; and to it, as the home and centre of all relations and contrasts, belong, if at all, substance and reality, rather than to the material objects whose entire nature consists of sensible contrasts and relations which are before a self, but not of it. In truth, however, mind and matter, subject and object, can as little exist apart, and have as little meaning in abstraction from each other, as concave and convex. They are two aspects of the one whole. The unity of the world, its common objectivity for you and me, is a mere reflection of the ultimate unity amid diversity of our minds; and as in the speculative sphere we lay down judgments that purport to be universal, so in the moral sphere the conscience at each step enacts rules that hold, not for him who enacts them alone, but for all; for that is what we mean by an action being right and a motive good. It is the expression of a common supersensuous self, which lies at the root of all civil institutions, and enshrines itself in law, written or unwritten. If, then, there be a God, our moral judgments, *pace* St. Paul, are as binding on him as on us. If he offends our elementary feelings of justice and mercy, then he is no God for us, but an evil demon.

Some metaphysicians have spoken of the universal mind which is realising itself in each of us as God. But God is usually conceived as a personal being, and the universal mind, or objectifying, creative thought, which works in us and through us is not a person, as each of us is, but something higher and vaster than all persons. We can perhaps say that the universe consists of a society of spirits, of which some may be more developed than others. More than this we cannot venture to affirm; and there is anyhow no need to suppose that there is one mind immeasurably transcending all the rest. The vulgar conception of a supreme God and Father is a naïve transference to the beyond of the patriarchal sovereignty of an earthly king. We see the animals below us on various rungs of the ladder of mental and moral development, and we cannot without presumption suppose ourselves to have reached the highest. There is, from this point of view, more to be said in favour of polytheism than is usually supposed ; and more of ultimate truth may underlie the Catholic cult of saints than underlies the cold abstractions of Mohammedan theology. The Christians themselves soon found it impossible to acquiesce in a God who is single and solitary, and invented three or four gods. Their only mistake philosophically is that they have not myriads. So far as our experience goes, spirits do not communicate with one another, except through material symbols; but it is no necessity of thought that this should be so. The association of spirits with material bodies, without which they would, so far as we know, co-exist unperceived one by the other, as might men deaf, dumb, and blind, and devoid of a sense even of touch, is perhaps a condition of soul-development; but it is also the evident cause of all those physical pains and discomforts which militate so profoundly against the idea of a monarchical providence, of a creative God both omnipotent and merciful.

We cannot, then, accept to-day the clause of the so-called Apostles' Creed in which the Church of Rome, about the middle of the second century, embodied its protest against Marcion: "*I believe in one God the Father, maker of heaven and earth.*" The visitor to the Vatican, as he traverses the long gallery which leads to the library and collection of sculptures, sees let into the wall, side by side with hundreds of inscriptions, mostly taken from the catacombs, a stone slab, on which are figured in deep incision a girl's upraised hands and forearms, from the elbows downwards. These divide into three columns of unequal breadth the following pathetic inscription: " Procope, lebo [*read* levo] manus contra deum qui me innocentem puellam sustulit quæ vixit annos xx. pos. Proclus." It is the grave-stone of a maiden who thus addresses her betrothed lover: " O Procopius, I raise my hands against God, who has snatched away me, an innocent girl. She lived twenty years." The mourning parent Proclus who raised this monument to his child felt with Marcion that the name of father ill suits a God who tramples on our affections, denies our dearest instincts, and has established in nature a kingdom almost wholly devoid of mercy and truth.

CHAPTER XVIII.

DEVELOPMENT

THOSE who to-day read the New Testament critically, and they are few, are aware of a deep chasm separating it, not only from modern ideas and civilisation, but even from the Churches around them. Differences hardly less profound divide the orthodoxy of the fourth century from the messianic Judaism of the first age. The question, accordingly, arose before the mind of John Henry Newman whether there is not an actual discontinuity between the dogmas of Catholicism and the faith revealed to the saints; and, in order to surmount the difficulty, he invoked the idea of development. The creeds and decisions of the Councils are, he argued, a mere unfolding and rendering explicit of the still unprecise and undefined data revealed to the apostles, and more or less completely enshrined in the Bible; and, in a work entitled *The Development of Christian Doctrine*, he tried to find in the New Testament the germs of later doctrines and customs—of the Trinity, the motherhood of God, the consubstantiality of the Father, Son, and Holy Ghost, of infant baptism, of Purgatory, and so forth.

Such a task seemed possible to Newman, partly because in his day criticism was unborn, partly because he could assume, without risk of contradiction, that the Fourth Gospel was the work of an apostle, and a faithful representation of the personality and teaching of Jesus; nor, in his day, did anyone, in England at least, dream of challenging the Pauline conceptions of the Messiah.

But to-day it is being made every day clearer and more certain that the writings of the New Testament themselves represent an evolution of ideas, beliefs, and traditions which took, in the case of the earliest of the documents some thirty, of the latest nearly a hundred, years.

During this period a hundred influences were at work to mould and amplify the primitive tradition of Jesus; and the four Gospels of our New Testament, and others of which we have but a few fragments, like the Gospel of the Hebrews, of the pseudo-Peter, of the Egyptians, were the result of the process. In our earliest surviving sources, the Gospel of Mark and the non-Marcan document, we can already trace such influences; and the former especially is seen on examination to be a selection from floating popular traditions, made by some credulous person with a bias for miracles. In his scholarly work, *Les Légendes Hagiographiques*, Father Hippolyte Delehaye, S.J. (Brussels, 1905), has a chapter entitled " The *Dossier* of a Saint," in which he shows how the brief and true account given by Eusebius of a martyr named Procopius, who suffered under Diocletian, was added to and recast by the professional compilers of Acts of Saints until it was no longer recognisable. All the stages by which the acts of this saint were exaggerated and falsified lie before us in the different manuscripts; and, if we had not got Eusebius' succinct and sober narrative of his trial and execution, we could hardly venture to affirm that Procopius was a historical personage at all, and not rather a creation of the mythoplastic imagination of hagiographers. The paragraph in which Father Delehaye sums up the difficulties which beset Bollandist editors anxious to winnow out the grain of truth in the Lives of Saints from the chaff of legend is so thoroughly applicable to students of the life of Jesus that I venture to translate it. It is as follows :—

> It is often a very arduous task to establish the title of a saint of the early centuries to the honours of public cult. Even when historical documents are not completely wanting, they have often undergone such alterations, through the combined efforts of legend and hagiographer, that we cannot make use of them without extreme precautions. Nor is our task accomplished when, by a rare bit of luck, the cause of the saint reposes on a relatively well-furnished *dossier;* for it is still incumbent on us to know how to class the pieces which compose it, to interpret them at their just value, to weigh the testimonies, to try to establish the degree of credence which each of them merits. Here we have a task both lengthy and of infinite delicacy, in the discharge of which many a pitfall awaits the novice in criticism who is insufficiently familiarised with hagiography.

Neither Jesus nor his disciples came before their public with cut-and-dried creeds, in the faithful reception of which lay a man's chance of salvation. One all-constraining belief alone possessed them—namely, that a mighty upheaval was at hand, that the divine father, in his omnipotence, was about to bring this age to an end and inaugurate for the Jews a new era of salvation. Luke (xix. 11), following a true tradition, assures us that, as Jesus with his disciples drew "*nigh to Jerusalem,*" in order to keep the Passover in the course of which he was destined to perish, "*they supposed that the Kingdom of God was immediately to appear."* Jesus had already, perhaps, gained the conviction that he was the Messiah, the man sent from God to inaugurate the new era, to part the sheep from the goats in the final judgment, to choose the elect from among the living, and to welcome, as they rose from their graves, the saints who slept. As Jesus conceived of the new kingdom, it was primarily a deliverance of Israel; yet not all Jews were to participate therein, but only those who had harkened to his own and to John the Baptist's summons to repentance. Thus although the promises had been made to Jews alone, yet the latter really lost their birthright so soon as moral qualifications began to be insisted upon by the judge. It was in this limitation of the future blessedness to those who had repented, and so won forgiveness of their sins, that lay the possibility and hope— nay, the necessity—of admitting the Gentiles. Their interests, however, almost certainly lay beyond Jesus's horizon. He was neither for nor against them, and just did not consider them at all. He can only be said to have made room for their admission in so far as his ideal state was to include those Jews alone who listened to his warnings, repented of their sins, and made their own in all purity of heart his ideal of a heavenly father who is merciful and loving.

So long as Jesus was alive the hopes of his followers must have been focussed on the new era about to be miraculously brought into being, rather than on him and his personality. He was to preside over it, indeed, when it came, to fill the chief throne, round which would be grouped the lesser thrones of his twelve apostles judging the twelve tribes of Israel; but he was the Messiah in promise only during the preliminary stage in which he was proclaiming its advent and preparing men morally for its membership. Some students, like the late Dr. Martineau, have argued that Jesus never regarded himself as the Messiah nor wished his followers to acknowledge him as such; but the evidence to the contrary is overwhelming. He was sentenced by Pilate in his quality as King of the Jews, or Messiah; and, without the prior conviction that he was such, his disciples could never have recovered from the shock of his death and have transformed their old faith in him into the new conviction that the divine father had raised him up into heaven, whence he was to come again and inaugurate the new kingdom.

Jesus, as he went up to Jerusalem, may well have had misgivings, for he must have been well aware that he had to face in Pontius Pilate a notoriously stern and merciless administrator, little inclined to be just or merciful towards Messiahs and messianic movements, but rather discerning in them a danger to the Roman Empire. Jesus's own attitude to the Roman authority was purely negative: "*Give unto Cæsar the things which are Cæsar's, and to God the things which are God's.*" He was not for taking up arms against it, as Judas the Galilean had done. There was no need to do so, for would not Jehovah, in good time, quietly brush it aside?

His death took his disciples by surprise, for they had not in the least foreseen it, or they could not have "*supposed that the kingdom was immediately to appear.*" Tradition, it is true, soon ascribed to Jesus himself discourses in which his death and resurrection after three days were elaborately foretold; but the evangelist, even while he reports these conversations, hints at the real truth when he adds (Mark ix. 10) that "*they kept the saying to themselves, questioning among themselves what the rising again from the dead should mean.*" It was only when his death overtook them, and visions of a Messiah cut off in his prime, and forsaken by themselves in the hour of need, began to haunt their remorseful imaginations, that they discovered his passion and death to be necessary moments in the scheme of Israel's salvation, duly foretold by Isaiah and the rest of the prophets. Even at the last supper, as we have seen above (p. 268), Jesus did not foresee his death. His visionary expectations of the advent of the kingdom had then reached their climax. He had been acclaimed Messiah by the multitude as he entered the holy city. Could Providence tarry any longer? He was so certain that the glorious consummation was imminent as to assure his disciples that this was the last time he would drink with them under the old conditions "*of the fruit of the vine. I will no more drink*" thereof, he says, "*until the day when I drink it new in the Kingdom of God.*" He does not know that his death is to intervene between then and now. When, therefore, the blow fell, it became incumbent on his followers either to resign their hope and abandon the movement for which they had given up all, or to modify the messianic scheme and make room in it for the crucifixion and death of their Messiah. They quickly took the latter course. New prophecies were invoked, of a kind to prove that the disgraceful death on the cross, which the unbelieving of their compatriots cast in their teeth, was foreordained of God, as a necessary episode in the working out of the scheme of Israel's salvation. The Messiah had all along been predestined to die and be raised from the dead to the right hand of the father, thence to return in glory and set up on a rejuvenated earth his eternal kingdom.

The minds of believers were already busy in this direction, when the persecutor Paul joined forces with them—a host in himself; for he soon discovered a new significance in the Christ's death, that of an expiatory and final sacrifice for the sins of mankind. Philo had long before taught that the just man is a ransom for the many, so that Paul merely made application to Jesus of an idea already current. Nevertheless, it was a stroke of genius; for it enlisted in behalf of the new messianic movement old sacrificial beliefs common to Jew and Gentile alike, and prepared Christians to regard as of providential design the subsequent destruction by Titus of the Jewish temple, with its pomp of burnt-offerings. Henceforth the crucifixion was nothing to be ashamed of; Paul openly gloried in it, and the author of the Fourth Gospel regarded it as the final glorification of Jesus. It is obvious, then, that Jesus himself had no idea of founding a new religion, much less of founding, like Mahomet, a book religion. He was devoured with the expectation of a divine kingdom, which he believed was to be miraculously set up on this earth before his own and his disciples' eyes, even within the lifetime of the generation that listened to him. His one desire was to gain over men's minds to this belief, and persuade them to repent and lead a new life before it was too late. He did not profess to reveal new rules and precepts for men's guidance in this present life, viewed as permanent and assured; for his own conviction, like that of his apostles and followers, was that which Paul expresses in the words:

"*But this I say, brethren, the time is shortened......the fashion of this world passeth away*" (1 Corinthians vii. 29, 31). The end was to come "*like a thief in the night,*" and the most one could do was "*to watch and pray.*" Marriage, family ties, property, law, police —nay, life itself—were all to be sacrificed and abandoned if, and in so far as, they stood in the way of the soul's preparation for the great event impending. To his own apostles Jesus said (Matthew x. 23) : "*Verily I say unto you, ye shall not have gone through the cities of Israel before the son of man come.*"

After the death of Jesus his disciples continued to proclaim that he must soon and suddenly return on clouds of glory from heaven and restore the kingdom to Israel. Following in his steps, they insisted on the necessity of repentance and moral preparation for the new era. This was the wedding-garment without which men would be excluded from the marriage-feast. But weeks turned into months, months into years, years into generations ; yet nothing happened. Meanwhile there was born of the waiting the church or *ecclesia*, organised under presbyters or bishops, fenced off from the world with catechumenate and baptism, fed with eucharist and agapé, endowed throughout its members with gifts and graces of the holy spirit.

And it is not perhaps untrue to say that the death of Jesus engendered Christology ; for his personality occupied a larger space in men's minds, and had more significance attached to it in the scheme of salvation, after his death than before it. In his earthly career he had been herald rather than agent. He had come in weakness and humility, but now was to come in glory and power. The legend of his Davidic pedigree was now added to the tradition, and also, though much later on, that of his miraculous birth. It also devolved on the teachers of the Church to demonstrate from the Old Testament prophecies that his death was part of a pre-arranged scheme, and that he was himself a pre-existent heavenly being temporarily revealed in our sinful flesh, then withdrawn to heaven, thence to re-appear in glory at the consummation or end of the age. Paul further discovered him to be the heavenly Adam and the Wisdom and Power of God — conceptions which figure largely in the Sapiential books and in the theosophy of Philo. In the so-called Pastoral Epistles he is declared to be the mediator between God and man—an idea equally found in Philo; and this train of speculation was crowned towards the end of the century by the declaration that he was the Logos or Word of God, which, as Philo says, comes down from heaven to earth and ascends thither again. Later on the thinkers of the Church derived from the same Alexandrine source both the name and the idea of a divine Trinity, for Philo taught that the divine being or nature is a three-in-one and one-in-three, and two of the persons with which he fills up his formula—namely, the king and father, and the son or Logos—are identical with those which Christian orthodoxy put forward in this scheme. It is plain that the Christians originated few ideas. The dregs of old Greek, especially Platonic, philosophy, filtered down to them through Philo and other Greek Jews of Alexandria; and they dressed up the homely Jewish Messiah in one figment after another, and finally concocted about him such empty rigmaroles of *a priori* notions as we have in the so-called creed of Athanasius.

We have already considered, in the preceding chapter, whether the conception of an omnipotent, and at the same time benevolent, God and Creator of the universe is either a probable or possible one. Let us now ask ourselves how much of the traditional fabric of Christianity is left standing to-day; how much of it, if any, an intelligent man can accept.

Properly speaking, you need to have gone through the phase of being a Jew and of believing the Jews to be the chosen race before you can embrace the messianic hope, and believe that Jesus was the embodiment of that hope. Now, why the Jews, rather than the Greeks or Romans, should be regarded as the one chosen people of a benevolent God, I fail to see. As much as anyone, I admit the Olympic grandeur of much of their ancient literature; and I recognise that their tribal deity, in spite of his bloodthirsty, capricious character and unrelenting cruelty to other tribes than his favourite Israel, was at least superior to the pagan Jupiter or Zeus, in so far as he was not a libidinous being, continually indulging in disgraceful liaisons. Of him there was no *chronique scandaleuse*, and even to his angels was denied what was the first privilege of pagan deities. Nevertheless, the sacrificial cults and taboos of the Jews were no better and no worse than those of other half-savage religions.

We may, then, admit the greater austerity of Hebrew theology; but what contributions to culture, art, poetry, philosophy, history, law, and political science had the Jews ever made comparable to those made by Greeks and Romans? To the mind of the late Mr. Darwin, as we saw—and he was a man who, more than most, looked at things as they really are—it was an initial and insuperable objection to Christianity that it has taken the Jews at their own measure, and granted as a postulate that they were, until the Christian era, the chosen people of God. The very idea, then, of a chosen people belongs to a forgotten mythology; and so do other cardinal notions on which Christianity reposes, such as the fall of man, original sin, and redemption. We are beginning to recognise that it is truer to speak of the rise of man than of his fall, and of original virtue than of original sin. We begin to realise that, if anyone needed redemption, it was Jahveh, and not Adam, nor even Satan, if, at least, the sole offence of the latter was that he deemed it, as Milton says,

<blockquote>Better to reign in hell than serve in heaven.</blockquote>

Thus the entire circle of ideas entertained by Christ and Paul are alien and strange to us to-day, and have lost all actuality and living interest. None, except a few ignorant ranters, believe to-day that the kingdom of God is imminent, and that any day Christ may appear on the clouds of heaven and set up the last assize, after which he will drive those who never believed in him down into hell, and establish on this earth an eternal reign of peace and prosperity for his elect ones. Jesus himself is seen to have lived and died for an illusion, which Paul and the apostles shared; and of this illusion the Church is the offspring, though for centuries she has striven to deny her true parentage. Jesus never claimed to found a religion, nor was he responsible for the emergence of the Church, save by accident and indirectly.

It barely needs to be remarked that the world-scheme of Jesus and his followers was other than our own, and purely mythological. Who to-day believes in a God who has a right and a left hand? Yet our clergy profess to believe in so many words that Jesus, when he rose from the dead and ascended into heaven, sat down at the right hand of God. So we read in Acts that Stephen, the first martyr, "*being full of the Holy Ghost, looked up steadfastly into heaven, and saw the glory of God, and Jesus standing on the right hand of God.*" And in the appendix of Mark we read that "*the Lord Jesus was received up into heaven, and sat down at the right hand of God.*"

Heaven, in the imagination of these writers, was an Olympus, suspended far above a flat and fixed earth, of which the nether parts were sometimes given up to the dead, like the classic Tartarus. Paul reckoned that there were several heavens, and was himself "*caught up even to the third*" of them, "*whether in the body or out of the body*" he "*knew not.*" He no doubt, like the authors of the Slavonic book of Enoch, of the Testaments of the Twelve Patriarchs, and of many other Jewish apocryphs of that age, shared the old Persian belief that there were seven heavens, in the highest of which sat the Almighty on a great white throne, surrounded by winged cherubim. Luke draws us a picture of the Christ's ascent into heaven in Acts i. 9: "*When he had said these things, as they were looking, he was taken up; and a cloud received him out of their sight.*"

The Irish mathematician, Sir William Rowan Hamilton, once allowed himself to be drawn into the speculation of how far out into space Jesus could proceed in a certain time if he was rising at the moderate rate which the above passage contemplates. When his calculations revealed to him that he would as yet not have reached the nearest of the fixed stars, he began, as a good Christian, to recoil from his speculation, and relegated the matter to faith, as a mystery beyond the reach of human reason.

From a religion which claims to be a final revelation we surely expect some teaching that we can lay hold of about the soul, about spirit, about immortality. But its founder had none. He looked forward to a miraculous epoch of material prosperity on this earth, in a land where the lost sheep of the house of Israel were to pasture once more under the immediate protection and guidance of Jehovah. This blessed era was to dawn at once, and the just among the dead were to rise from their graves and participate in the flesh with those who should be still alive when it opened. The Church has tried, lamely enough, to interpret these millennial beliefs of the first age with reference to a life which awaits us all beyond the grave; but any such idea was foreign to the mind of Jesus. He was probably incapable of conceiving of a purely spiritual existence in detachment from the body; and if he ever asked himself, as he probably never did, about the nature of spirit, he must, like others of his age, have decided it to be an attenuated form of matter, similar to the wind, of which we perceive the effects and hear the sound, though in itself it remains intangible and invisible. Small blame to Jesus, if he was no philosopher. What is really amazing at the present day is that bishops and deans should be quarrelling over the question whether this Galilean prophet was omniscient or not. The Bishop of Birmingham, Dr. Gore, has written a learned treatise on the point, and gingerly concludes that he was not omniscient, because he was not *au courant* with the latest results of higher criticism; but he insists that Jesus was anyhow infallible, like a modern pope.

It only remains to address a warning to those who desire to make a speedy end of orthodox Christianity, in the belief that, if they could make a *tabula rasa* of the European mind, something much better would instantly take its place. I would advise such dreamers to enter a museum of anthropology, like the Pitt Rivers collection in Oxford, and survey the hideous goblins and ghouls still worshipped by savage races all over the globe. Let them only visit Perugia, and inspect the collection of ancient, medieval, and modern Italian fetiches collected there by a Professor Giuseppe Bellucci. There is no difference between those of the present and those of past ages. Perhaps we ought to be grateful to the Catholic Church in Latin countries for having established cults so respectable as those of the Virgin and the saints; for it is certain that, in default of them, the Latin peasant would relapse into a fetichism as old as the hills around him. You can turn Spanish and Italian peasants into anticlericals, but you seldom turn them into Rationalists. They may give up Christianity; but they only believe all the more firmly in the evil eye, and in all the debasing practices which attend the belief. In the same way the Irish peasant, if you robbed him of his Catholicism, would at once lapse into the cult of hobgoblins; for this, in spite of the effort made during centuries by the Church to eradicate it, lies everywhere a very little way below the surface, and belongs to the inmost convolutions of his brain.

This is not to say that in our own land, where real emancipation is more possible, we ought to compromise with falsehood, and go into the Church and recite creeds which we no longer believe, merely because it is held respectable to do so. Those who cannot accept a creed literally do best to avoid it altogether; and I believe that the intellectual atmosphere of Oxford and of England at large would to-day be clearer and more wholesome, if men like Jowett and Stanley had, like Newman, boldly left the Church, given up their orders, and followed wherever clear thinking might have led them. There could not then have been related of Jowett such a *bon mot* as this, that when he publicly recited the creed in Balliol College chapel he surreptitiously interpolated the words *used to* before the word *believe*, and began thus: "I *used to* believe," etc.

There is too often a want of candour about the discourses and works of our orthodox English clergy which leaves on our minds a disagreeable impression. They ought to write as scholars and men of learning, but their tone is that of apologists. They lack thoroughness and sincerity, and are for ever pulling up their horses just as they seem about to leap. The result is that, instead of clearing their fences, they are left floundering in the muddy ditch of deanery and prebend. When Anglican bishops meet together in council they talk and write as if religious life was impossible unless it be based on a quiet, but wholesale, suppression of truth. They certainly deserve the stinging rebuke which Mommsen inflicted when, in his discussion of the census of Quirinius (see p. 191), in his work, *Res Gestæ D. Augusti* (Berlin, pub. 1883, p. 176), he expressed a fear lest his historical researches should be exploited, for their own ends, by *homines theologi vel non theologi sed ad instar theologorum, ex vinculis sermocinantes*—that is, "by men who are theologians, or who, without being even that, yet, after the manner of theologians, chatter from their chains." And the chains are quite imaginary, for such a reign of terror as the present reactionary pope has created in the Catholic Church is inconceivable in the Anglican. I used to know a dog over whose head his master needed only to make a few passes, as if he were tying him up to a fence, and nothing, not even his master's call, could induce him to move. He believed he was tied up, without being so. The docility of those who, at ordination, pledge themselves to a number of propositions which had a meaning and application four hundred years ago, but have lost it now, is only to be paralleled by this example of canine scholasticism.

ADDITIONAL NOTES AND CORRECTIONS

P. 38.—*The task of a purely Jewish Messiah.*

It is worth while to compare the histories of later Jewish Messiahs with that of Jesus, and to remark how constant and unvarying in character continued to be the expectations and aspirations of this downtrodden race—the earliest, perhaps, of all races to develop a national self-consciousness and patriotism. As an example of such invariability, we may select the career of one of the latest of the Messiahs, Sabatai Levi, who was born A.D. 1625, and, to the utter confusion of his adherents, turned Mohammedan in 1666. A good sketch of his career is to be read in a contemporary work entitled *Théâtre de la Turquie*, written by Michel Felure, and printed in Paris in 1682. Sabatai first established a reputation as a teacher and prophet among the Jews of Salonica and Stamboul. Thence he went to Smyrna and Jerusalem. While he was in the holy city, a maiden of Galata had a vision of an angel clad with light and girt with a flaming sword, who warned her that the true Messiah was come, that he would shortly manifest himself on the banks of the Jordan, that all must get ready to receive him, and repair to the sacred stream to meet him. The Rabbis credited her vision, and numbers of Jews before long forsook house and home and chattels, and embarked for the Holy Land, where a German Rabbi of Gaza, Nathan Benjamin, had already assumed the *rôle* of precursor and prophet of the new Messiah. When Sabatai reached Gaza, Nathan at once recognised him and proclaimed him to be the Messiah, though he himself for a time protested that he was not. His protests only renewed the enthusiasm of his followers, who, seeing in them nothing but a proof of his humility, threw themselves at his feet and hailed him king of the Jews. Sabatai returned to Smyrna, whither, after two or three months, followed him emissaries of Nathan, bearing a letter fallen from heaven, in which God himself approved of the new Messiah's claims, and commanded all Israel to welcome him. This letter was read in the synagogue of Smyrna, and excited such enthusiasm that Sabatai gave way, and no longer declined the homage of his compatriots. Thenceforth he dressed in robes of silk and gold, and carried a sceptre in his hand; his walks abroad became royal progresses in which crowds of Jews escorted him, laying down carpets on the earth for his feet to tread. In all the Jewries of Turkey his miracles were talked of; and the further it was from Smyrna, the more marvellous were the tales told of him. The very children fell into ecstasies and raved of his prodigies. Some of his followers declared that he partook of food but once a week; others that he had never held relations with women, though, as a matter of fact, he had been married for years. A single word from his lips availed to open a prison gate and set at liberty a Jew confined therein; and one day, when he was preaching in the synagogue, a Jewish doctor of healing beheld him transfigured and suffused with light. So brilliant was the glory that the doctor was struck dumb for a while, and was unable to reply to the question addressed him by the Messiah. It concerned the interpretation of a passage of the Jewish Scriptures; and, when the doctor explained it of the new Messiah, the latter promised him a post of authority so soon as he should take possession of his new kingdom.

Sabatai next betook himself to Stamboul, in order to proclaim his kingdom there. He arrived February 6th, 1666; but the magnificent reception designed for him was a failure; for the Turks arrested, flogged, and cast him into prison. Brought before the Grand Vizier and questioned by him, Sabatai denied afresh that he was the Messiah, and alleged that the honour had been thrust upon him. Nevertheless, when he was subsequently imprisoned in the castles of the Dardanelles, far away from Stamboul, Jews of both sexes and all ages flocked from all over Turkey, bringing him gifts of money and eager to do homage to him as their king. Michel Felure even gives the text of a letter which purported to have been addressed by Sabatai in prison to his followers, and which runs thus: "The only and first-born Son of God, Sabatai Levi, the Messiah and Saviour of Israel, to the beloved people of God, peace! Forasmuch as ye have been made worthy to behold the great day looked forward to by Abraham, Isaac, and Jacob, for the salvation and redemption of Israel and the fulfilment of the promises which God made to your fathers by the prophets as touching his beloved son, let your sadness and bitterness of heart be turned into joy, and your fasting into feasting and rejoicings; because ye shall no more weep, my dear children of Israel, since God has vouchsafed to you consolation unspeakable.....Abate your fears, for ye shall have dominion over all nations; and I will set you in possession, not only of all that is seen on earth, but of all that the sea encloses in her abysses. All is reserved for your consolation."

The ministers of synagogues all over Turkey began to insist on fasts and public prayers in preparation for the advent of a Messiah thus recognised in Stamboul and Smyrna; and Felure asserts that in Aleppo, where he was living at the time, the Jews would go three or

ADDITIONAL NOTES AND CORRECTIONS 365

four days together without food, even babes at the breast being made to fast; while the fervour of some reached such a pitch that they cast themselves naked into the rivers, though it was midwinter. Felure also attests that Sabatai sent briefs of investiture with kingdoms and thrones to certain of his followers, assigning in particular the realm of Portugal to the Jewish doctor of Smyrna already mentioned. But a bitter disillusioning was in store for the believers. In July, 1666, the Sultan haled Sabatai before him at Adrianople; and when he denied afresh that he was the Messiah or had ever announced himself as such, he was offered the alternative of death or conversion to Islamism. He chose the latter; and Felure testifies to the despair with which the apostasy of their Messiah filled the Jews of Turkey.

The story of Sabatai has much in common with that of Jesus. An angel of light predicts the Messiah to a maiden, and that Messiah is to appear on the Jordan. The faithful forsake all in order to meet him and baptise themselves. He has his precursor and prophet. He begins by refusing the honour thrust upon him, but ends by accepting it. He is accredited by a message direct from heaven. Crowds escort him and strew his path with carpets. He gets credit for working miracles, for extraordinary fasting and asceticism. The very children in arms acclaim him. He is transfigured, like Jesus, and shines with glory. He promises "thrones" to his disciples in his future kingdom. He claims to be the Son of God, and addresses his followers in terms which at first sight seem to be borrowed from the canticles of the first chapter of Luke, but may quite as well be imitated from the very source which probably inspired Luke—namely, the prayer-book of the old Jewish Synagogue. The more we bear in mind the stability of the religious beliefs and conditions of the East, the less we shall suspect the good Michel Felure of having coloured his picture of Sabatai Levi with pigments taken from his own Christian paintbox.

P. 157.—*A day of rest for man and beast.*

Let me not, from my use of these words, be supposed to approve of that hypocritical invention of Puritan ignorance called "the Sabbath"—a day of enforced misery and tedium for young and old; the only day on which the poor have leisure for recreation, for hearing music, for games, for visiting museums and galleries of art, and yet the one day on which all this is made impossible for them. This inhuman confusion of Sunday with the Jewish Sabbath is impossible in Mediterranean lands, where the name Sabbath survives as the designation of the Saturday. In the early Church the Sunday was a day of feasting and recreation, not of sour misery and debauchery, as it is in Scotland. The Puritan Sunday is responsible for the worst and most degrading features of the English public-house and Scotch whisky-hell. Nor are the minor taboos of the British Sunday less curious than those of any South-Sea Islander. I have known persons who would listen on it to the melodies of Moody and Sankey, but not of Schumann or Schubert; would knit, but not use a sewing-machine ; would play patience, but not whist ; draughts, but not dominoes ; bagatelle, but not billiards ; who would fish, but not shoot ; bicycle, but not row ; row, but not play cricket or football ; would devour the unedifying legends of the Jewish Patriarchs, but not read the *Times* or one of Thackeray's novels ; would freely talk scandal, but not join in a political or ethical discussion.

P. 188.—*An old Greek manuscript in the Vatican Library.*

I refer not to any codex of the Gospels, but to a MS. of the Dialogue of Timothy and Aquila, edited by myself for the Clarendon Press.

P. 231.—"*Ruffinus*" or "*Rufinus.*"

P. 231.—*The rays of light from heaven entering Mary's ears.*

An old Jesuit missionary in Siam, Guy Tachard, in his book *Second Voyage au Royaume de Siam*, printed in Paris in 1689, repeats, p. 253, a similar story about the birth of Buddha from a Buddhist source, as follows : " A young girl had withdrawn into a lonely forest to await the advent of God, and there led the most austere of lives, avoiding all human intercourse. One day, when she was engaged in prayer, she conceived in a most wonderful way, without losing her virginity ; for the sun, by the ministry of his rays, formed the body of a child in her womb during the fervour of her prayer. Some time afterwards she was amazed to find herself big with child ; and although she was sure of her virtue, yet, being ashamed of her condition, she plunged deeper into the forest in order to avoid the eyes of mankind. She reached at last a great lake between Siam and Cambodia, where she was delivered without pain or travail of the most beautiful babe in the world. As she had no milk to suckle it with, she entered the lake to lay it on the leaves of a plant which floated on the water's surface. However, nature provided for the safety of the child, who was the God, long awaited, of the universe. For his mother having laid him on the bud of a flower, the flower spread its petals of itself to receive him, and then closed upon him as if to form his cradle." The text proceeds to relate how certain kings, jealous at hearing the common folk say that the true King of Kings was born, sought for the child in order to slay it ; but a good hermit fled with it into the kingdom of Cambodia. Even if this legend has been coloured by Christian influence, its ready acceptance by the Siamese shows how easily such tales of virgin births can grow up, and how engrained they are in the human mind.

P. 238.—*Only known to himself.*

So, in Revelation xix. 11, "*he that sat on the white horse, called Faithful and True,*" also had a name written which no one knew except himself. The same conceit of a secret name, "*which no one knoweth but he that receiveth it,*" is met with in ch. ii. 17 of the same book. The King of Siam had a proper name of his own which none but the highest mandarins might utter, or even know, so sacred and mysterious was it. No Hindoo woman to-day will disclose, if asked it, the name of her husband. The Valentinian heretics believed that the name descended on Jesus in the form of the dove at his baptism.

P. 239.—*His name was used by exorcists otherwise strangers to him.*

Note here the story in Acts xix. 13 of "*the strolling Jews, exorcists who presumed to name over them which had the evil spirits the name of the Lord Jesus, saying, I adjure you by Jesus whom Paul preacheth.*" There follows the anecdote of the seven sons of Sceva, a Jew and chief priest, who did the same. "*And the evil spirit answered and said unto them, Jesus I know, and Paul I know; but who are ye? And the man in whom the evil spirit was leaped on them, and mastered both of them, and prevailed against them, so that they fled out of that house naked and wounded.*"

P. 242.—*M. Salomon Reinach.*

Read "M. Theodore Reinach."

P. 248.—*Executed in heaven.*

We should notice in connection with magical knots the story told in Acts of the prophet Agabus, who "signified by the Spirit" (ch. xi. 28) "that there should be a great famine over all the world, which came to pass in the days of Claudius." The same prophet, in Acts xxi. 11, *came down* from Judæa to Cæsarea, and, "*taking Paul's girdle, he bound his own feet and hands, and said, Thus saith the Holy Spirit, So shall the Jews at Jerusalem bind the man that owneth this girdle.*" In the preceding chapter Paul had said to the elders of Miletus: "*And now, behold, I go bound by the Spirit unto Jerusalem.*"

It is difficult not to suppose a connection between the behaviour of Agabus, engaged in prophesying by virtue of the spirit within him, and "the widely-spread habit of tying up the limbs of a medium," described by Mr. Andrew Lang in his book, *The Origins of Religion*, essay ix. (on "Savage Spiritualism") and essay x. (on "Ancient Spiritualism"). He shows from Eusebius's work on *Evangelic Preparation*, v. 9, that the medium of the ancient Greek was swathed or tied up when the "control," the god or spirit, was to speak through him. Presumably Agabus chose Paul's girdle by way of interesting the spirit in its owner. Mr. Lang notes that the Australian Blacks, the Eskimo, the Dènè Hareskins, the Davenport Brothers, and the Neo-Platonists of antiquity have all been equally convinced of the need to tie up a medium's hands and feet when the god is about to take possession of him. When Paul declared at Ephesus that he was *bound by the Spirit*, Agabus's prophecy was not yet delivered. Paul, therefore, at that time was only bound in the ordinary way in which things and persons bewitched or laid under a spell are said to be bound.

P. 296.—*The spirit or soul of a man remains by his corpse for a period of three days.*

This belief is quaintly illustrated in a story told by Damascius (about A.D. 450) in his life of Isidore. The Huns, under Attila, fought in the Campagna against the armies of Rome. The battle was so fierce and prolonged that no combatants were left alive on either side. But the fray did not then cease, for the spirits of the slain proceeded to fall on one another; and for three days and nights a ghostly battle raged over the waste plain on which their bodies were stretched unburied. And there were those, says Damascius, who were witnesses of the phantom warfare, and heard the war-cries of the dead as they continued, with unabated fury, to rain blows upon one another.

INDEX OF SUBJECTS

(A double asterisk signifies that the reference is to the Additional Notes.)

ABYSSINIAN Christians, their superstition about names, 236
Adoptionism of Ebionite, of early Spanish, Armenian, and other Churches, 174, 178
**Agabus, Christian prophet, why bound, 367–68
Agapeti, technical term for the spiritually married, 217
Allegory used by Stoics in interpreting Homer, 330
—— by Aristobulus and Philo in interpreting Old Testament, 331
Altar, its taboo sanctifies gift or victim laid on it, 259
Anahite, her feast became the Virgin's in Armenia, 229
Anglican clergy, their timidity, 338, 361
Antichrist identified in the East with Nero, 193
Anti-Semitism of Marcion, 329
Aphraates on spiritual wives, 219
—— his Christology, 184
Apollonius of Tyana, his exorcisms, 143
Apostles of Jesus upheld the Law for Gentile converts, 7
Apostles, call of the Four naïvely described by Mark, 29
Apostles' Creed levelled at Marcion, 341, 346
Aquinas, St. Thomas, on Incubi and Succubi, 234
Aramaic, the original language of the Gospel traditions, 59
Archelaus of Kharkhar on natural birth and baptism of Jesus, 325
Arianism, evil significance of its defeat, 185

Aristides Rhetor, his visions, 290
—— on binding and loosing of the god Dionysus, 245
Aristobulus allegorised the Old Testament, 331
Armenian dissenters, 262
Athanasius, the so-called Creed of, 356
**Attila, legend of in Damascius's life of Isidore, 368
Augustine on infant baptism, 315

BAPTISM of Jesus, in non-Marcan document, 132
—— its significance in the earliest Gospel, 165 *foll.*
—— in the Acts of Archelaus, 325
—— age of Jesus at, 177
—— Jesus spiritually anointed and elected therein, 180, 325
—— ancient form of, 317
—— postponed for dread of postbaptismal sin, 323 *foll.*
Baptismal crown worn for eight days, 319
Basilidians feasted the baptism of Christ, 175
Bath Kol, or voice from heaven, in Talmud, 167
—— Bishop Lightfoot upon it, 168
—— Philo upon it, 168
Batiffol, Abbé Pierre, on Encratites, 225
Bellucci, Professor, his collection of Italian fetishes, 360
Berkeley's philosophy, 344
Bibliolatry, mischievous effects of, 338
Binding and loosing, a magical conception, 245 *foll.*

INDEX OF SUBJECTS

**Binding of Agabus, an early Christian medium, 367–68
Birth of Jesus denied by Docetes, 226 foll.
Bishops, their origin, 313 ; their succession, 328
Blessing, use of hand in, the same as in exorcisms, 323
Blood, conceived of as the life, 257; ghosts consume blood, 257; why shed for remission of sin, 265
Blood-brotherhoods, 258
Breathing as a mode of transmitting the holy spirit, 323

CATECHUMENATE, rite of, 314
Cathar rite of *Consolamentum* a survival of death-bed baptism, 317
Cathars continued the tradition of Marcion, 334
Cause, idea of, applies only within the world of experience, 342
Celtic Church, spiritual wives in, 219
Chivalry influenced by early Christian encratism, 222
Chosen People, idea of a, mythological, 339 ; involved in Christianity, 356
Christianity a mere development of Judaism, 356 ; assumes the Jews to be the chosen people, 329, 357
Christmas feast, its history, 176
Christology and dogmatic definitions originated with death of Jesus, 354 foll.
Chrysostom, John, on the argument from prophecy, 209; deprecated spiritual wives, 224
Church or *ecclesia*, idea of it absent in Non-Marcan document, 135
—— as virgin bride of Christ, 220, 223
—— the, born of the waiting for the Second Advent of Christ, 354
Churching a child on fortieth day from birth, rite of, 314
Codex Amoris of Andrew, 222

Conception through the ears, see Virgin
**—— of Buddha through rays of sunlight by a virgin mother, 366
Confirmation, or sealing with the Spirit, 319
Conjugal relations incompatible with baptism, 316
Consecration by holy names, 243
Cosmogony of early Church, 357
Crucifixion in Plato and in Philo, 130
Cyprian of Carthage prohibits spiritual wives, 217
Cyrenius or Quirinius, his census, 191

DANAE, Justin Martyr illustrates from her case the virgin birth, 196
Dante and Beatrice, 219
Darkness at hour of crucifixion paralleled from pagan sources, 284 foll.
Darwin, Charles, on Jewish origin of Christianity, 329
Davidic pedigree of Jesus, accepted by Paul, but repudiated by Jesus himself, 187
Delehaye, Hippolyte, on hagiographic legends, 348, 349
Delphic spirit, why unclean, according to Origen, 234
Demiurge, or author of nature, evil, 341; Paul's comparison with a potter, 341
Demons recognise Jesus, 30
—— ignored in Fourth Gospel and by Philo, 69
—— Mohammed, like Jesus, accused of being possessed by, 70, 148
—— of disease, 143
Development of Christological ideas in the New Testament, 348
Docetism, 226
Dositheus, his list of the seventy disciples, 90
Doublets in Mark, 51 foll.
Dove symbolises the spirit in Philo, 167
—— was white according to Lactantius, 171

INDEX OF SUBJECTS

Dragon in the Jordan trampled on by Jesus at baptism, 172
Dreams and visions, importance anciently attached to them, 289

EARS, conception by Virgin through, 230 *foll.*
—— in Plutarch, 230
—— in Philo, 231
—— in Ephrem, 231
—— in Ruffinus, 231
Ebionites believed in baptismal regeneration of Jesus, 172
—— denied the legend of the birth, 206
—— their Gospel, 206
Ecclesia, a spiritual unity, 254
Eclipse of sun at crucifixion, 284
Enoch, Book of, its picture of Messianic kingdom, 295
Ephrem on Virgin's conception through her ears, of the *Logos*, 231
Epiphanius on the two Maries, the spiritual wife and real wife of Joseph, 225
Epiphany feast, its history, 176
Essene sacrament, 271
Essenes abjured marriage, 211
Eucharist of Paul, 251 *foll.*
—— how it became a fetish, 265 *foll.*
—— account of in the Synoptic Gospels taken from Paul, 267, 277
Eusebius on the seventy disciples, 89
Evil eye, 324
Evocatio, rite of, 237
Evolution, idea of, applied to revelation, 335

FAITH-HEALING in Gospels, 63 *foll.*, 146
Family ties sacrificed by Jesus, 154, 160 *foll.*
Farrar's *Life of Christ*, 140
Fascinatio exemplified in Jesus's cursing of a fig-tree, 249
Fish, how symbolic of Christ, 173
Fleshly resurrection of Jesus ignored by Paul, 294

Frazer, Dr., his *Golden Bough* cited, 238, 248, 250

GALATIANS, Epistle to, 16
Gentiles, how they came to be admitted in Christianity, 350
God, idea of eating hi min Paul, 275, 278
Gore, Bishop, on mind of Christ, 359
Gospels compilations, 22, 27, 58
Gregory of Nazianzen on fit age for baptism, 316
—— of Nyssa on spiritual wives, 217
Greville, George, on Irvingite gift of tongues, 93
Grotta Ferrata Monastery, sculpture at, of baptism, 173

HAMILTON, Sir William Rowan, on ascension of Jesus, 358
Hands, laying on of, origin of rite, 322
Harnack, Professor, on Luke, 103
—— his reconstruction of the non-Marcan document, 107 *foll.*
Hebrews, the Gospel of, on baptism of Christ, 171
Hegesippus on James's vision of the risen Christ, 305
Hermas, Shepherd of, on spiritual wives, 217
Herod Antipas, 37
Herodotus on oaths, 258
Hillel called by the Bath Kol, 168
Hippolytus on Messianic movements in Pontus and in Asia, 216
Horoscopes and baptism, 316

IDOL-OFFERED flesh infected with diabolic spirit, 260
Ignatius on the Virgin Birth, 205
—— of Antioch on the eucharist, 261
Immaculate conception of Mary, history of the doctrine, 229
Immanence of Christ, early doctrine of, 254, 275
Incubation in temples, 291

INDEX OF SUBJECTS

Infant baptism, unknown in early Church, 315
Inquisition, Roman, 279
Irving, Edward, his speaking with tongues, 93

JEROME on spiritual wives, 214
Jerusalem, early Church of, presided over by relatives of Jesus, 206
Jesus, tenuity of the tradition about him, 1, 139
—— reserved his kingdom for Jews, 5, 13
—— why condemned to death, 45
—— sublimated in Matthew and Luke, 62
—— accused by his own family of being possessed, 71 *foll.*
—— how much junior to John the Baptist, 142
—— reborn in baptism, 172 *foll.*
—— his age at baptism, 177
—— his gradual deification, 180
—— by whom buried, 297
—— his death, its influence on growth of Christology, 352 *foll.*
Johannine Gospel denies by implication both Davidic origin and virgin birth of Jesus, 189
—— —— its exaggerations, 229
John the Baptist, senior to Jesus, 142
John's Gospel a romance, 20, 62
—— —— denies intercourse of Jesus with evil spirits, 69
—— —— its exaggerations, 77
—— —— its appendix, 78
Jonah, the sign of, 34 *n.*, 128
Josephus on demons, 143
—— on resurrection of the just, 294
Jowett, Benjamin, his opinion of the Gospels, 1
Judaisers and Paul, 8
Judas Thomas, Acts of, their teaching on marriage, 225
—— —— twin brother of Jesus, 207, 255
—— of Galilee, his revolt, 192
Justin Martyr on Virgin Birth, 180, 196

Justin Martyr regarded Jesus as an archangel, 226
—— —— on the demons which would waylay the soul of Jesus, 309

KEYS of heaven and hell, a magical conception, 248
King of the Jews, Jesus condemned as such to be crucified, 45
—— —— the claim of Jesus to be, not offensive to Jews, 46
Kingdom of God conceived of by Jesus and his followers as a restoration of Israel in Palestine, 38; also by Philo, 40
—— —— not to be brought about by force, 161
—— —— believed to be imminent by Jesus and his Apostles, 350, 354
Kinship, Arab's idea of, 255
—— strengthened by common food, 256
Koran, resembles primitive Christianity in not deifying Jesus, 185

LACTANTIUS on the dove, 171
—— his protest against deification of Jesus, 183
—— illustrated the Virgin Birth from mares, 196
Law, Jewish, not to be imposed on Messianic converts from among the Gentiles, 7
Logos, Old Testament epiphanies of, 226
Loisy, Abbé, on burial of Jesus, 297
Luke, how he used his sources, 23, 61 *foll.*, 84 *foll.*, 105
—— invents the call of the seventy *de suo*, 86
—— a picturesque story-teller, 102
—— Ad. Harnack's estimate of him, 102
Luke's narrative of birth of Jesus, how originated, 190 *foll.*, 200 *foll.*

MAGI, visit of to Nero, 193
Magic, homœopathic, 263, 275

INDEX OF SUBJECTS

Magical character of early Eucharist, 265, 275
—— attributes of Eucharist in Paul, 261, 275
Marcion regarded Jahveh as an immoral Demiurge, 330
—— rejected allegorisation of the Old Testament, 331
—— his Antitheses, 332
—— denied birth and baptism of Jesus, 333
—— denied Jesus to be Jewish Messiah, 339
—— denied the goodness of the author of nature, 341
Marett, Mr., on use of names of power, 244
Mariolatry, 75
Mark's Gospel, its author knew nothing of the legend of the Virgin Birth, 186
—— —— used by Matthew and Luke, 21; summarised, 28 *foll.*; and characterised, 32
—— —— a compilation, 56
—— —— contains many doublets, 51 *foll.*
—— —— supplied their historical plan to Matthew and Luke, 60
Martineau, Dr., on Messiahship of Jesus, 351
Mary conceived of as the spiritual wife of Joseph, 224
—— conceived through her ears, 330
Matthew, how he used his sources, 23, 61 *foll.*
—— eliminates human traits of Jesus reported by Mark, 61, 64 *foll.*
—— exaggerates or invents miracles, 76, 79
—— probable date and authorship of his Gospel, 136
Matthew's pedigree of Jesus affirmed the paternity of Joseph, 188
—— Gospel on birth of Jesus in Bethlehem, 192
**Messiah, the, Sabatai Levi, in the seventeenth century, 363 *foll.*

Messianic expectations banished marriage and family, 215
—— character of Jesus concealed according to Mark, 30 *foll.*, 170
—— —— patent from the outset according to Luke, 83
—— —— evidence about it of non-Marcan Document, 134
Millennial beliefs, interpreted by Church in reference to a future life, 150, 359
Minucius Felix attests the mere humanity of Jesus, 181
—— on morals of early Church, 210
Mohammed, 18, 38
—— unlike Jesus, created a book religion, 353
—— his spittle sacred, 148
Mohammedan theology, its empty abstractions, 345
Mommsen, Theodor, on orthodox theologians, 361
Monophysites, their Docetic view of Christ's flesh, 232
Monotheism, its self-contradictions, 340 *foll.*
Mother, child, and dragon in Revelation, 204
Muratori on spiritual wives, 214

Name, magical use of, 235
—— equivalent to personality, 235
—— of Jesus, magically used in exorcisms, 239 *foll.*
—— of Father, Son, and Spirit interpolated in Matthew xxviii., 19
Name-giving on eighth day after birth, 314
Names, holy, localised in sanctuaries, 243
Nero, belief in his return after death, 294
Newman, John Henry, on development of doctrine, 347
Nile, of blessing the, in January, 175
Non-Marcan Document overlaps Mark, 57

374 INDEX OF SUBJECTS

Non-Marcan Document consisted chiefly of sayings of Jesus, 107
—— —— to be reconstructed out of Matthew and Luke, 107
—— —— does not mention death or resurrection of Jesus, 127
—— —— a Galilean document, 131
—— —— absence of miracles in, 133
—— —— anterior to all Church organisation, 135
—— —— were the sayings it contains authentic? 137

OATHS ratified by mutual sucking of blood, 258
Oil, sealing with, origin of rite, 320
Oliphant, Laurence, on spiritual wives, 220
Opus operatum, its meaning, 326
Ordination, origin of, 322
Orphic legends of descent into hell coloured Christian creed, 286
Ovid on demons, 324

PARABLES used by Jesus to conceal his meaning, 33 *foll.*
Parthenos, or virgin, in Isaiah vii. 14, its meaning
Paul, his negative attitude towards Jesus, 2
—— his ecstasies, 3
—— an epileptic, 4
—— his conversion, 4 *foll.*
—— his universalist ideal of Jesus as the Messiah, 6, 18
—— flouted the genuine Apostles, 8 *foll.*
—— ignored Jesus's teaching, 9
—— on virgins or spiritual wives, 212
—— believed in blood sacrifice as only mode of atonement, 274
—— and Thekla, Acts of, on virgins, 215, 254
Pearl, why Jesus was the, 232
Pedigrees of Jesus, their origin, 188
Penitence, history of the rite of, 321

Peter, his relations with Paul, 11, 14
—— Gospel, its account of the resurrection, 308
—— —— authentic details in it as to flight of the Apostles at the crucifixion, 309 *foll.*
—— —— shared with Luke a lost source, 281, 283
Peter's vision of the risen Jesus, 291
Philo on virgin births, 199, 211, 231
—— his allegorising of the Old Testament, 331
—— his idea of the Trinity, 355
—— his Messianic aspirations, 40, 150
—— rejected popular belief in demons, 69
—— urged on converts the necessity of sacrificing family ties, 154, 156, 158
—— on symbolism of dove, 167
Pilate, Acts of, ignores the virgin birth of Jesus, 208
—— Philo's description of him, 280
—— his treatment of Messiahs, 351
Pitt Rivers Museum, 360
Plagiarism not held disgraceful by authors of New Testament, 22
Pliny the Elder on use of spittle, 144
Plutarch on virgin births, 195
—— on conception through the ears, 230
Porphyry on evil spirits connected with flesh eating, 257
Priesthood, emergence of, in the Church, 322
Procopius, Martyr, his *Dossier*, 348
Progressive revelation, the idea of, criticised, 336 *foll.*
Prophetic *gnosis* in Matthew, 80
Proselytes abandoned family ties, 155
—— in Asia Minor, 4
Protevangel, its narrative of the Virgin Birth, 202

INDEX OF SUBJECTS

Ra, his secret name stolen by Isis, 238
Rationalism of early Christianity, 159
Regeneration of Jesus at baptism, 172 *foll.*, 175
Resurrection, Paul's account of it, 16 *foll.*
—— it transformed Jesus into Son of God and universal Saviour, according to Paul, 18, 178
—— subjective character of it, 44
—— not alluded to in Non-Marcan Document, 127
—— Luke's account of it criticised, 100
—— gradual growth of belief in, 287
—— originated in Peter's vision, 289
—— of the flesh, an old Egyptian belief, 295
—— why timed on Sunday at dawn, 300
**—— after three days, 368
—— of Jesus, belief in not universal in the earliest Church, 305
Rings, use of in exorcisms, 324
Risen Christ, appearances of merely subjective, 292

Sabbath diffused by Jews, 157
**—— of the Puritans, 365-66
Sacrifice and kinship, 256
Sacrifices, Jewish, their cessation, 353
Sacrificial idea of Jesus's death, discovered by Paul, 353
Salt, use of in baptism, 320
Sanday, Professor, on Virgin Birth, 186, 200
Sayce, Professor, on magical use of names, 248
Scourging, columns of, 325
Second coming, belief in its immediacy, 45, 151
—— —— coloured the teaching of Jesus, 154
—— —— was it contemplated at the last supper?, 269

Sermon on the Mount, 152 *foll.*
—— —— preached in view of approaching end of the world, 162
Seventy, call of the, an incident invented by Luke, 86
Sleep, how far analogous to death, 343
Solomon's ring as a Christian relic in Jerusalem in fourth century, 324
Son of Man, 39
Spirit, Holy, his place in the legend of Virgin Birth, 210
—— holy, its odour, 100
—— —— its luminosity at Christ's baptism, 171
Spiritual wives, institution of in the Church generated legend of Virgin Mary, 224
Spittle, use of, in healing, 148
Star of the Magi, 193
—— in the East, paralleled, 169, 193
State, negative attitude of Jesus towards, 153, 351
Strangled meats, meaning of rule against eating, 258
Suneisaktai, technical term for spiritual wives, 218
Surrogate, use of term in magic, 263, 275
Swete, Rev. Professor, on Mark iii. 21, 72

Table of devils parallel to the Table of the Lord, 261, 276, 277
Taboos on names, 236
Tacitus on oaths of Armenians and Iberians, 259
Tarsus, Paul's native city, 4
Teaching of the Apostles, its account of eucharistic meal, 273
Tertullian on infant baptism, 315
—— on magic use of names, 242
—— on the veiling of virgins, 233
Tertullian's idea of the conception of Jesus by the Virgin, 230
Testaments of Patriarchs quoted, 169
Therapeutæ of Philo, 211
—— their holy meal, 272

INDEX OF SUBJECTS

Thiasoi, or trade-guilds of Roman Empire, their common meals, 273

Three days, resurrection after, how to be explained, 293, 296

Thyestean banquets alleged against Christians and Jews, 259

Timothy and Aquila, Dialogue of, 286

Tomb, empty, story of in Mark, 299; in Matthew, 302

Tongues, gift of, in Paul and Luke, 92 *foll.*

Trial of Jesus, narratives of, distorted by hatred of Jews, 279 *foll.*

Trine immersion, a pagan rite variously explained from three days' entombment of Jesus or from Trinity, 319

Trinity, idea of, in Philo, 355

VATICAN Museum, monument therein of Proclus, 346

Veil of Temple rent, meaning of, 285, 287

Vespasian heals the blind and lame in Alexandria, 144

Victor, Henry, Professor, his *Atharva Veda* cited, 247

Virgil on mares conceiving by the breeze, 196

Virgil's prediction of a virgin birth, 198

Virgin Birth unknown to the author of Mark's Gospel, 186, 206
—— —— rejected by early Christians, 180
—— —— illustrated by Lactantius from mares, 196
**—— —— of Buddha, 366
—— —— of Julius Cæsar, 196
—— —— Justin Martyr upon, 196
—— —— in Philo, 194
—— —— of Plato, 194
—— —— a *via media* between the Docetes and Ebionites, 228
—— Mary, relative lateness of her feasts, 229

Virgins' ears to be protected against assaults of demons, 233

Virgins or spiritual wives in Corinthian Church, 211
—— in the Shepherd of Hermas, 217
—— in the Greek Churches, 218
—— in Carthaginian Church, 217
—— in early Celtic Church, 219
—— among Cathars, 219

WATER, living, use of in baptisms, 319

Wellhausen's appreciation of Mark's Gospel, 46

ZEUS Sebazios, 324

Zoroaster, his legend parallel to story of Christ's baptism, 177

www.ingramcontent.com/pod-product-compliance
Lightning Source LLC
Chambersburg PA
CBHW071438300426
44114CB00013B/1483